1985 Cowboys Schedule

Date	Opp.	Site	Time
		Preseason	
Aug.	10	**Green Bay**	8:00
Aug.	17	at San Diego	6:00
Aug.	26	**Chicago**	7:00
Aug.	31	**Houston**	8:00
		Regular Season	
Sept.	9	**Washington** (Monday)	8:00
Sept.	15	at Detroit	1:00
Sept.	22	**Cleveland**	12:00
Sept.	29	at Houston	12:00
Oct.	6	at New York Giants	9:00
Oct.	13	**Pittsburgh**	12:00
Oct.	20	at Philadelphia	1;00
Oct.	27	**Atlanta**	12:00
Nov.	4	at St. Louis (Monday)	8:00
Nov.	10	at Washington	4:00
Nov.	17	**Chicago**	12:00
Nov.	24	**Philadelphia**	3:00
Nov.	28	**St. Louis** (Thanksgiving)	3:00
Dec.	8	at Cincinnati	1:00
Dec.	15	**New York Giants**	12:00
Dec.	22	at San Francisco	1:00

THE OFFICIAL
1985 DALLAS COWBOYS BLUEBOOK
VOLUME VI

by Steve Perkins
& Greg Aiello

Taylor Publishing Company
Dallas, Texas

Photographs courtesy of The Dallas Cowboys,
The Dallas Cowboys Cheerleaders and
The Dallas Cowboys Weekly.

Published in cooperation with The Dallas Cowboys

1550 West Mockingbird Lane, Dallas, Texas 75221

ISBN: 0-87833-474-2

Printed in the United States of America.

Contents

THE VIEW FROM TEXAS

Texas E. Schramm is seated at the vortex of the Dallas Cowboys' ups and downs, and since there have been many more of the former than the latter, the seat has mostly been comfortable indeed. But in 1984 his club has rolled a nine and a seven, which turned out to be the equivalent of boxcars and "next good shooter coming out." The numbers meant no playoff games.

That is calamity time in the Dallas corral, and here the Cowboys President answers a few of the more obvious questions on several related subjects, as follows:

BLUEBOOK: A lot of people are always ready to leap up and proclaim that the Cowboys are no longer a club in the top echelon in the NFL, but this year for the first time there seems a sense that people within the Cowboys organization feel that could be so, that the 9-7 season *shook* things around here. Do you feel that?

SCHRAMM: I think the 9-7 season affected people, not so much for the fact that it was 9-7, but because until the last two games of the year, the signs weren't encouraging. Most people were aware that the year before, 1983, the team was not as good as its record. That became very glaring at the end of that season. Everybody was very hopeful that would be turned around in '84. And rather than being turned around, it was compounded. It was hard to put a finger on what caused the difficulties in '84, because it was so easy to point to the quarterback situation, where Hogeboom did not live up to the expectations of many, and White, when he was called upon, really couldn't produce, as he had in previous years. But — without an offensive line, that was decimated by injuries, and without any real wide receivers, it was very difficult to see where the problem was or whether there was hope of correcting it.

I think the way the team played the last two games opened a glimmer of light, because we could have won the last two games, and we played the defense to win the last two games.

BB: If you win those last two games, you win the division, right?

SCHRAMM: I know we would have been 11-5, which is a very pleasing record and you would be in the playoffs. And who can say how lucky you might get as those games move along? But I think the reason there is more concern and more intense effort on everybody's part to do more is that for the first time people thought they were not looking at a winning football team. That's why I feel more optimistic now than I did two months ago.

BB: Why?

SCHRAMM: Because I think that we can make some changes. I think there is a possibility we will be stronger defensively. I think we can correct the passing game. I think that we'll have some receivers. And I think we will have a very much improved offensive line, because I think they are going to go with some bigger players, some younger players, and some more intense players. If we can stay away from the injuries, there is going to a big, big change.

Most people were aware that the year before, 1983, the team was not as good as its record. That became very glaring at the end of that season.

I think there is more a feeling on our coaching staff, with Tom Landry and everyone, that we went a little too long with a pattern of success and that now we're prepared to move ahead and look at things differently and play differently. There's an old axiom, "Don't fix it if it's not broken." Well, we were kinda in the "don't fix it if it ain't broken" syndrome. Now we are going to start doing some things we should have done two years ago. It might be healthy for everybody to go into a season scared for a change.

BB: Do you think it's important to get back to establishing a Number 1 quarterback?

SCHRAMM: I've been in — I guess I have to admit — the National Football League for 35 years, and I've seen everything work as far as quarterback is concerned. There's no hard and fast, impregnable rule that you can only have one quarterback. It all depends on the situation. In our situation maybe it is necessary that we get the one quarterback and go with him. But that's because of the personalities and the abilities of the people. I can point to a number of teams that have had two quarterbacks and have used them successfully. But you have to have a certain kind of chemistry.

BB: Do you think that Gene Lockhart will set the tone of the defense for the next several years?

SCHRAMM: Yes. I think that Lockhart, because of the competitive nature of his play, is going to lift the defense to that kind of competitiveness. Just as Bill Bates will contribute in so doing. And I still have a lot of hope in players like Jeff Rohrer and Steve DeOssie, and at this point I'm very, very hopeful that we've found the person we're looking for in our second draft choice.

BB: Jesse Penn.

SCHRAMM: A hitter. Fast. And when you look at the defensive line, Jim Jeffcoat is only going to go up. He has the potential to be the best defensive end we've had.

Look at our last draft. Everybody was extremely anxious to get a receiver, including myself, and we would have done some pretty drastic things to get one, and the one we wanted was Eddie Brown. But that we didn't accomplish that may turn out to be a big blessing in the long run, because we probably had a stronger draft, as we drafted, than we would have if we'd given up some important choices to get that single player.

BB: You dug yourself a pretty big hole before the draft, making so much of the fact you had to get a wide receiver. There hasn't been a wide receiver go early in the draft since Paul Warfield, has there?

SCHRAMM: Paul Warfield. We had him signed, sealed and sitting in our hotel room somewhere.

BB: Who made that deal, Buddy Dial for Scott Appleton?

SCHRAMM: Well, I did, I guess. But it wasn't for Scott Appleton, it was Dial for our pick and Pittsburgh took Appleton (for the 1964 season). But that's an indication of what I say happens to you when you feel you want something and you need something, and you go beyond what is the norm, what is reasonable. We could have had Warfield *and* Mel Renfro, who luckily was still there in the second round. Dial didn't pan out.

Those kind of manipulations seldom happen anymore. We've had bad luck, and anybody can have that. I've looked back at some of the teams — the big team now is San Francisco — they have made just as bad first choices over the last seven years or five or whatever period you want to pick up. You can take any team and look for one specific thing and you'll see the same results that we have experienced.

BB: Well, then, what is the answer?

SCHRAMM: Anybody who feels they've got a brilliant approach to the draft is dreaming, because the draft is just a matter of percentages. It's totally percentages, and the people who work the hardest, spend the most

time, spend the most money, and make the greatest effort will make the fewest errors over a period of time. But anybody is going to have good years and anybody is going to have bad years.

BB: You changed your approach to the draft the last two years by drafting football players instead of athletes with great athletic ability who had the *potential* to be great football players. Is that correct?

SCHRAMM: We've looked a little bit more at the competitive angle, the toughness, yes, the football ability. But you have to realize that we were in a period for many, many years when we were drafting at the end of the draft. When you draft at the end of the draft, the kind of players that win the Super Bowl are not sitting there as proven players at the college level. So what you're looking for is the great athletes, the players who have a lot of athletic ability and who for one reason or another — injury or playing out of position — haven't gotten quite as much attention at the college level.

BB: And players from Henderson State.

SCHRAMM: But not only that. And so, rather than take a player that you know can make your football team, and probably contribute, but is probably never going to be a great player, then you go over and gamble with the guy that has the great natural ability. A player who can help you get to the Super Bowl, because the Super Bowl is your only goal. Now, when you drop down a little and you're trying to build your squad back up again, then you start looking a little bit more for the football players.

BB: And that's what you did in this draft.

SCHRAMM: That's what we've done the last two years. If you're a contender trying to make the playoffs, you're trying to make sure that your first four players are going to be able to play for you. Because if you go three years and you get four a year, you have 12 who are playing, and you're going to improve your football club. But where we were for 15 years, the only answer to a successful season was a Super Bowl. And when you played in the Conference Championship and lost, and people said, 'Well, you're going to have a better year next year,' then we were looking for a specific thing, looking for somebody who could put you over the edge. Obviously, when you do that and you're drafting somewhere in the 20s, you're out in Las Vegas, you're throwing the dice. And whenever you're throwing the dice, the odds are against you. And it will catch up with you.

BB: What do you say to the proposition that the fine way the team ended up the season last year, as far as effort and attitude are concerned, will carry over to this season, and yet all the losers — for many years the Bears and the Cardinals — would win four of their last five and think they had it going, then next season *lose* three out of their first four? Isn't it dangerous to count on a carryover?

What we have to do is not lose to the Buffalo's and not lose some of the other silly games that we have dominated in the past.

SCHRAMM: We still have people who know how to win. It's like the pro on the golf course. There are people who have won and know how to win, like Ray Floyd. Golfers can shoot well but they have to get over the hump of knowing how to win. We know how to win and we expect to win. And what the last two games showed is we have the quality and the ability to win against two of the best teams (Washington and Miami) in the league. It's that simple. We still have the ability to compete at the championship level. What we have to do is not lose to the Buffalo's and not lose some of the other silly games that we have dominated in the past. If you have to split with the biggies, that's one thing, but don't give away games to the others.

BB: Is the setup of the league different now, where it's possible to be out of the playoffs one year and you can go to the Super Bowl the following year?

SCHRAMM: That's happened a lot lately. For example, you can have a problem at receiver, as we have had, and all of a sudden people show up out of your rookie group, where receivers can play. All of a sudden that weak position is a strength. Two years ago who had ever heard of (Mark) Duper and (Mark) Clayton at Miami? And all of a sudden, they are the greatest weapon in the National Football League. Two years ago the Miami quarterback was David Woodley. What transformed Miami? Three people alone — Dan Marino, Duper and Clayton. And they're in the Super Bowl.

Now, we will have 18 or 20 receivers at training camp — and we've got some burners. And when you look at receivers, you have to remember Drew Pearson was a free agent. You know, if you've got a Drew Pearson sitting there, and you've hit a Mark Clayton, who was an eighth-round draft choice, all of a sudden your quarterbacks might look pretty great like Marino looked.

The encouraging thing is that our quarterbacks, and the receivers, worked three days a week during the off-season, beginning in March right on to training camp.

BB: And you have Duriel Harris, who came aboard in the middle of the trip last season.

SCHRAMM: Duriel Harris runs about as great routes as anybody you could see, has the great speed and the great quickness, and if he concentrates and can hold onto the ball, he can make a big difference.

You only have to have a few little things happen to you to become a really good football team. San Francisco is a classic example of that.

COWBOYS AT THE CROSSROADS

The writers had come down through the stands to the sidelines behind the Dallas bench to attend the last two minutes of a 21-14 Cowboys loss at Miami. The writers were not feeling too happy, not that they were tuned to live and die with the Cowboys, but it is simply more fun to write about a team when it's in the NFL playoffs. And the way things stood, Dallas was out. A victory here would have given the Cowboys a ticket to ride, as a wildcard entry, and they had once ridden that route all the way to a Super Bowl in this same stadium.

Danny White threw a pass from his own 34-yard line toward the far side, some 55 yards away, and the writers saw the action as through a picket fence, between the standing players in front of them. There was a flurry of bodies over there as the ball came down, a stunned split second of silence from the 75,000, then Tony Hill was running into the end zone with the ball aloft, his arms forming a "V." A writer grabbed Frank Luksa by the arm and pulled him around to announce, "The Cowboys are going to the Super Bowl, Frank!"

"How come?" said the unflappable columnist.

"They pull off a deflected pass for a TD, they got to be destined to go."

"Huh," said Luksa.

The lucky deflection was only half of it. Early in his pass route, Hill had been bumped out of bounds, and for his catch-and-run to be an official touchdown the ball had to have been touched by the defense — and it had been, by a Miami linebacker.

Of course, less than a minute later, from his own 37, Dan Marino threw a short pass to Mark Clayton coming across the middle and he ran with it straight upfield for the winning score. On the play, two Dallas defensive backs, one after the other, slipped on the uncertain Miami turf and fell down.

That was the symbol of the 1984 season: The Cowboys fall down. For the first time in 10 years, Dallas would not be in the playoffs — for only the second time in 19 years. What was preserved, at 9-7, was their NFL record of consecutive winning seasons all those years, third in all of sport annals, behind the New York Yankees streak of 39 winners and the Montreal Canadiens' 32. (But the Yankees and the Canadiens have not been winning much lately, it's been noted.)

So now the NFL calendar has been turned a year forward, and vociferous Cowboy haters from coast to coast are ready to raise shouts of glee. The late Douglass Wallop once wrote a bestseller entitled "The Year the Yankees Lost the Pennant" (later the hit Broadway musical, "Damn Yankees"), in which the hero had to sell his soul to the Devil to get the home team through. (And there still remain suspicions that Miami's

The reason this year is critical is that we must build the backup positions that we've had for years.

Marino reverted to a 55-year-old Joe Hardy during the second quarter of January's Super Bowl.)

But, are the Dallas Cowboys now just another NFL team, one of those with an uncertain future? A non-contender to remain just a few men shy of playoff caliber? New Orleans Saints management once mistakenly estimated that the team was "just three players away" from becoming a champion, and of course an irreverent TV man remarked, "What they didn't tell the fans was that the three players are the Father, the Son and the Holy Ghost." (Catholic New Orleans absorbs those kind of wisecracks without an eyeblink.)

Or was that 9-7 season just a glitch on the computer, or an aberrance that can be adjusted by reducing an overload here and upping power shortage there? The man at the controls, as always, is Tom Landry, and he is not going to send you out the door to cheer wildly up and down the streets.

And yet — "We have enough of the good, top players to do the job for us," the coach says. "Our defense, the way it came together at the end of the year, is strong enough to get us back in the Super Bowl — with the right help from the offense. But of course defense is where you start if you want to win a championship."

But Landry will agree that 1985 is a pivotal year for this proud franchise. "The reason this year is critical," he says, "is that we must build the backup positions that we've had for years. This is the thing that has sustained us all that time, that we had excellent backup people who could step in and play when you had retirements, or when you had injuries during the season.

"This is where we're really weak right now. We don't have the real depth throughout our football team that will enable us to do that at this point. It's mainly because retirements are accelerating, more than we had all through the '70s. We were always ready in the '70s to fill in at any position, except for Ed Jones, when he went to boxing, and we had to give up quite a bit (first- and second-round draft choices) to get John Dutton in here.

"But every other time we had that situation, there was always somebody to step in there and produce. When a team has depth, it has a comfortable feeling, a confidence in the whole scheme. Hey, if a guy goes out, who cares? Not that they didn't care — just that they know they can replace somebody. And, boy, that's a comfortable feeling when you have that."

It seems that the great assembly line that kept replenishing talents suddenly hit a slowdown a few years ago, and the void is beginning to hurt. From D. D. Lewis stepping in for Chuck Howley down to Doug Cosbie taking over from Billy Joe DuPree,

Cowboys' fortune was in the very best of hands.

But now it seems that two areas of the team have been hit severely — wide receiver and outside linebacker. Drew Pearson was in an auto accident and forced into early retirement and Butch Johnson, after tearing his Dallas welcome into shreds over a number of years, was traded away. And, finally the past winter, Doug Donley's chronic bad shoulder was deemed unable to pass the muster of a team physical, leaving another gap.

"We need to have more depth in our pass receivers," Landry says, "more potential speed backing up Tony Hill and Mike Renfro, our two starters. The injury situation last season made things critical — Hill getting hurt in the first game and not being healthy for half a season. Donley was very disappointing, because we figured on him being our starter. He demonstrated in the first game (vs. Los Angeles Rams) he could still catch the ball even with his arm being restricted a bit. Then he comes up with a hamstring pull, and things kept happening to him all year. He was just not durable enough to withstand 12 or 16 games as a starter.

"Renfro is a good clutch receiver, a good professional. But his not knowing the system, the matter of confidence between him and the passer, the timing — all those things along with Donley and Hill having problems left us almost void of production at wide receiver.

"We want to get back to a four wide receiver-set on some passing downs. We just didn't have four wide receivers. We have to pick up somebody who can play there this year. The thing about wide receivers, and defensive backs, too, is you have more of a chance getting them late in the draft or as free agents, because there are so many more of them. A Drew Pearson you can find later, which is why you see so few first choices used on receivers or defensive backs. You can see a running back who runs well, like an Eric Dickerson. You know a great runner when you see him — but everyone else does, too."

(Playing the percentages, and looking for another Drew, the Cowboys signed more than 20 free-agent wide receiver prospects to examine in training camp.)

Turning to the other trouble spot, outside linebacker, Landry said, "Our linebacker situation was where we thought we were in great shape, best in a number of years, but then Bob Breunig goes, and Billy Cannon goes, and (Anthony) Dickerson played out his option, so that put us in a bad spot again with linebackers, as far as depth is concerned."

Veteran Breunig's back problems forced him into retirement at season's end, and a neck injury suffered at mid-season by Cannon, 1984's No. 1 choice, was so severe it ended his career aborning.

Landry sees the coming season as a critical year on another front, "because we have to make a decision at quarterback, to see who is going to

be our quarterback of the future, a very important decision.

"We still feel strongly that Gary Hogeboom can be one of the outstanding quarterbacks in the league. Last year wasn't an opportunity for him to prove that, other than that he started as great as anybody ever started (33 completions) at L.A. But in the games after that, he never had good sound receivers running for him out there — and not the same ones every time. Therefore, you have to hedge a little bit, whether he can be a great player or not. I don't think he had a real chance to prove he could be a great quarterback, because I think quarterbacks have to have great receivers, too."

It was suggested to Landry that Danny White, in his 10th NFL season at age 33, should be at the peak of his powers. "Under different circumstances, yes," the coach said. "Now he has to recover his confidence level. If you have confidence everybody's behind you, you go on and reach a high level. Danny has to learn to play within himself. The trouble with a lot of quarterbacks, a lot of players, when they get as conscientious as Danny is, he wants to be Superman in a game. He wants to do a lot more than he needs to do to win a football game. And that's because he wants to prove that a lot of people who have not backed him are wrong. It works negatively against your performance, because you're forcing things. But Danny has the ability to take us a long way."

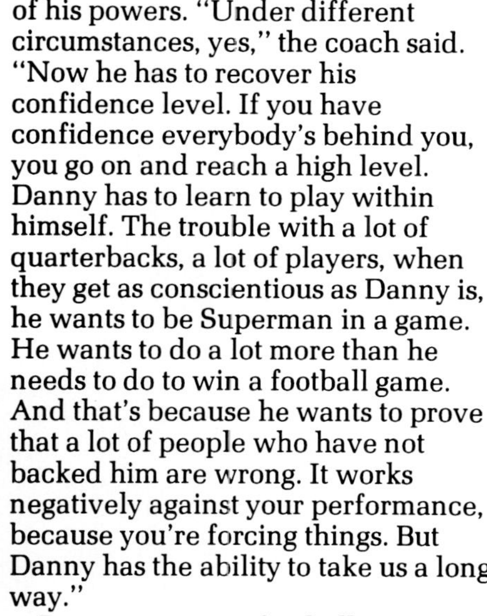

But man — even football man Tom Landry — cannot live by Xs and Os alone, and thereby hangs the strongest tale of the Cowboys 1985 adventure. A year ago, in the aftermath of a one-game exit from the playoffs, Cowboys players were sniping at each other, splitting sentiments on who should be the quarterback, etc. The overall atmosphere was palpably bad, and Landry commented on it in Bluebook V: "Attitudes can be changed. The timetable you use is the only problem."

As it turned out, the "timetable" went to the 12th game of the season before disaster and "humiliation" at Buffalo brought the hoped-for change.

"The team's attitude made a rather radical change after Buffalo (a 14-3 defeat by the theretofore winless Bills)," says Landry. "That usually happens if you have pretty good character in your players. If they have a loss, an embarrassing loss, they're either going to rebound very strongly from it if they have a certain amount of character — or they won't. That's an indication of the quality you have, and it was a positive recovery from that game. We saw a team that was better the last four games there than any we've had in two or three years.

"Attitude-wise, the way they were playing, the way they were supporting each other, the way they felt — that's what you're after. If we can maintain that in the coming season, we are going to win a lot of games."

THE SEASON OF THE DUELING QUARTERBACKS

When last we left Danny and Gary at the end of Bluebook V, they were engaged in a power play whose result only Fate and Tom Landry could determine. The suspense was excruciating.

How did the master of their fates put it? "Gary Hogeboom is trying his best to move into the starting role. We have a very competitive situation and that's not bad." And: "Gosh, you couldn't ask for better statistics from your quarterback than what Danny has had. But statistics don't always tell the way things are."

And so we coasted through training camp and four pre-season games until the final Monday before the league opener when Landry faced a battery of TV cameras and tape recorder mikes and announced The No. 1 quarterback: "Pozderac."

See, even the head coach feels the pressure of a quarterback battle.

But if the drama and suspense was drawn out, Dallas fans did not have long to wait for the final result. Monday Night Football, as it always tries to do, led off *its* season with a Cowboys game, this one at Anaheim, California against the Los Angeles Rams. The home team had the greatest runner in pro football, Eric Dickerson, and a strong-armed veteran quarterback, Vince Ferragamo, who once pitched his way into the Super Bowl. What the Cowboys had mostly was a lot of disarray.

And that's the way the game began. The Dallas No. 1 quarterback didn't see a blitz and fumbled the ball away at his own two. Dickerson scored in one play from there. Hogeboom next threw an interception to set up one field goal, and Tony Dorsett caught a pass and then fumbled it away to set up another. Dallas trailed 13-0 in the first quarter.

But Hogeboom was far from doing anything wrong. This night he would set a club record of 33 completions (old record, 31, by Danny White), and one of the early ones knifed 19 yards through a pocket of Ram defenders to Doug Cosbie for a touchdown. A lot of bad things had happened to the Cowboys, and still they trailed only 13-7 at the half.

Happily, it was also a night when Ferragamo could hardly hit the ground with his hat (11 for 33, four interceptions) and Dallas made him pay for the wildness. Dextor Clinkscale's first interception led to the Cosbie score, and he stole another in the third quarter, leading to a Rafael Septien field goal. A Mike Hegman interception allowed Septien to kick another, this time from a whopping 52 yards away, and the score was knotted at 13.

An ebullient Hogeboom said postgame: "Football is a team game and if there ever was a team game, it was tonight. We kept turning the ball over and our defense kept giving it back."

One of the things I learned last year was to play within my limitations, but I learned I could throw the ball past people . . .

An Everson Walls interception at the Dallas 19 provided impetus for the winning Dallas drive, which ended with Dorsett spinning and whirling up the middle, behind a block by Timmy Newsome, for a seven-yard TD.

It remained, however, for Randy White to make the play of the game and probably save Dallas from any overtime efforts. White had been a mysterious holdout all summer (most of it spent fishing in East Texas) but had signed a new contract and reported for duty exactly a week before this game. And in the fourth quarter, with the Rams at fourth-and-one on the Dallas 39, White demonstrated why he is being paid more money. He stopped Dickerson for a one-yard loss — and the Dallas win was sealed.

Typically, White described the play this way: "Ron Fellows forced from the outside to keep him from sliding that way and Eugene (Lockhart) came in and mopped up on the tackle."

GARY HOGEBOOM: *Trying to get ready for that Monday Night game, with everyone wanting interviews that first week, I was trying to get everything prepared along game-plan lines, so I would know what I had to do when I got out there. A blessing was that the Rams play a straight zone defense and that helped a lot. After we got behind 13-0, it was just a matter of settling down. It was pretty hectic, being my first game — I missed a Willie Blitz, from the back side, on that fumble at the goal line. One of the things I learned last year was to play within my limitations, but I learned I could throw the ball past people, like that game. That's going to get me in trouble sometimes, but most of the time I think it will work out good.*

Almost from the moment Tom Landry had seen the dates and times of the Dallas schedule for 1984, he professed amazement at what the league had asked his team to do. "You just don't ask a team to play on a Monday night on one coast and then on a Sunday on the next coast." The week of the New York Giants game, Landry repeated that view, but by now his remarks were tinged with alarm.

On the way home from a 28-7 thumping at the Meadowlands, Landry said to writers: "I've been telling you for weeks that we're back with everybody else this season, and it's not going to be easy, not like any other season."

The Rams were viewed as title contenders, the Giants as longshots, but it was the latter who did a number on the Cowboys.

Quarterback Phil Simms hooked up with Byron Williams on a 62-yard touchdown pass, when Everson Walls missed a tackle and Williams ran the rest of the way untouched. Hogeboom's lone interception of the day set Walls up to be victimized again, this time on a little stop-and-go route by rookie Lionel Manuel for a 16-yard TD pass.

An oddity of this game is that Dallas was never playing as badly as the score indicated. Strange things just kept happening. For example, at the New York six, Hogeboom is told to throw a little swing pass to Newsome, but before he gets his arm back, linebacker Lawrence Taylor arrives and separates him from the ball. Another linebacker, Andy Headen, picks it up and goes 81 yards for a third Giant touchdown.

Then the Cowboys come back later in the quarter with a drive that reaches the Giants' 10, and Hogeboom tries to run the same play, the short pass to Newsome. Taylor hits him again, unblocked, to cause another turnover. "We made Taylor all-NFL in one game," says Landry, not sweetly.

Well, Dallas has come from 20 points down at halftime and won before, so why not from 21? Ron Fellows stifles the answer by fumbling away the second half kickoff, and on first down Simms passes for an 18-yard TD to tight end Zeke Mowatt. Dallas has never come from 28 down.

Hogeboom completed 21 of 43 passes, but was sacked five times. "What I was afraid would happen because of the schedule," said Landry, "well, it happened. Nobody was alert."

GARY HOGEBOOM: *"We were talking about that in Quarterback School this spring — how two plays like those Taylor plays can have such a significance on a game and that's the way the season went last year. If we'd had it within ourselves, we could have come back and won that game, so you can't blame everything there. Against New York and the defense they have you don't get down there that much, and they did something we didn't expect them to do, blitz Taylor, but considering how good Taylor is you've got to expect it.*

"I remember Timmy (Newsome) broke open down the middle and had his guy beat by three yards and the guy just tackled him. We got the interference at that spot, but two plays later Taylor caused the fumble and they were going the other way with a touchdown."

There are certain teams in any era of the NFL that are guaranteed to cure what ails a contender, teams these days like Indianapolis, Tampa Bay, Buffalo. Well, strike Buffalo; it is not a good example for this chronicle. But one such team is Philadelphia, and it was the Eagles who came to town to open Texas Stadium's league play.

Still, the 23-17 Dallas victory was not a laugher. It was, in fact, a victory brought about by a hoax.

The first three Cowboy offensive drives were stifled into field goal attempts, one of those a miss, so a Ron Jaworski-Mike Quick connection of 16 yards put Philadelphia in front, 7-6, just before halftime.

But not quite close enough before halftime. Hogeboom used the last 2:28 of the second quarter to move Dallas 62 yards in eight plays, the last 25 for the TD to Ron Springs, wide open in the end zone down the middle.

Septien kicked a 30-yarder in the third quarter (to go with his earlier boots of 47 and 51), but the Eagles had managed a field goal of their own, so Dallas was sitting on a shaky 16-10 margin when Landry reached once more into his famous hat for a bit of trickery. It was the pass that Drew Pearson used to throw, thrown this time instead by the new fellow at his position, Mike Renfro, for a 49-yard TD to Doug Donley.

Quick later got another touchdown on a pass that was tipped up in the end zone by Ron Fellows, but the Dallas defense did not allow the Eagles a first down on their subsequent three possessions.

"When your regular stuff isn't getting you anywhere," said Landry, not a bit sheepishly, "you have to use anything you've got. You win football games any way you can. If we didn't have that problem, we'd be Super Bowl contenders right now, instead of trying to be."

Hogeboom threw 22 completions in 40 attempts for 320 yards, but had one intercepted. "His stats speak for him," said Eagles coach Marion Campbell. "He's a good quarterback with a great arm."

GARY HOGEBOOM: *This one meant a lot to me because it was my first as a starter in Texas Stadium. It was one of my better games, but it was a close game. We didn't score a lot of points. I hit Springs down the middle on a touchdown pass, but other than that we scratched the ball around, didn't do a lot of running, and most of all didn't get the ball in the end zone.*

A 20-6 victory over Green Bay brought the Dallas record to 3-1, but the manner of winning brought some evident truths about the ball club. "It's not a powerhouse offensive team," said Landry. "For us to win, we've got to make turnovers defensively."

For a while in this one it seemed neither side could score, on the first seven alternating possessions. But Hogeboom found Doug Cosbie open down the middle for a 36-yard gain, then directed Dallas the remaining 41 yards, ending in a one-yard run by Newsome.

The Dallas defense continued to allow Green Bay to go nowhere, due mainly to the re-emergence of Randy White, the late starter who missed training camp. Now, four weeks into the season, he was hanging up some familiar numbers — five unassisted tackles, five other assists, two quarterback sacks, and countless "harries" when he was in the passer's face. Packer starter Lynn Dickey retired at halftime with back spasms after throwing for only 28 yards.

White's work was helped by a "kitchen sink" pass rush. "We had 10 different blitzes in our game plan," said safety Michael Downs. Dickey was trapped five times, and replacement Randy Wright, a rookie, went to the turf six times more. This action also produced four interceptions.

But the Dallas offense never turned the game into a runaway. After that first quarter TD drive, Dallas netted only two field goals until the fourth quarter. Meanwhile, the offense had even been giving some points back. A Hogeboom screen pass was lobbed too short and Green Bay defensive end Robert Brown grabbed it at the Dallas five for an easy six. Downs blocked the extra point, but the Cowboys' 13-6 margin was nothing to brag about. When it was mentioned to Randy White that perhaps his platoon was due part of the offense's pay checks that week, he said, "Hey, when one area's not working, we pull it up and pat each other on the back. We're all in this together."

Tony Dorsett added a seven-yard touchdown run at the beginning of the fourth quarter, but his numbers for the day overall were quite discouraging — 20 carries for a 2.2-yard average.

GARY HOGEBOOM: *This was sort of the scenario of all last year. We didn't score a lot of points. A guy can have a good game, but if you don't score points, it doesn't mean a whole lot. That's our objective — we need to put the ball in the end zone when we get down there. The one play — you tend to try to forget the bad plays — but I remember the screen pass for Dorsett. I just didn't get it over the guy and he ran it right into the end zone. I don't think I'll ever throw that pass again without recalling the Green Bay throw.*

On a sun-kissed day in Soldier's Field, the Cowboys accomplished one of their rare true grit victories of the season. Setting the tone at the outset was the healthy Bill Bates, out since training camp with a bruised hip. That is, he did it on the first Dallas punt, slamming returner Jeff Fisher loose from the ball at the Chicago 22.

Ominously — and typical of the club's offensive dash — Dallas had to settle for a 44-yard Septien field goal, but it was to be Septien's three field goals through the afternoon that made all the difference at the end.

The Cowboys, as a good many other teams this season, were in the way of Walter Payton's pursuit of Jim Brown. He ran 25 times for 155 yards, and the fact that all of this led only to 14 points on the scoreboard was largely due to the Bears having a sore-handed starting quarterback, Jim McMahon, and no backup to speak of.

When the Bears got the ball, McMahon threw only once on their TD drive, handing off to Payton for 29 yards, and running the final 16 himself.

It's been a Tom Landry dictum through the years, if you want to know if your team is "ready to play" that Sunday, "Watch the kicking teams and they will tell you." Evidently, Bill Bates had told 'em.

Two plays after McMahon's touchdown run the Cowboys responded with a touchdown of their own, a 68-yard advance by Tony Dorsett with a screen pass. "That's the first time we used it in the game," Hogeboom said, "and they came with a blitz. I had to get rid of it quick, and I threw it before Tony turned around. I really threw it high, because I didn't want anybody tipping it up again."

Dorsett said: "I saw Herb Scott get the block on his man and then Kurt (Peterson) and I just weaved our way through the rest of them."

Soldier's Field was where Tunney took Dempsey's title, but this action was more like toe to toe. Payton scored on a 20-yard run to end Chicago's next possession, and Dallas bounded right back with bang-bang plays by Newsome. He took a flip-turning hit, but held on to catch a 25-yard throw from Hogeboom at the Bears' two-yard line. Newsome rammed home from there on the next play.

The 17-14 halftime Dallas lead was extended by the two additional Septien three-pointers, so that when backup quarterback Rusty Lisch was throwing into the Dallas end zone from the five-yard line at the end of the game he wasn't throwing a possible winner.

"This is a big win for us," Landry said. "Our team is still trying to gain confidence, and this is a good team we beat, a definite contender in their division." The Bears' shortcoming at quarterback, with McMahon hurt, was to be their ultimate undoing in the NFC Championship at San Francisco, denying them a Super Bowl appearance.

GARY HOGEBOOM: *The Bears play a lot of different defenses, a five-man line, a lot of changes. It was a game where I really got down to keying the defense because I had to know what they were doing. I underthrew a couple of passes that could have been touchdowns to Newsome, swing passes, but there was the screen pass. Any time you get the ball to TD on the outside, you're going to have something big happen. He improved so much as a receiver last year, I can see him getting better this year and we can really use that."*

Landry's remark about the Chicago victory being helpful to the team's confidence was puzzling on the surface, because Dallas had negotiated better than a fourth of its season and owned a 4-1 record. A panel of NFL writers, who provide rankings on the 28 teams through the year, had Dallas No. 5, behind Miami, San Francisco, the Raiders and the Redskins. But Landry knew what he was talking about, as usual. From this point onward, the Cowboys would win five games and lose six.

The first of these six was dealt out brutally at Texas Stadium by the St. Louis Cardinals, 31-20, in a game that was not as close as the final score.

They definitely outplayed us all around, and I think this game showed us St. Louis is going to be up there in contention for a few years to come.

The major culprits were quarterback Neil Lomax and wide receiver Roy Green. Lomax completed eight to Green overall, and included among those were touchdown plays of 70 and 45 yards, plus another 44-yard gain that reached the Dallas three.

"Lomax did a good job of reading our blitzes," said Landry, "and switching to another play."

The Cowboys tried to keep up, and they had matters at 13-14, partly through Cardinal largesse. A fake punt that failed to realize a first down, led quickly to a 31-yard TD burst by Dorsett. The ever-reliable Septien contributed 35- and 36-yard field goals.

But Lomax and Green tore the game apart in the third quarter with their two long plays. Danny White came on in the fourth quarter and created a drive that closed the score to 31-20. Hogeboom had gone 13 of 28, with two interceptions, and Landry said he would start again the following week at Washington. "He is not going to beat the league overnight," Landry said. "How he reacts and how he comes back will tell you how good a quarterback he will be."

GARY HOGEBOOM: *I remember going into that game we felt they had some defensive backs who were suspect. The week before (Dan) Marino had done a number on them. But it turned out they had good DBs and they shut us down. They definitely outplayed us all around, and I think this game showed us St. Louis is going to be up there in contention for a five years to come."*

The usual crystal-shattering uproar of the RFK Stadium crowd greeted Dallas through all the pre-kickoff ceremonies, but the Cowboys quickly quieted them by taking the ball zip-zip for a 7-0 lead. Dorsett ran 14 yards, Hogeboom threw to Mike Renfro for 31 and 13 to Doug Cosbie, and Dorsett skipped 29 yards for the score.

This one was decided early in Washington's favor, however, by two badly thrown Hogeboom passes. The first was picked off in the left flat by linebacker Monte Coleman, and the next one he threw soared over Timmy Newsome's head when he was wide open for a touchdown that would have put Dallas back on top. "Those two plays turned the game," said Landry. "You can't turn the ball over to Washington. That's their game. And any break we got (blown coverage on Newsome) we had to take advantage of."

"They get on top of you," said Danny White, who again saw late action, "and they *lay* on you."

Dallas trailed only 17-7 at the half, a mere nothing to the 20-point deficit at RFK that they once overcame. But on the first play of the third quarter, Joe Theismann rolled right and threw back left to Calvin Muhammad breaking clear deep down the middle. It was an 80-yard TD play, and it killed the Cowboys. White's late "salvage job," his term, produced a Dorsett score for the final 34-14 margin.

One bright spot was the return of Tony Hill, out since the Los Angeles opener, for nine catches and 134 yards.

GARY HOGEBOOM: *When I think back to that game I think of a play where we were third-and-four and on about their 30-yard line and their defense had a wide-open gap in the middle — the two tackles were playing real wide in a 4-0 defense where there's no middle linebacker — and I gave (Tom) Rafferty the nudge that we were going to have a quarterback sneak. Then we fumbled the exchange. That was the key play. We were up 7-0 and we were going down for another score. On the Newsome play, I dropped back and looked for my key and nobody was there, and instead of relaxing and just getting him the ball, I wanted to throw it to him as quick as possible so nobody could catch him. That's just something you've got to learn."*

The New Orleans Saints were in the middle of a rueful season (3-4) when they came to Texas Stadium and they knew just who could fix that. A win over the Dallas Cowboys goes over big back in New Orleans, more so even than other places. Bum Phillips' team came out gunning, and by *halftime* had rushed for 191 yards. The Cowboys Flex was geared to stop either George Rogers or Earl Campbell, but it was someone with the unlikely name of Hokie Gajan who ripped off a 62-yard touchdown run.

Field goal kicker Morten Andersen booted one in from 49 and another from 50, and the Saints held a 20-6 third-quarter lead. Overall, in the memories of Dallas fans dating back 20 years, the Cowboys were presenting one of their all-time inept performances.

And then Gary Hogeboom threw another "linebacker" pass like he'd thrown at Washington, and this time linebacker Dirt Winston took it 43 yards — for a 27-6 New Orleans lead. Hogeboom bruised his wrist on a helmet in throwing that interception, and Danny White came into the game.

Ineptitude remained the order of the day, however, until the punt return team galvanized Dallas out of its lethargy. Chuck McSwain blocked the punt and the Cowboys recovered at the Saints' three, from where Tony Dorsett quickly scored. White directed a long drive that ended with a 12-yard TD shot to Renfro, making it 20-27.

Suddenly, New Orleans is penalized for holding Randy White, and on the next play there is no holding him as old Kenny Stabler elects to pass from his nine-yard line. White knocks him loose from the ball, which rolls into the end zone, where Jim Jeffcoat leaps over everyone and falls on six Dallas points. Tie game; sudden death.

The overtime seems pre-ordained. Cowboys' ball. Pass interference to the Saints 47. A 15-yard throw from White to Renfro. A 41-yard field goal by Septien. It was the first time, in all the Dallas comebacks, that the Cowboys had come from 21 points down.

GARY HOGEBOOM: *I can remember two things in that game. Throwing an interception to their linebacker, on a play that was a mis-read between me and the tailback. That's when I hurt my hand, a bone in my wrist, and Danny came in and played the next so-many games.*

DANNY WHITE: *You've got to win a game or two like that sometime to build your confidence so the next time you're behind you'll feel like you can win it. One of those games where everybody contributes — the offense scores, the defense scores, the specialty team scores. Talk about a team effort!*

Dallas walked over the Indianapolis Colts, 22-3, with Danny White at quarterback, and he was again the starter when the Giants came to Texas Stadium the following Sunday. An oddity of this season had come into play. With all of the Cowboys' fits and starts, even at quarterback, the ball club entered the Giants game at 6-3 and alongside St. Louis at the top of the NFC East standings.

The Cowboys offensive line, riddled with injury, allowed five sacks of their quarterbacks, first White until he got a shoulder cartilage separated, then Hogeboom. They also committed three holding penalties and Landry, who sends the plays in, was moved to say: "It's tough to get anything going when it's something-and-20 all day."

The Dallas defense dented the first two Giants' scoring drives into field goals. On a third, Bob Breunig stripped the ball carrier at the Dallas six.

A Gary Allen punt return of 16 yards reached the Giants' 30 and Hogeboom threw down the middle to Tony Hill for a 7-6 halftime edge.

Giants quarterback Phil Simms threw a nine-yard touchdown to Lionel Manuel and hit that rookie with another for 53 yards, to set up a field goal and a 16-7 New York lead. Danny White tried to return at this point, but was unable to throw unhindered by his injury, so

Hogeboom came in again and ran out the clock. The Giants added another Ali Haji-Sheikh field goal for the final 19-7 score.

But the oddity in the standings remained. Dallas sustained its tie for first, knotted up with St. Louis, Washington and the Giants, all at 6-4.

DANNY WHITE: *What I remember is that while you can throw with pain, you can't throw very well when two bones in your chest are rubbing against each other.*

'First Place' Dallas nevertheless went to St. Louis in somewhat bedraggled fashion, losers in three of their last five, led by a somewhat discredited Gary Hogeboom at quarterback. St. Louis had beaten Dallas soundly, more soundly than anybody, and were heavily favored to do an encore at Busch Stadium.

But whatever else happened, Dallas had determined that Lomax-to-Green would not burn them again, as in the first game. Green was double-covered throughout.

Michael Downs started things going the Dallas way by blocking a Neil O'Donoghue field goal attempt at midfield. Ron Fellows ran it down to the Cards' 11 and fumbled forward to Dennis Thurman at the four. Ron Springs ran it in on two carries from there.

The Cardinals then took a break of their own, when Mike Renfro fell down as Hogeboom threw to him for an interception at the Dallas 29. Nine plays later, Lomax hit Pat Tilley to tie the game.

An Ottis Anderson fumble at the Cards' 41 was covered by Mike Hegman, then cashed by James Jones on an eight-yard pass from Hogeboom. Hogeboom directed a drive from his own two-yard line against the clock, throwing to Tony Hill and Doug Cosbie and getting first down runs from Dorsett and Springs, so Rafael Septien could kick a 35-yard field goal, giving Dallas a 17-7 lead at the half.

Lomax decided to throw into Green's double-coverage in the third quarter and reached him for 19- and 24-yard gains in a 62-yard move, ended by a one-yard toss to tight end Randy Love.

An O'Donoghue field goal of 30 yards tied the score at 17, and only a controversial offensive pass interference call against Green nullified a 39-yard TD play that would have put the Cards back on top by seven.

A Victor Scott interception at the Cards' 37 lined up Dallas for the winning score. Hogeboom lofted a neatly-timed pass to Ron Springs, who had beaten his man cleanly down the sideline, for a 26-yard touchdown.

The Cowboys could gloat over this one. "All you heard," said Dennis Thurman, "was 'Dallas is doomed' and 'lose this one and the season is over.' They were so eager to write us off."

In fact, the weekend's results left the NFC East standings in familiar shape: Dallas and Washington were tied for first.

GARY HOGEBOOM: *This was a game where St. Louis was talking a little beforehand and they were the favorites, and that doesn't happen a whole lot — hasn't happened while I've been here. We were still in the playoff hunt and knew we had to win this one. It was snowing and raining before the game, but we went out and did it. The defense played great to stop Green and those guys. The throw to Springs was the same one I missed in Chicago twice, to Newsome.*

So next the Cowboys shuffled up to Buffalo, and shuffled out again with heads down. The 14-3 defeat, by a team that had lost all 11 of its games, and one field goal against a team that had yielded an *average* of 29.5 points all season.

This one will go down as the all-time worst loss to a worst team, in Cowboys' annals for the regular season. "I am totally embarrassed and humiliated," Tony Dorsett said in the postgame locker room. "If we're not going to play ball, we might as well pack it up and take it home."

On the first play of the game, Greg Bell busted 85 yards on a play that went inside left guard, and that turned out to be the winning touchdown. Septien kicked a 30-yard field goal in the second period, and just before the half Dallas mounted its only other scoring threat of the 41-degree day.

Hogeboom threw for 12 yards to Ron Springs, for 23 to Doug Cosbie, and for another 23 to Mike Renfro. And then he threw a completion to Cosbie in the end zone, but nobody in a striped shirt raised both arms skyward to signal six. Cosbie was flagged for pass interference, pushing off the defender. He had laid a hand on the defender's hip as he turned to catch the ball. Whatever, that was the extent of the Dallas offense for the day.

In the fourth quarter it finally sank in on the Buffaloes that they might not lose to Dallas, 7-10, the way they had lost No. 10 two Sundays before to Cleveland, 10-13. When this wondrous thought blossomed, they got another touchdown, on a little three-yard toss to hero Greg Bell.

The ultimate cruelty of the day was that Dallas *still* was in a tie for the NFC East leadership, with the Redskins and the Giants.

GARY HOGEBOOM: *It's funny, but pre-game, throwing the ball, was the best I'd ever felt. The weather was nice and cool out, like it used to be at Michigan. After that questionable call on Cosbie's touchdown, we were desperate, we were throwing all the time, and we couldn't do anything. For myself, that was the end of playing. What Tom told me was, 'I'm happy with what you've been doing, you've handled everything right, but right now I need a change. I'm going to go with Danny and see what we can do.' I had to put myself in his position and realize he was doing what he thought he had to do to be a winner.*

The Hogeboom adventure had ended, after he had started 10 of the 12 games. He had completed 53.1 percent of his passes, thrown seven touchdowns and 14 interceptions. Now Danny White would take over for the stretch run, and for a while there it looked good in the win-loss columns.

Dallas beat New England, 20-17, with four seconds to spare. The defense sacked Patriot quarterback Tony Eason 10 times and Michael Downs got the first six Dallas points with an interception return. Still, when the Cowboys had to have it, White took them downfield against the clock so Septien could kick the 23-yard winner.

Then next Sunday at Philadelphia, it was almost the same thing. Dennis Thurman put the first six on the board with his 38-yard run with an interception. The offense had a big stroke when White threw seven yards to Ron Springs and Springs turned it into a 57-yard TD by splitting right down the middle of the Eagles' secondary. But White threw four interceptions, balanced out by two that Ron Jaworski threw and two fumbles the Eagles gave away.

Still, Dallas was 9-5, tied atop the NFC East with the Redskins and the Giants, and as the cynics said, their future was all in front of them. So they went stumbling into it — Washington at home and Miami on the road.

DANNY WHITE: *We controlled the Philadelphia game, but I personally didn't have a good game — four interceptions. Really frustrating. Murphy's Law was working, every time something different went wrong. One of those games where you get on the bus and say, 'Let's get out of here before something else happens.' It kept us from really blowing them out.*

It was all laid out for them: If Dallas could beat both Washington and Miami it would clinch the NFC East title. They could take a week off

while the wild cards battled, then host one of the division-round games at Texas Stadium.

And everyone agreed the Cowboys gave it their best shots. Playing better than they had all year, they drove with the opening kickoff and scored on a six-yard pass from White to Doug Donley.

Then suddenly — Doomsday Defense, with rookie Eugene Lockhart at middle linebacker and sack-hungry sophomore Jim Jeffcoat at defensive end, rose up to sack Joe Theismann eight times in the game. Washington got only two field goals the first half, while White added a bootleg-rollout pass to Cosbie from the two-yard line, and Renfro caught a deep corner throw and danced quickly past two Redskins to complete a 60-yard touchdown.

Dallas led 21-6 at the half. Like a phoenix risen from the ashes of a zany season, could the Cowboys yet pull out a title? No.

On the first Dallas possession of the second half, White threw for Donley slanting across the middle. But White thought Donley would keep going, and Donley thought White would see him pull up in an opening. Meanwhile, the ball was in the air. Cornerback Darrell Green plucked it out of the air at the Dallas 32 and raced it into the end zone: 21-13.

Chuck McSwain was knocked loose from the ball on the ensuing kickoff, and Theismann threw to Calvin Muhammad for a 22-yard touchdown: 21-20. Inside of four minutes of the third quarter, the Dallas lead had shrunk to one point. Still in the same period, Timmy Newsome fumbled the ball away at the Dallas 21, and Mike Moseley put Washington on top with a 21-yard field goal.

The Cowboys fought back one last time, and with 9:41 left in the game White found Tony Hill for a 43-yard TD bomb.

The Redskins moved in seven plays, the last three from the one-yard line, where Lockhart and Downs and Jeff Rohrer stopped John Riggins twice before he finally got across by disputed inches on a third try. Washington 30, Dallas 28.

It finally came down to 1:58 left on the clock, Dallas with the ball on its 29, needing only a 50-yard Septien field goal to win. But Dallas never got a first down.

DANNY WHITE: *We played the first half of that game as well as any half I can remember since I've been with the Cowboys. Defense played well, offense made the big plays, scored the points against a great team. We had things coming together psychologically. I made a comment at that point, 'boy, it would be nice if this was the second or third game of the year and we had some time to smooth out our execution.' We were playing like a team that had just started the season.*

The way the convoluted tie-breaking numbers worked out, the Cowboys were still alive when they kicked it off at Miami. All of the league games had been played except this Monday Night finale and the alternatives were both stark and bright: Dallas wins and it's in the playoffs as a wild card; Dallas loses and the joker is dealt to the Giants.

The stage was set for the wildest, wooliest, heart-breakingest game of the season.

For the longest time, neither team could do much right. A Ron Fellows interception at the Miami 43 went for naught when White threw an interception into the end zone. Miami's phenom, Dan Marino, who would finish the regular season this night with a record 48 touchdown throws, got the 45th on a toss over the middle to Mark Clayton, who took it 41 yards.

But that was it, in what seemed a strange and lethargic game, 7-0 Miami into the third quarter. The Dolphins went 81 yards then, ending with a three-yard pass to tight end Bruce Hardy, and Dallas did not appear capable of accomplishing anything to match a 14-0 margin.

When ex-Dolphin Duriel Harris got open in the end zone, Miami had to wrack him to prevent a 23-yard TD, and Newsome plunged over from the one-yard penalty mark. Then Downs stole a Marino pass and ran it 25 yards to the Miami 21, and Newsome soon crashed over again, this time from the four. It was midway in the fourth quarter and Dallas was even, 14-14.

But in the last two-and-a-half minutes of the Cowboys' season, Marino made believers of them all. He threw a 39-yard touchdown right past the upraised arm of a blitzing Michael Downs.

And when Tony Hill caught a weird, ricochet pass a moment later for a 66-yard touchdown, it seemed Fate was wearing dark blue and silver.

Fate was only fooling. Marino threw across the middle to Clayton again, Ron Fellows fell down on the slippery, spongy Orange Bowl turf, and so did Downs. The Dallas hopes went 63-yards thataway, with only 50 seconds left in the game.

Said Danny White at the time: "I know this — the way we ended this season is a lot better than the way we ended the last one — though it may take our guys 'til sometime next year to realize that."

DANNY WHITE: *We started that game like we ended the Washington game, kinda hit and miss. Our team last year had to rely on big plays. We weren't the ball-control, take-it-down-the-field team we had been in the past. That's a dangerous way to run an offense. When we got that play to Tony, I felt like we had won the game. The momentum was ours, and we were so really close to being a good team.*

Our team last year had to rely on big plays. We weren't the ball-control, take-it-down-the-field team we had been in the past.

Frank Glieber

A PRO, A FRIEND.

(The following is the eulogy given by Tex Schramm at the funeral of Frank Glieber.)

I'm here because I knew Frank a long time, maybe longer than most, not as long as some of his family. But I speak for all of you because I loved him. I loved the man.

We started together in Dallas. Frank was here when the Cowboys began in 1960 and there has always been a special relationship between Frank and the Cowboys.

When I came to Dallas, Frank was a disc jockey. That didn't hinder him in his efforts to become a sports reporter. Even though we weren't the hottest ticket at the time, Frank came to us in 1960 and said he wanted to broadcast our games. We got together and started a beautiful 25-year relationship.

It wasn't long before the networks discovered him, although he didn't lose his roots in Dallas. He became important to the networks and well-known nationally because there was no sport he didn't know and no assignment he wouldn't take. It wasn't necessarily because he had grown up with those sports. He just would accept any challenge as something that would further his career in sports broadcasting.

He worked and he prepared. No matter what the event was, Frank would say, 'Sure, I can do it.' And he would read and learn about the sport. When the light came on and they pointed and he started, you would have thought he had been involved in that sport all his life. That was being a professional.

Being called a professional is the highest accolade anybody in the broadcasting and entertainment business can receive. When his compatriots, his peers, look at him and say, 'He's a professional,' it's something very special. Frank Glieber was a professional.

He didn't receive much attention from the national media because he had the consummate professional approach of subjugating his own personality to the event he was broadcasting. He made the event the big thing. That was what the people were interested in. He wasn't interested in the people coming away and saying, 'Frank Glieber.' As a result, he had the greatest respect from the top network executives. They knew. That's why he was at CBS for 23 years. He did the Masters golf tournament for 17 years and would have done it for another 17 years.

His fellow broadcasters respected him. They knew he would be there when things got tough. And he was appreciated by the people behind the cameras and mikes — the producers, directors and cameramen — because they knew they were going to get a professional job from Frank Glieber. That's why he is held in such high esteem and with such love by the people he worked with.

Remember, Frank is unusual. There are millions of people who would love to be a radio or television commentator. There are thousands who try. There are only a handful who make it. Frank Glieber made it.

He also was great with the athletes, the people on the field of glory, because he was fair. When he interviewed somebody, he would talk to them. He tried to let them say the things they wanted to the fans. He didn't interrogate them. He talked to them.

He could get to the essence of an issue in his commentaries without making worldwide pronouncements. He treated the stars just like he treated the fans and, as a result, both loved him. He had the respect of everyone.

There was another thing about him. He always came home.

Everyone joked that when an event was over, it was always Gliebs who was out of there first trying to get the first plane back to Dallas. That was because he enjoyed his family. He wanted to come home.

And the big national television sportscaster, who was talking to the whole country on Sunday, was up at six o'clock Monday morning talking to the regular folks in the Dallas area on the radio. That's another reason he was special. Six or seven in the morning, he was talking to those thousands of people who had to get up, even if they didn't feel like it, and go to work. But Frank was there with them, talking to them right after talking to everybody in the United States the day before.

Then on Monday evening he did that crazy little radio show with me, which was fun, and during the week he would find time to be Tom Landry's straight man on television. And he would do commercial spots and public service announcements and luncheons and banquets and anything for anybody here in Dallas. Money wasn't the important thing. When Thursday or Friday came he was back on the road as a national sportscaster.

But he never changed. He was loved and respected because he had humility, compassion and understanding. He kept his work and family in perspective. In the last few years he got a tremendous kick watching sons Mitchell and Craig play football at Richardson High School. That was bigger than the Super Bowl to Frank.

But Frank is gone.

Remember one thing. He was happy. He was doing what he wanted to do, and he loved every minute of it. He loved it to the hilt and he loved it to the end. The last thing he did was cover the NFL draft at the Cowboys office.

From all of us here and from all of his many, many other friends who enjoyed listening to and visiting with him, Frank, you will never be forgotten and you will always be loved.

TONY DORSETT EMERGES AS A LEADER

TAKING CHARGE

It was mid-November and the stop-and-start Dallas Cowboys had again gone dead in the water. This time, experts around the NFL were whispering America's Team might well sink, carrying with it all the hoopla and hollerin' of its Silver Anniversary celebration. They had just suffered their fifth loss of the 1984 season, yet there were those quick to call this particular one the most devastating defeat in the club's modern history.

Struggling to hold to the NFC East leadership, Dallas had gone to Buffalo with an opportunity to finally put some distance between itself and the other division contenders. The Buffalo Bills were widely regarded as the most ineffective team in the National Football League — and had the record to prove it. In 11 previous outings they had not won a single game.

In professional athletics there is a proven theory which suggests that capable teams, having problems with various phases of their game, can best resolve said difficulties by a show of muscle against a weak opponent. Call it the Bully Principle. Rarely, in today's parity-locked NFL, does a team get such an opportunity. But in Buffalo the Dallas Cowboys had a gold-plated chance to iron out the wrinkles, experiment, and gain the needed measure of confidence a clear-cut victory produces. The odds-makers said they would win by no less than a couple of touchdowns.

Rather than embrace the opportunity, Dallas dropped the ball with a thud heard 'round the league. The Bills, scoring on the first offensive play of the afternoon, managed their first win of the year, 14-3, and in the Cowboys locker room you could hear a pin drop. Except in front of the locker of team captain Tony Dorsett, who had been held to 70 rushing yards by a defense no one had been writing poems about.

Generally quiet and reserved, Dorsett was fuming. "I'm totally embarrassed. I'd like to stick my head somewhere and hide. We came into this game, knowing that we had to force the issue with a team like this. And, for whatever reason, we didn't. If we're not going to play any better than we did today, we might as well pack it up and take it home."

Members of the media, taken aback by Dorsett's sudden outburst, could not take notes fast enough. In his eight years in the league, the former Heisman Trophy winner had spoken out about the number of times he was called on to carry the ball, had been critical of management during heated contract squabbles, and vowed never again to talk with a particular Dallas columnist, but never had they heard him engage in such a tirade about the attitude of the team for which he plays.

Finally, the Captain had spoken.

"I've always felt I was a person who best led by example," Dorsett says. "And, the truth is I still feel that way. I'm not, by nature, a rah-rah kind of guy. It just doesn't come natural to me. But that day in Buffalo was one of the all-time lows for us, for me. Something had to be done; something had to be said; and I felt it was my place to do it. I was embarrassed not just for myself, but for everybody on the team, our coaches, our fans. I knew we were better than that."

The record will show that Dallas did, in fact, improve as the season wound to an end. The final 1984 record (9-7) was not good enough to maintain the long-standing string of playoff appearances, but there was reason for some small measure of optimism about things to come. In the last month of the season the highly-publicized player squabbles were quieted, the quarterback controversy disappeared from the headlines, and a new team unity seemed to build.

Now, after agonizing months of reflection on the Silver Season failures, the Cowboys are preparing to go to the post again. A new campaign awaits; one which could well be the most important in a decade for the Dallas franchise.

And if the team is to rise to a challenging position in '85, it can be said that it will have to do so on the shoulders of Dorsett. Long established as one of the game's premier runners — he is, by Tom Landry's admission, the team's offensive catalyst — his role will expand this season.

At age 31, the coaches feel Dorsett has reached a point in his professional career where he can provide the much-needed team leadership that has been absent since the retirement of people such as Roger Staubach, safety Charlie Waters, lineman Larry Cole and linebacker D.D. Lewis.

"I don't think there's any question that he's matured a great deal in that area," says Landry. "Tony is at a point now where he is able to recognize the importance of leadership. It's something many players don't fully understand for a long time.

"I think last year he was more visible in that area than anyone on our team. We had a good group of captains (All-Pro Randy White served as defensive captain and Bill Bates was the captain from the specialty units), but it was Tony who stepped forward and led vocally. He took a position — and that was a very good sign."

Backfield coach Al Lavan agrees: "Tony's response to the instability on our team last year meant a lot to us. It became very obvious that being a captain was important to him. The things he had to say after our loss to Buffalo were, really, out of character for him. Ordinarily, he's very quiet, very private. But he saw the need for someone to do something and took on that responsibility.

"And I thought his reaction to the injury problems we were having in the offensive line said a great deal about his maturity and his interest in the overall team concept. He responded, not by criticizing, but by assuring everyone that he would do his best to get the yardage he could. A lot of running backs with his talent would have made it clear to the press that the reason they weren't having the 100-yard days was because of the problems in the line. But Tony said nothing and did his job.

"What I saw last year was a guy who grabbed the mantle of leadership and ran with it. His presence in practice was felt more than ever. There was a new lilt and liveliness about him I'd never seen before, and the team responded to it. And on Sundays everyone saw how he was fighting and scratching for every yard he could get. That weekend in Philadelphia, when he was knocked cold in the first half, then came back to play so well in the second half, opened a lot of eyes, believe me. Determination like that rubs off. By the end of the season everyone was looking to Tony for leadership, and he was responding in every way he could."

In some ways, in fact, the 1984 accomplishments of Dorsett may one day be reviewed as the most impressive of his Cowboys career. There were no All-Pro citations or Pro Bowl invitations despite his 1,189 yards rushing. Yet in light of the team upheaval and personal tragedy he dealt with, it was a year both Landry and Lavan judge one of Tony's best.

"I was amazed at how well he performed during the two-week period when his father had a heart attack and then died," says Lavan. "Tony was able to work out just two days during that period of time, traveling back home (to Pennsylvania) to be with his father in the hospital, then to help with funeral arrangements after he passed away. Yet on Sunday he performed at a very high level. The ability to do so, I think is the highest tribute to his talent."

Dorsett, for that matter, has endured a great deal during the course of his NFL career — everything from death threats and unfavorable publicity to loss of loved ones and domestic difficulties — without effect on his playing ability. And by doing so he has climbed to seventh on the all-time league rushing ladder with 9,525 yards in eight seasons. And, there are those who feel new leader Walter Payton, who has spent 10 years with the run-oriented Chicago Bears, had better establish some lofty figures in the next few seasons if he hopes to hold the title he claimed from Cleveland's immortal Jim Brown last season. Payton ended the '84 season with a career total of 13,309 yards and questionable knees. Dorsett, as healthy as he was the day he came into the league, could well have a number of productive seasons left and should climb into a challenging position.

Tony, however, insists he's not chasing any such status. "I'm sure I'll move up (in the rankings) as time goes by, but Walter and I are about the same age — even though he's been in the league longer — and we'll probably be ending our careers at about the same time. So, my thinking is this: The most important thing for me now is to concentrate my energies toward helping the Cowboys get back into the playoffs where they belong. The yardage and the records and all will take care of themselves."

Whether or not he ever climbs to No. 1 on the all-time charts, Dorsett has clearly made his presence felt in the NFL. The legendary Brown, who was displaced by Payton last season, makes no bones about his admiration for Tony's talents:

"He's an artist, the best 'little' back in the game. His acceleration is remarkable and he has that great balance. And now he seems to have the determination to do well on every play. There was a time when I'd watch him play and he seemed to be daydreaming at times, not really motivated. Then there would be times when he was really something to watch. If it was a big game with something on the line, he'd really be motivated and motoring. Now, I think, he goes into every game that way. Maybe he doesn't have the line in front of him that he once had, but he's giving more. As I've said for several years, there's no light back in the game who can touch him."

Lavan makes a valid suggestion that perhaps Dorsett is, in fact, motivated by the fact he's worked behind an offensive line with injury and experience problems in recent years. "Adversity," Lavan says, "seems to bring out the best in Tony."

Certainly it is something he's had his share of experience dealing with.

It was January, 1978, and the most

celebrated rookie ever to appear in a Super Bowl patiently stood signing autographs in the courtyard area just outside the hotel meeting room which was his destination.

It had been the same since he and his Dallas Cowboys teammates had arrived in New Orleans to prepare for Super Bowl XII against the Denver Broncos. No sooner did the young running back leave his room at the Airport Hilton, than enthusiastic fans, young and old, sought his attention. They wanted to say hello, to wish him luck, to stand near him and have his signature on photos, programs and scraps of paper. Clearly it was great to be young and a Dallas Cowboy. Dorsett's life, it seemed, has become one endless celebration.

Just a season removed from winning the Heisman and leading the University of Pittsburgh to the national collegiate championship and a victory in the Sugar Bowl, he had enjoyed a 1,000-yard season and Rookie of the Year honors in his first NFL campaign. And there was the Super Bowl title which he felt confident he and the Cowboys would claim in a matter of days.

If Dorsett seemed almost giddy, it was understandable.

Then in one frozen moment, one he clearly recalls to this day, the fun and games turned to fear. The excitement and expectation turned to anxiety and concern.

It had taken only one brief phone call to erase the relaxed smile which had been his trademark. Midway through the holiday-like Super Bowl Week an anonymous phone call had come to the temporary offices the Cowboys had set up in one of the hotel banquet rooms. The cheerless whisper on the other end of the line voiced a message of terror. The secretary who had answered the call listened to the brief, one-sided conversation for just a few seconds, then sat motionless, speechless as the line went dead. Then she began to cry.

After gaining her composure she went in search of someone in a position of authority. Where was general manager Tex Schramm? Vice-president Joe Bailey or Gil Brandt? Her fellow workers quickly recognized the look on her face as one of sheer panic. The call, obviously, had been something far out of the ordinary. "Someone," she finally said, "wants to hurt Tony. He said he was going to 'get' him. He knows where to find him and he said he was going to take care of him sometime before the game Sunday. He said there would be no Super Bowl for Tony Dorsett." Then she began to cry again.

What exactly had the caller meant? Get him? Take care of him? Did he have kidnapping in mind? Or was it a death threat? The Cowboys management chose to consider the worst and deal with it accordingly. There was, however, really very little they could do except quietly alert local authorities and the NFL security personnel who were already on round-the-clock watch. Chances are, they were told, it was nothing more than a crank call. On the other hand, there was always the grim possibility that this one might be for real.

In a case like that you want to think it's just some kook who will never be heard from again. But you have to think of the other possibilities, too.

It was decided that Dorsett's movement would be watched carefully, that security personnel would be close by whenever he was in public. They moved him to another room, just in case someone did have a copy of the Cowboys room list and knew, in fact, where he was.

To make the move, however, required a step they didn't want to take. Dorsett would have to be told what was going on. Amazingly, it would not be the first time they had been forced to go to him with such information.

"The first thing that ran through my mind," Tony remembers, "was that I couldn't believe it was happening again. And not at the Super Bowl, of all places. There we were, trying to get ready for the biggest game of the year and I'm running around, changing motel rooms, because some nut calls and threatens to — what? — kill me.

"In a case like that you want to think it's just some kook who will never be heard from again. But you have to think of the other possibilities, too. It was a frightening experience."

Equally as frightening was a situation he had been forced to deal with midway through the regular season.

Despite the refreshing talent he displayed on the football field, Dorsett had dealt with several instances of bad publicity during his first pro season. The people of Dallas obviously appreciated the fact that he ran for 1,007 yards in his first campaign, but there was occasional angry criticism of his off-the-field life. And there was, among the working class, more than a little disenchantment over a 21-year-old kid who had signed a reported $1.2 million contract, drove a Mercedes with personalized license plates, and publicly wondered if he would be treated fairly by the fans and media in Dallas.

Shortly after his arrival in Dallas he was involved in a fracas in a local disco. It was headline material in the Dallas papers. In many sections of the city judgment was passed on Tony Dorsett long before he was given a chance to prove himself.

One Sunday, just hours before the Cowboys would play in Texas Stadium, a call came to the stadium offices. The voice on the phone warned that Dorsett's life would be in danger if he played that afternoon. Officials at the stadium immediately went to work, preparing to divert any possible disaster. And, as the stadium's plan for such matters is outlined, things were carried out quickly and quietly. Local authorities were alerted as were members of stadium security. Plainclothesmen were stationed at critical points throughout the stadium and a number were issued sideline passes so they might be near Dorsett when he was on the field.

"I didn't even know anything about it until halftime," Dorsett says. "There are always a lot of people milling around the bench area, wearing suits. You never know who they are. You don't even think about it, really. But when we came out of the tunnel for the second half, this guy stopped me, showed me a badge, and told me what was going on. He told me when I was on the sidelines to be sure I stayed in a group, not to sit alone on the bench or stand by myself. He assured me everything was under control, but to just be careful. Then he told me not to worry

"If I hadn't been so scared I would probably have laughed. To be honest, I didn't even remember a lot about the second half of that game. Fortunately, it was just somebody calling to get their kicks. Nothing ever happened and I eventually forgot about it. I suppose things like that are going to happen when you're in the public eye. But it's not something I like to talk about. The last thing I want to do is give some nut an idea."

Such stories did not make their way to the sports pages. There was no film at 10, telling of such pressures. The general public, in fact, knew very little about the adjustments Dorsett, a certain star of the future, was making as he tried to fit into a team already well stocked with stars of the present.

What the man on the street knew was what he saw on Sundays and read in the paper. From those two sources he was able to draw two conclusions: Dorsett was a remarkable athlete and he lacked maturity.

Even in times of personal loss, he was big news. When a girlfriend died of a rare nervous disorder, sensational headlines were streamed across the pages. Grieving, Dorsett confided to several teammates that he was considering giving up the game. He also said he felt the press was trying to run him out of Dallas.

The press, however, wasn't his only complaint. Dorsett spent the first several years of his Dallas career bitter about the fact he wasn't being used properly. Other backs in the league, he pointed out, carried the ball 25, sometimes 30 times in a game. An 18-carry afternoon was a busy day for him.

"All my life," he says, "I had been the guy the team looked to for offense. It was that way in high school and later at Pittsburgh. I've always thrived on the pressure of being expected to come up with the big play. And for a running back to do that, he's got to get his hands on the ball a lot. In college I carried 30 times a game. Sometimes it took that many for me to finally break one. I thought I should do the same as a pro. I just couldn't understand why I wasn't being used more and it frustrated me. So I spoke out about it from time to time."

The complaints fell on deaf ears. If Dorsett was to enjoy his career with the Dallas Cowboys, it would have to be within the structure of Landry's philosophy.

It was following the 1980 NFC title game against Philadelphia, when he touched the ball just 13 times and gained but 41 yards, that Dorsett's attitude began to change.

"I did some serious soul-searching that day," he says. "After that game I had doubts that my career was going anywhere. And I made up my mind to change that. I came away from that game more hungry and more determined than ever to make myself a better football player."

An impressive resolution, indeed, for a young man who had been enjoying 1,000-yard seasons since his sophomore year in high school.

Taking Landry's off-season program seriously for the first time, he spent the summer months at the Cowboys practice field, lifting weights, doing sprints and eagerly awaiting the new year. In '81, he was convinced, the NFL would see a new Tony Dorsett. Landry, in fact, saw it long before the public, recognized a new spirit of dedication, and first named Dorsett as one of the team captains. He also decided to let Tony test his added strength and conditioning by allowing him a larger role in the Dallas offense.

I've always thrived on the pressure of being expected to come up with the big play.

The results were obvious: Averaging nearly 22 carries per game, Dorsett gained a club record 1,646 yards, losing the NFL rushing title to New Orleans' George Rogers in the final week of the season. For the first time in his five-year career he was afforded All-Pro honors, was voted the NFC Player of the Year in one poll, and established himself as the Cowboys' all-time rushing leader.

The "new" Tony Dorsett had begun to emerge.

"I finally realized that I'd been cheating myself by not working hard in the off-season," he says. "Now, I realize just how important it is. What I know now is that if you work hard enough you can convince yourself that you can do anything you set your mind to do."

It was that overdue work ethic that gained Dorsett entry into the select company of the Paytons and Dickersons and Simmses. Today, no list of superstar running backs is complete without mention of Dorsett.

Still, there are those who reserve judgement, waiting to see if the mature Dorsett is, in fact, the genuine article.

One of approximately 400 letters he receives weekly during the course of the season had, without the slightest hint of warm salutation, taken him to task. The source of the writer's obvious displeasure was a frank admission by Dorsett that he had never had any intention of playing for the Seattle Seahawks. Not even if they had drafted him following his senior year at Pitt.

Reacting to a magazine article which had once again rehashed the stunning trade the Cowboys negotiated back in 1977 to secure the draft rights to Dorsett, the letter writer said, "Anyone who says he would refuse to play for a loser has to be a loser himself."

Two days later, however, another letter arrived, bearing the same Madison, Wis., postmark and handwriting. "Dear Tony," it read, "I've been thinking about the things I said to you in my letter the other day. I want to apologize, because I think you are one of the greatest players in the game today.

It was yet another change of heart, another re-evaluation of Anthony Drew Dorsett.

In truth, "new Tony Dorsett" stories have become something of a cliche in the last couple of years. Journalists, still trying to determine what makes the millionaire Flip Wilson look-alike tick, write of the better-conditioned, more durable, more dedicated athlete. Still, he remains something of an enigma to most of the outside world.

"Tony doesn't talk much about it, but his public image is very important to him," says his secretary Marge Fenney. "For all the things he's able to do on the football field, he's still basically a very shy person. But he's working on being more open, more receptive. Really, he's no different from any of us; he wants people to like him."

"I suppose I got off on the wrong foot when I first came to Dallas," he says. "I came across as a loudmouth rookie, predicting I'd run for 1,500 yards and all that. I had no idea, really, what it was going to take to make it in pro ball. I like to think I've learned a few things since then. I'm more serious about a lot of things now — my job and my life. And I like to think I'm a little more alert to the people around me.

"I've learned there are a lot of things that can destroy an individual if he's not careful about how he conducts himself. I've learned some of it the hard way; I've had a few incidents in my life that helped educate me."

Such is the maturing process.

"You know, Tony has received a lot of criticism for various things since he came here," says Cowboys quarterback Danny White. "But I don't know of a single person on this team who has ever resented him. He's never been one of those who goes around beating his own drum, making everyone else aware he's the star of the team. The truth is, I find it remarkable that he's handled all the attention he's had so well. He's spent his entire football career under incredible pressure. He's lived in a fishbowl all his athletic life."

And, says the unwritten law, life in such a dwelling is subject to constant, sometimes unfair, scrutiny. The indiscretions of the man on the street, however large or small, are no big deal to the masses. Tony Dorsetts' are news items.

"I think I've come to accept that now," he says, "and I've learned how to deal with it. I just happen to be a very private person who works in a very public profession. For a long time I didn't really understand that. I think now I do."

And there is indication the public is coming to understand — and accept — the gifted runner. In several recent national polls, wherein youngsters are asked to list the role models they most admire, the name of Tony Dorsett is generally mixed with those of rock singers, movie stars and other athletes.

And there's evidence he's gained a newfound popularity in the city he calls home. It was following the 1981 season when the Dallas-based All-Sports Association presented him its most prestigious award.

Receiving the trophy, Dorsett spoke softly and with obvious sincerity: "It is difficult," he said, "for me to tell you what this award means to me. It is the first I have ever received here in Dallas. For a long time, the Heisman Trophy has occupied the most special place in my trophy case. I'm going home tonight and place this one right alongside it. That's how special it is to me."

With that, he received a standing ovation.

BILL BATES KNOWS NO OTHER WAY

FULL THROTTLE

"Billy has been fighting too much on the playground. He needs to be less aggressive around the other children."

note written to the parents of Bill Bates by Faith Swindle, first grade teacher, Prattville, Alabama

"I guess I just know what it takes for me to be able to play football. That is to hit. That's how I've been brought up. I'm not going to change my style."

Bill Bates, Dallas Cowboys safety

It was to have been one of those training camp battles that not only created headlines but new enthusiasm among the rank and file. No man's job was safe, head coach Tom Landry had already announced, and since there was well deserved concern about the capabilities of the Dallas Cowboys secondary, the strong safety position promised an interesting confrontation.

In one corner was Dextor Clinkscale, something of an enigma; a guy who spoke softly at times, angrily at others. He hangs out with professional boxer Donald Curry, break dances with the best of them, and is on a first-name basis with pop singer Michael Jackson.

The question, however, as the 1984 season preparations got underway, was his ability to perform as a full-time, start-to-finish member of the Cowboys' defense. He'd proven he could make the big play on occasion but there was more than a little concern about his eagerness to fit himself into a position where he would, on a Sunday-to-Sunday basis, be taking the good with the bad.

Ready to battle him for the job was a second-year Tennessee free agent named Bill Bates. He, too, had charisma — and celebrity friends,

like movie star David Keith who made it a point to attend most Cowboys games regardless of where they were being played. But Bill was easier to figure. He had developed into something of a cult hero in his rookie season as a member of the specialty teams and pass prevent defense. His speed was questionable and more than one member of the coaching staff worried about his size. Still, he was aggressive, a hitter; one of those rare players who makes sparks fly with his contagious enthusiasm. Bill Bates was a graduate of football's Old School, a kid who played the game at full throttle every minute he was on the field. Landry made no secret of his admiration for the young man's hell-bent style of play. During the previous year's playoffs, in fact, Tom caused the lifting of more than one eyebrow when he suddenly elevated the rookie into the starting lineup.

The purpose was clear. Bates was a player who made the team's adrenalin flow. And that, Landry felt, was sorely needed. It was, then, that intangible but vital characteristic that made Bates a strong contender for the starting job.

Then a pre-season hip injury put him out of the running.

Clinkscale won the battle by default and some wondered if Bates, the Success Story of '83, was one of those pro athletes destined to be a one-year sensation; a victim of the sophomore jinx which had stunted all too many fast-starting careers.

For four games last year, Bates stood on the sidelines, on injured reserve and dressed in civilian clothes, feeling no part of the Cowboys' celebrated Silver Season. It was frustrating, trying.

"I'd never gone through anything like that," he reflects. "Once, in high school, I cracked some ribs but I was still able to play. In college, I hurt a knee slightly and had to miss one game in four years. I'd just never had to cope with a major injury before and it wasn't easy. During the week, you stand there, watching everybody getting ready for the game. Then on Sunday you do some more standing around. You don't feel a part of it all. It gets to you pretty quickly."

And, as Bates stood and watched, Clinkscale went about his chores as the Cowboys' strong safety in a workmanship-like manner. In Bates' mind, they had been even in their battle for the job when he was injured during that exhibition game against Green Bay. By the time he was finally healthy and elevated back to an active role, he knew his rival had put too much distance between them to be made up in the

'84 campaign.

"I suppose there were several ways I could have looked at the situation," he says. "The easiest would have been to hang my head and feel I'd been cheated out of a fair chance to be a starter. But that wouldn't have gotten me anywhere; nor would it have been any benefit to the team. The truth of the matter was that Dextor was doing a good job. And you don't take someone out of the lineup who is playing well. In fact, the entire secondary was playing well — and it would have been foolish to disrupt what it had going. I decided the thing for me to do was make my contribution wherever, whenever I could and hope to get another shot at challenging him when training camp opened again."

Thus it was as a member of the specialty teams that he stepped on the field for the first time in '84. Racing downfield after a Danny White punt, he hit the receiver, forcing a fumble on his first play back. By game's end he had played well enough to earn a game ball. Clearly, the layoff had affected neither his enthusiasm nor his talent for making the big play.

By the time the Silver Season, one of the most disappointing in modern Cowboys history, had ended, Bill Bates again stood as one of the positive hopes for the future. His go-for-broke style of play earned him a place in the Pro Bowl which, after too long, was finally recognizing the contribution of special team players. Most All-Pro teams also included him in their rosters. And for the second year in a row, the NFL Alumni Association voted him the Special Teams Player of the Year.

Which is not bad for a youngster whose abilities as a four-year starter at the University of Tennessee didn't gain enough attention to get him drafted by anyone. In fact, only the Pittsburgh Steelers, Seattle Seahawks and Cowboys showed interest in signing him to a free agent contract.

"Johnny Majors (the Tennessee coach) called me," recalls Cowboys player personnel director Gil Brandt, "and told me if we didn't sign Bill Bates that my wife and I could forget about coming to the Kentucky Derby or ever visiting in the Majors home again. He was joking, of course, but he was obviously serious in his belief that Bill should get the opportunity to

play pro ball. I've never known a coach who had stronger feelings about one of his players."

Majors' pressure, needless to say, worked to the Cowboys' benefit. "Bates," says Brandt, "is one of those college players who really causes you a problem. You go out and watch him play and you like everything you see, except he's lacking in one area. You want a defensive back who will run the 40 in 4.5 (seconds) and you know the best he's going to do is about 4.7 or so. But, when we ran him through our standard series of athletic tests — jumping, hand-to-eye coordination, back-pedaling, breaking on the ball — he scored close to some of the people we felt were No.1 picks. That's why we forgot about the 4.7 business and went after him as a free agent."

Which, history will show, is one of the best decisions the Cowboys scouting department has made in recent years. Bates is now firmly established among the team's blue ribbon list of free agents — Everson Walls, Cliff Harris, Drew Pearson, et al.

And, as Dallas prepares to regroup for the 1985 season, hoping to return to the playoffs after a year's absence, Bates will again launch his bid to climb another notch up the professional ladder. Though he obviously thrives on special teams play and 4-0 duty, he would like to be a starter. Once again he is eager to battle Clinkscale for the job.

"It will be an interesting battle," says secondary coach Gene Stallings, "one that can only benefit our team. Any time you have strong competition at a position, you're going to be better for it. And, yes, I fully expect to see Bill make a strong run at the job. He's one of those players who seems to always be doing something that helps you win football games.

"You can go to a game, not even really knowing much about football, and have your attention drawn to Bill Bates. He'll be the first one down on a kickoff, making the tackle, forcing a fumble or delivering a real hit. He's around the ball when a fumble occurs or he picks off an interception when you badly need one. A coach can't take credit for things like that. Some players just have that special kind of ability."

The first to recognize all this was Tom Landry. Since Bates' arrival, the Cowboys coach has made little attempt to hide his admiration for the aggressive manner in which his pupil approaches the game. "Bill," he says, "is one of the few people we've ever had on this team that you have to hold back a little. You have to tell him now and then not to be quite so aggressive. Most guys have to be told to be aggressive."

While Landry says he's been pleased with the progress of Clinkscale, he also admits the need to have a player of Bates' enthusiasm and ability on the field. "When you have a player like that," Landry says, "you're hurting the whole team if you don't have him out there. What we need is more aggressive play, more hard tackling. When you have a competitor of Bill Bates' caliber, it is tough to keep him out. Bill's going to push Dextor hard because he's an ultra-competitor. He knows how to play the game tough and in an intimidating manner. When you have a player like that he's always going to pressure the guy in front of him.

Whether Dextor can keep him out of the lineup this year, I don't know, but he's going to have to play awfully hard to keep his job."

There are those, in fact, who have gone so far as to suggest that Bates might be the resolution to the long-standing problem the Cowboys have had at outside linebacker. He's tough, a sure tackler, and moves well; so why not?

"If he were a little bigger," Landry says, "he might be an ideal outside linebacker. But today, with teams using the double tight end sets so much, they could isolate him just about whenever they wanted him. There's just no way you could free him to do the things he does best from that position. If things were like they were back when Chuck Howley and D.D. Lewis were playing, it might be something worth looking at. Back then, you could do some flip-flopping and keep a small, fast linebacker away from the blocking of the larger tight end. But not today."

Thus Bill Bates, a little too small, a step too slow, must make his mark as a safety. Which is fine with him. A young man who follows a strict mental code, he is obviously confident about his chances.

"I prepare for training camp the same way I prepare for a game," he says. "I simply can't afford to let myself think I can't do it. They say for every negative mental picture you have, you should have at least ten positive thoughts. That's what I try to do. I've done it while standing on the sidelines, waiting for my chance to get into a game, I've done it while getting ready for practice, and I'll do it during camp this summer. It's all a part of the confidence-building process that's such an important part of this game.

"In the last couple of years I've gained some confidence. I feel good about my ability. I now have enough experience to where I feel comfortable with the things we're trying to do. On the other hand, I have what Charlie Waters used to refer to as a healthy respect for failure. I know it can happen if I don't work hard; if I don't approach my job with the same degree of aggressiveness I've had in the past."

His first grade teacher might not like it, but such an observation is music to Coach Tom Landry's ears.

Where the Questions Are

OFFENSE

Once again, a major question confronting the Cowboys is: Who will be the starting quarterback? But perhaps that query does not have the all-important aspect it had a year ago. In effect, it went unanswered last season, but along the way enough other shortcomings made themselves evident so that the quarterback's identity carries less weight.

Still, Landry says the decision on quarterback is critical. It's critical because "it will determine who will be our quarterback of the future."

Whoever it is, things are going to be doubly-tough for the guy who ends up Number 2. Gary Hogeboom said, "Once you've worked for something long and hard and achieved it (the starter's role), you just can't accept anything else," and "I know Danny feels the same way I do — Number 1 has got to have the job, no matter what. Switching quarterbacks doesn't work."

Danny White merely said early last winter he would take his chances in the battle at quarterback through camp and the pre-season.

A little historical note here might help those who seek the answer in a crystal ball. Tom Landry does not think it's such a big deal to have an unhappy Number 2 quarterback. When Roger Staubach won the job from Craig Morton midway through the 1971 season, it wasn't until 1974 that Morton demanded to be traded, well into the fall. Of course, neither of these two quarterbacks is Morton, but Landry is still Landry.

That quarterback question was expected to work itself out, finally. As Jim Shofner says, "The quarterback position wasn't much of a factor last year."

There are several mysteries about the offense of far more import: Who will be the four wide receivers? Will the offensive line be a weakness or a strength? Where, with the help of better blocking up front, will the running game (24th in league yards last season) pick up some added juice?

The wide receivers may, in fact, answer a lot of the quarterback questions. "Passers," says Shofner, "are a little bit at the mercy of who's catching that thing." Split end Tony Hill no longer claims to be "The main man — just get the ball to me" as he did a year ago. "This is the new quiet Hill," he says.

Mike "The Quick" Renfro owns flankerback until someone takes it away, and he has been working since March, three or more times a week, with the quarterbacks. So has Duriel Harris, last year's trade acquisition out of Miami via Cleveland. "He runs great routes," says Hogeboom. "He's going to contribute a lot."

Behind those three is the mystery man, the joker who jumps up out of the deck and spits cider in your ear, as Drew Pearson did one summer so long ago. It could be draftees Karl Powe or Leon Gonzales, or one of a host of free agents such as Bobby Leach of SMU or Mel Lattany, the trackman.

Newsome is the key this season. His development is the key to having a more productive offense.

Tight end belongs to Doug Cosbie, who was hampered last year by a sore knee and by being the obvious target too many times on third down. But he remains a Pro Bowler, backed up by second-year men Fred Cornwell and Brian Salonen.

At running back there is the kingpin, Tony Dorsett, ready at the least suggestion to burst past 2,000 yards in a season. But what is new is the fullback, Timmy Newsome, in his sixth year finally getting his chance at the starting fullback job.

"Newsome is the key this season," says backfield coach Al Lavan. "His development is the key to having a more productive offense. He needs to provide us with the real tough, move-the-pile kind of running. He's always been the kind of guy that things happen with him, when he's in a ball game. And he's a third-down receiver. He can make the difficult catch, like Preston Pearson did for us. You didn't have to hit Preston in the numbers to get him the ball, and Timmy's the same — just throw it out there and he'll get it."

Newsome himself spent all off-season considering his new roles and responsibilities. "It's my chance at getting my hands on the football for a whole year," he says. "The biggest factor is experience, and I know what's expected of me — that's the biggest plus."

Behind Newsome are Norm Granger, the second-year man "who must prove himself in the summer," says Lavan, and Todd Fowler, the emigre from the U.S. Football League. Sometime fullback Ron Springs was a question mark, for other reasons.

But who is behind Dorsett in the depth chart? James Jones and Chuck McSwain are listed, but can Jones complete his remarkable recovery from what appeared to be a career-ending knee injury three years ago? As insurance Dallas took the 6-0, 195 pound Robert Lavette in the fourth round of the draft.

"Granger has very good running ability," says Lavan, "something like that of Robert Newhouse in that he has very quick feet, his instincts are good and he catches the football. He hasn't had much opportunity to show what he can do, nothing at all in the regular season."

And down in the engine room, the base source of power for the running game and protection for the pass, is last season's disaster area, the offensive line.

"I don't believe I've ever been through that many injuries," says assistant head coach Jim Myers. "I know I never have started five guards before, and I don't believe anyone else has either." Herbert Scott, now retired, and Brian Baldinger were the guards who were pressed into duty at the tackle positions, and center Tom Rafferty was a guard in his early days.

Strange things kept happening to the offensive linemen, traditionally one of the NFL's low-risk positions. Tackle Jim Cooper will probably never live it down that he slipped on some confetti on the dance floor at a night club named Confetti and broke his ankle and tore some tendons. And Cooper wasn't dancing; he was on his way to the men's room. Center Tom Rafferty was hobbled, but played anyway, with a "turf toe." Guard Kurt Petersen missed five and a half games. Tackle Phil Pozderac went down and came back playing on two knee braces.

Well, that was the bad news. The good news, expectantly, for 1985 is that out of this cauldron of adversity has emerged a much more experienced, and certainly more versatile, offensive line.

The key to its solidity and its excellence is guard-tackle Howard Richards, also one of the injured. In doctoring his knee injury, doctors discovered a chronic pain-producing condition that had never been tended. "If you've ever wondered about his toughness," said salty Dr. Marvin Knight to Myers, "don't wonder anymore. He's played right through that pain for a long time."

The game of musical wheelchairs in the offensive line seems to have ended for a while. Richards, in particular, is happy to hear that Landry and Myers want to station him at guard, period. The development of the towering Pozderac at tackle has led to that move for Richards.

"Richards started out like something fantastic at tackle, before he got hurt," says Myers. "He hasn't yet proved what was expected of him, but he's been moved back and forth so much he hasn't had a real chance to develop at one spot."

What was expected of Richards was a lot, because he was the club's Number 1 draft choice five years ago. "The first year I went through most of that, especially not playing at all. But I played for Herb (Scott) in '82 and got a lot of experience then, and in '83 when we shuttled plays, and '84 I

started a lot of games — and I felt very comfortable, and that I was making a contribution."

Now he's ready to emerge, after what he calls "the nightmare of the offensive line in '84," to be the next All-NFL star of the unit. "After that nightmare, we're all emotionally and spiritually prepared, because everybody's now had a taste of it."

With everyone healthy, there will be considerable elbowing for the five starting spots. Baldinger, for example, is listed Number 2 at both right tackle and center, though he was originally a guard. Baldinger, it should be noted, was one of the few offensive linemen in the NFL last season to incur a personal foul penalty. It's the way he plays the game.

"Baldinger told me," says Myers: "'If you'd left me at center I'd beat out Rafferty. If you'd left me at right guard I'd beat out Petersen. If you left me at right tackle I'd beat out whoever was there.' So, I told him, 'I don't want to hear anything else from you. I'm going to give you your choice, and I've never done this with a football player — you pick it, center, right guard or tackle.' He chose left guard. Actually, he played better at tackle than anywhere. No end he played against overpowered him."

Digging deeper into the depth chart, Myers singles out John Hunt: "He was a guy that surprised all of us, when we had to start him (at guard) in Philadelphia. He has a knack, I don't know how else to put it. Some guys are big and strong and fast but never do anything; Hunt just has the knack. His strength is in his legs and he needs to build his upper body, and when he does that he's got the ability to do things at guard."

Adding to this mix were draftees Crawford Ker (third round) and Matt Darwin (fifth). Ker is projected as a 290-pound guard and Darwin plays both center and guard.

Aside from their own departments, Cowboys coaches are enthusiastic about the team's prospects for '85. "We're coming off the best attitude we've had in a long time," says Myers, "and that's a big plus. If we'd had that attitude the previous five years we would have been in two or three more Super Bowls. Everybody putting their heart in it, togetherness, playing as a team. It's what you've got to have, and I think it will stick with us."

Al Lavan puts that subject this way: "At the end of last season, our guys demonstrated and came to believe they needed to and could play together. That's something we haven't had since I've been here (1980). They still feel very good from a psychological standpoint, they know that they played together and cared about each other. It's a nebulous thing, but it's precious."

While the offensive show was still in dress rehearsal, in the background was the notion that the *dramatis personae* may not have been completed. The specter of trades, like the rumors of war, hovers over the team. What can the Cowboys offer, what can they afford to offer, to gain significant help? Would they trade away future draft choices, which they value no more highly than eye teeth?

"You would only give up draft choices," says Landry, "based on what you felt the team was going to do with the help you were going to get — whether it would put you over the hump or not, or improve your chances for the championship. That is what the 49ers have done so well lately, with the help they've picked up from San Diego and elsewhere."

For the moment, whatever the 49ers have done seems to be a guide, because they are the Super Bowl champions.

QUARTERBACKS' BOX SCORE

OPPONENT	START	FINISH	WINNER
at L.A. Rams	HOGEBOOM	HOGEBOOM	DALLAS 20-13
at N.Y. Giants	HOGEBOOM	HOGEBOOM	GIANTS 28-7
PHILADELPHIA	HOGEBOOM	HOGEBOOM	DALLAS 23-17
GREEN BAY	HOGEBOOM	HOGEBOOM	DALLAS 20-6
at Chicago	HOGEBOOM	HOGEBOOM	DALLAS 23-14
ST. LOUIS	HOGEBOOM	WHITE	ST. LOUIS 31-20
at Washington	HOGEBOOM	WHITE	WASH. 34-14
NEW ORLEANS	HOGEBOOM	WHITE	DALLAS 30-27 (OT)
INDIANAPOLIS	WHITE	WHITE	DALLAS 22-3
N.Y. GIANTS	WHITE	HOGEBOOM	GIANTS 19-7
at St. Louis	HOGEBOOM	HOGEBOOM	DALLAS 24-17
at Buffalo	HOGEBOOM	HOGEBOOM	BUFFALO 14-3
NEW ENGLAND	WHITE	WHITE	DALLAS 20-17
at Philadelphia	WHITE	WHITE	DALLAS 26-10
WASHINGTON	WHITE	WHITE	WASH. 30-28
at Miami	WHITE	WHITE	MIAMI 28-21

Start-to-Finish Wins-Losses: Hogeboom 5-2, White 3-2
Losing Starts: Hogeboom 4, White 3.
Losing Finishes (did not start): White 3, Hogeboom 1
Winning Finish (did not start): White 1.

Boosting Back Up to Doomsday

DEFENSE

There at the end it had begun to come together — 57 sacks of the quarterback all year, but 26 in the last four games. They came on like gangbusters, the safeties blitzing, the linebackers pounding and the pass rush swooping in like so many birds in a Hitchcock picture.

"Gee," said Tom Landry, "our guys played so hard those last two games and lose 'em."

You boil it all down, this "carrying over the attitude" from the end of last season to the beginning of this one, and the essence is Defense, and the Dallas defense was playing so well the last few games of '84 that it was only a step or so from being all the way back to Doomsday.

New York Giants quarterback Phil Simms corrected someone this spring in an estimation of the NFC East: "Don't you count Dallas out, not as long as they have that defense coming in from everywhere. You don't know how they're coming, but they're in there."

And the Giants beat Dallas twice; and Simms never saw Dallas after Nov. 4.

"Defense wins championships," Landry said a long time ago, and he was asked what would happen if you had a great offense and only a mediocre defense, how that would work out, and the coach replied, "You would get beat."

Now Landry is saying for 1985: "Defensively, I believe the way we played and the attitude we played with toward the end of the year would indicate that we have a defensive team that could complement a good offensive performance and put us all the way to the Super Bowl."

"Toward the end of the year," quarterback Danny White recalled one day, "Landry saw something he liked and he started telling us what a good team we were. We need more of that."

If the defense keeps its foot to the floorboard, the team will get more of Landry's high praise, his equivalent of the high five.

Even with the 9-7 record, last season the Dallas defense ranked seventh overall and fifth against the pass. Bear in mind when considering those rankings that 10 NFL teams reach the playoffs, and that the offense ranked 11th.

How did this happen, that the Cowboys' defense could advance to championship-contender level during a 10th-year crisis when nobody got a playoff check at all? The platoon had its standout talents — interceptor Everson Walls, one-speed-flat-out Randy White, and Ed Jones knocking down a record number of passes like a badminton player swatting shuttlecocks.

But suddenly last season three new ingredients were added. Michael Downs, perhaps galvanized an extra bit by public threat of demotion, had an All-Pro season at free safety. There arrived at middle linebacker, a fellow much bigger than Bill Bates but with a similar mode of operation. When Gene Lockhart arrived at the scene of a ball carrier, you could hear it. And finally, there was Jim Jeffcoat, a nugget among the dross of recent first-round draft choices. Jeffcoat ended up with 11½ sacks of the quarterback, the same number recorded by a player of larger note, Giants linebacker Lawrence Taylor.

Downs was in the limelight on the safety blitz, for which he has uncanny timing, and he was the team's leading tackler and leading interceptor. "Mike's strength," says defensive backfield coach Gene Stallings, "is that he's awful smart. That's his longsuit. He is in the right spot, doing the right thing, the way Charlie Waters was."

. . . It's how you play together as a team that counts, and that's what we have to remember.

But Downs does not wish to hear too many accolades just now. "One year does not a career make," he says. "I'm just concentrating now on the things that didn't go well last year. I felt more comfortable last season, more confident in my position on the team. But we've learned that it's not a matter of individuals — it's how you play together as a team that counts, and that's what we have to remember."

Bill Bates and Dextor Clinkscale were set to battle over the strong safety job, and Walls is expected to rebound from a relatively off season when interceptions fell through his fingers like grains of sand.

But the key to another stepped-up notch in the defense is the other cornerback, Ron Fellows, who weathered his first season as a starter. "He had a good year," says Stallings, "but he can still be better. He hasn't reached his peak by any means. He has the quickness and speed to cover man-to-man and the toughness to make the tackles."

The fifth-man theme belongs to Dennis Thurman, who gave up his corner job to Fellows and reverted to his natural position at free safety, where he possibly pressured Downs into that big year. Thurman is still a key man in the defense on passing downs, making big plays, doing "everything we asked him to," in Stallings' phrase. The coach adds: "He gets our guys lined up right, which is no small thing because we see so many formations and play so many people and combinations of defenses. It's not all that easy to get everybody in the right spot to cover the right people."

More often than not it's the middle linebacker the defense looks to in order to set its tone, bare its soul, and Gene Lockhart seems born to play that role, pressed into the starting job as a rookie when Bob Breunig's back forced him to the sidelines. "I think he has the potential to be an All-NFL middle linebacker," says Landry. "I think the thing we'll know soon is

how, with his experience, he'll adjust to his keys and all the things he has to do to play defense real well. Right now he has great instincts. If he's out of position, he knows how to get back in position and make the play, make a false move and then recover from it. That's what you don't teach, that's something a linebacker has, the knack of getting to the right place. Some of them never have that and therefore they're never great linebackers."

Lockhart admits now that he couldn't allow himself too much time to worry about the intricacies of Landry's Flex Defense last season. Then it was as if he'd been thrown into the pool for his first swimming lesson and turned out to be a natural swimmer. "I just went to the ball," he says. "Whenever I found myself hesitating or waiting on something to happen, a different key, I was lost. But by the end of the season it started clicking for me. The people around me helped me get there."

Lockhart is equally aware of the intangibles of his job. "I feel responsibility, all right, because the middle linebacker is more or less the quarterback of the defense, but the rest of it is just part of my nature. I'm an emotional person, very enthusiastic. I enjoy playing football. I'm constantly talking to people, trying to fire people up all the time. That's just the way I was brought up to play football."

Lockhart, naturally, is optimistic about the season, with a proviso. "We came through adversity last year," he says, "and finished uphill. We carry that through, we're really going to be hard to handle. Everybody's got to take care of their job and not worry about someone else doing their job — that's what team unity is all about."

Alongside Lockhart, however, there is uncertainty. Second-year man Steve DeOssie will be given a chance to compete with veteran Mike Hegman on the left side, traditionally the "strong" side because most offenses send running plays to their right.

The rightside linebacker was expected to merge, coaches hoped, during the pre-season. "Jeff Rohrer," was the first name mentioned by Coach Jerry Tubbs at the outset. "He's a fighter, a hitter, a hard worker, not too fleet of foot, but he might be able to do it. Then there's Jimmie Turner, who did a good job on the kicking team, has good speed and has shown some blitzing ability."

This spot was owned by Anthony Dickerson last season, but Dickerson was unsigned past the option of his contract and a mystery all his own.

Tubbs is very high on second-round draftee Jesse Penn, whom he rated as the best outside linebacker in the college crop. "Penn could be a help to us in the 4-0. He could be one of our two linebackers in that defense because his strength is pass coverage and he could contribute to the team that way right away. He's quick, he's got good body control and he'll hit."

(No rookie has started for the Cowboys at linebacker since Lee Roy Jordan played the right side next to middle linebacker Tubbs in 1963 when Dallas was not exactly looking to get into the playoffs and when, in fact, there *were* no playoffs, just an NFL championship game.)

An early season bonus this year in the defensive line is bound to be Randy White, who is an unlikely source for improvement until you recall he was absent all of last year's training camp. "He was probably our best-conditioned athlete from the off-season program," says Landry, "and that conditioning was still with him when he reported late as he did, or he couldn't have played as well as he did. But I don't care what you do staying in condition, you need to recreate your competitiveness by getting hit and absorbing punishment. You get that no place else except in training camp. So it took Randy about five games or more before he really could start playing."

From then on, with White as his usual constant self, attention began

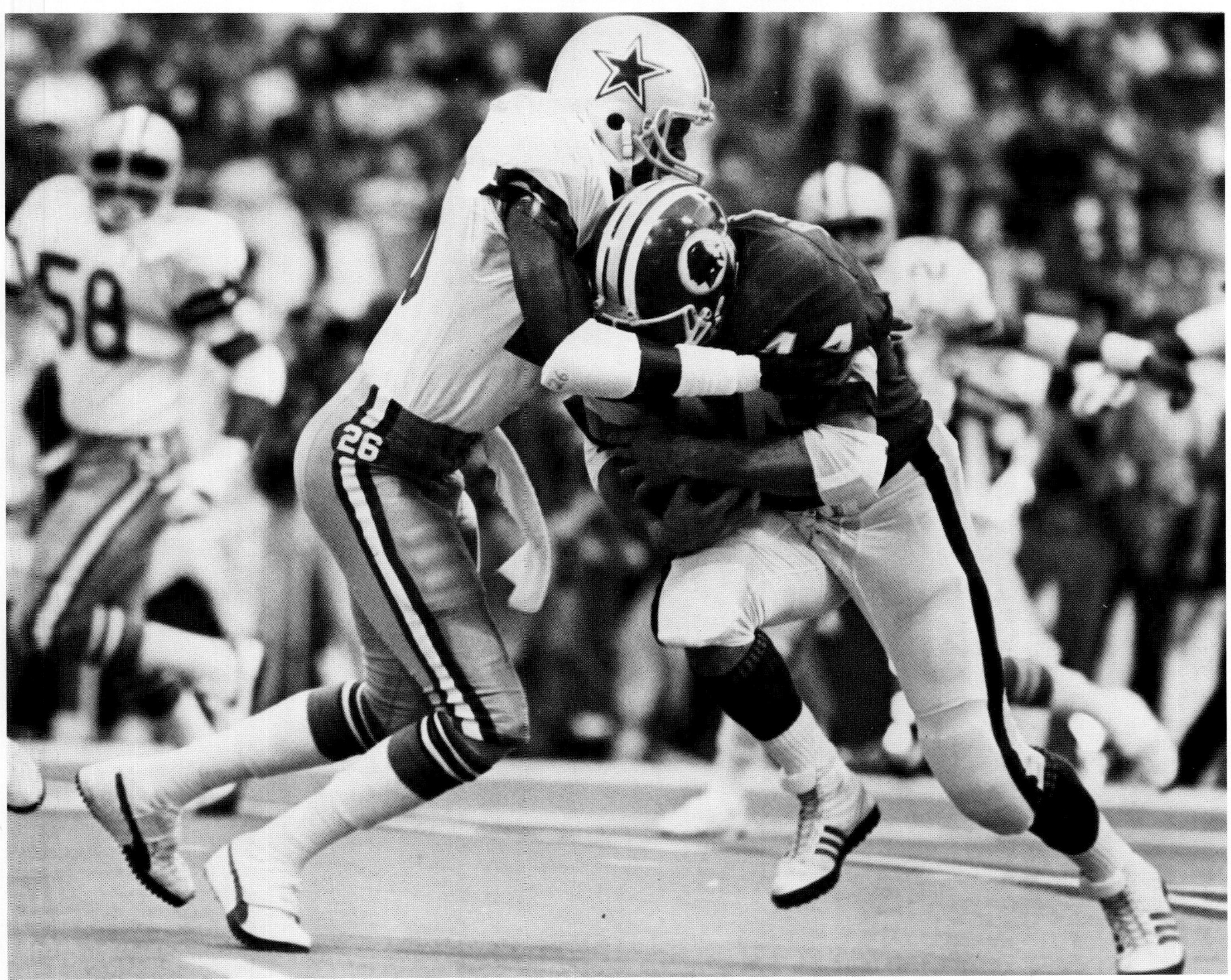

focusing on the new guy at right end, Jeffcoat. Now he turns away plaudits with an explanation: "That's what can happen to you when you're playing alongside Randy White."

"Jeffcoat was one of our biggest pluses down the stretch," says defensive coordinator Ernie Stautner. "He turned in great jobs over the last four or five games. It wasn't a surprise, exactly, because when I rated him as a draft prospect I rated him high on his athletic ability. But you never know — and it turns out he has a big asset, that he won't take anything off anybody."

Another asset of Jeffcoat's is a dedication to hard work. Prior to the '84 season he spent months in an aerobic dancing class and hour after hour lifting weights at the practice field. This off-season Jeffcoat spent more months aerobic dancing and more hours lifting weights. "I'm trying to become more flexible," he says of the dancing, and do you wanna make something of it? "My second year," he says, "I wanted to assert myself, to prove that I belonged in that line, with that defense. My third year, this one, I want to prove that I can improve even more."

An interested fan of Jeffcoat's is Harvey Martin, the right defensive end on the Cowboys' 25-year team. "I noticed the two Washington games," said Martin. "The first one, up there, the turf is hard to get traction for a pass rusher and Joe Jacoby handled Jim pretty well. But the second game, at the stadium, he *owned* Jacoby. Another thing he's already learned — on a running play to the other side, you can hustle and make the tackle from behind the runner. I used to do it all the time. Jeffcoat's doing it sooner."

Jeffcoat, incidentally, is doing everything sooner than Martin, who hadn't progressed as far in *his* second year out of East Texas State. But Jeffcoat doesn't buy Martin's compliment about the Jacoby battles, either way. "The turf shouldn't bother a pass rusher," he says. "I notice it doesn't bother Randy White. I had a better game against Jacoby the second time because I was able to use some of the things I'd learned in the first game."

All in all, the defense is ready to tee it up, and it is not asking any favors from the offense. Gene Stallings is still sizzling that Dallas didn't beat Buffalo 3-0. "We let them score two TDs," he says. "You want to hold a team to a field goal — and *block* that one."

RELIABILITY: SEPTIEN'S TRADEMARK

AUTOMATIC

Exasperating seems to be the proper word to describe one's feelings when, immediately after flipping on a light switch, a little crackle is heard and the light goes off.

Not only does the room continue to stay dark, but now you are faced with the chore of replacing the burned-out light bulb, which, more often than not, is located in some hard to reach locale.

How exasperating!

It is always taken for granted that when the switch is thrown, the light is going to come on and stay on. It is automatic.

Light bulbs, of course, seldom get their due. They do their job time and again and finally, as they inevitably must, they have a mishap. It is when they let you down that you notice them.

Such is the way it is with place kickers in general and with Rafael Septien in particular.

Septien in particular, of course, because he has the kind of reliability that is treasured within the National Football League.

Twenty kickers in the NFL were called upon to make at least 25 field goal attempts during the 1984 season. And of those 20, only one had a higher success ratio than did Septien.

The native of Mexico City made good on 23 of 29 attempts for a percentage of .793. Paul McFadden of the Philadelphia Eagles was at .811.

And to stretch things a bit further, Septien has missed only 11 field goal tries in the past two seasons. Last season alone the St. Louis Cardinals' Neil O'Donoghue missed 12.

So reliability has become Septien's trademark and reliability is the most cherished quality a place kicker can secure.

That reliability, however, can

really be seen when considering Septien's efforts in key situations and from distances that most people feel a field goal should really be made.

Of course, most of those who grumble when a player misses a comparatively short field goal have never tried to kick a football over their garden fence, much less between the goal posts with all of those other guys trying to keep you from doing it.

Anyway, during Septien's eight-year professional career he has converted 110 out of 123 attempts from 40 yards or less. That is an astounding success ratio of .894.

Last year Septien tried 18 from 40 yards or less and he missed just one. He tried 13 the year before last and didn't miss any.

Septien did not get to kick in the playoffs last year, but it figures that if he had he would have been outstanding.

He holds the NFL playoff record for most field goals made in a row and for the best career percentage. Between Super Bowl XIII in 1979 and the 1982 NFC championship game he kicked 15 consecutive field goals and nobody has ever had a longer success streak. Septien's field goal percentage of .857 is also a playoff record.

The Cowboys obtained their current place kicker in 1978 when the Los Angeles Rams made what has proven to be a ghastly mistake. They released Septien after the final preseason game that year and he was quickly snapped up by the Cowboys.

Dallas did not enjoy as much success in 1984 as has been customary, but it was not because of Septien. When drives bogged down, on he came to salvage something.

A glance at some of the games a season ago reflect how much he was needed. In the season opener against the Rams, a game in which Gary Hogeboom received a tremendous amount of attention, it was Septien who kicked a 31-yard field goal late in the third quarter to get the Cowboys within three points. Then he kicked a 52-yarder to tie the game in the final period.

Dallas managed a six-point victory against Philadelphia a few weeks later and Septien contributed three field goals, including the first six points of the game on efforts of 47 and 51 yards.

On the last day of September the Cowboys were outgained by the Chicago Bears and Dallas was penalized for 115 yards. But the only points scored during the second half of that game were scored by Septien, securing the Cowboys' nine-point win.

Then, with Dallas badly needing a victory against New England on

Thanksgiving Day after suffering an embarrassing loss to Buffalo just four days earlier, Septien kicked a 23-yarder with four seconds to play to bring about a 20-17 decision.

As the seasons go by and hopes rise and fall, there has been one constant about the Cowboys during the 1980s.

Rafael Septien has scored in 118 games in a row — the third longest such streak in NFL history. Before the season is out he could move into the top 20 list of all-time scorers.

He has, indeed, become very much the reliable light bulb for the Dallas Cowboys — providing service and getting only a small share of the attention he deserves. And it is comforting for the Cowboys to realize that he should continue to shine brightly for years to come.

WAYMER

The Dallas Cowboys Cheerleaders

SIDELINE SUPREME

Though the Dallas Cowboys have always had sideline cheerleaders, the phenomenon as it is today really didn't begin its rise until 1976.

In the 1960s, the cheerleaders for the Cowboys were high school students from the Dallas area and very small in number. The 1970s saw an upswing with the introduction of young women 18 years and older and a new idea in uniforms. Super Bowl X in January 1976 seems to be the turning point as TV cameras found their way to the sidelines and a new attraction was added to professional football.

The Dallas Cowboys saw the opportunity and a decision was made to increase the number of the squad by holding open auditions in the spring of 1976. Approximately 250 girls made their way to Texas Stadium and the number of applicants has increased significantly over the past 10 years as over 1400 young women applied this year.

The auditions are held over a month and a half beginning late March, and are based on a three-stage system of preliminaries, semi-finals and finals. The basic requirements are as follows: (a) 18 years of age at the time of your audition (there is no age limit); (b) High school graduate (GED accepted); (c) Attending school or holding a full-time job; and (d) If selected and don't live in the Metroplex, you must relocate. Young ladies come from all over the United States by plane, bus, train and car to audition in search of a dream.

Each year, present squad members are given a bye into the finals where they then must compete in the hopes of reclaiming a position for the current year. As with the football team, no one is ever secure about a position from year to year.

1977 was a World Championship year for the Cowboys and the DCC reaped a portion of the benefits. A majority of the country has made them the sweethearts of America. Thousands upon thousands of people congregate wherever it is announced that two or more will appear — whether in Pittsburgh, PA; Hobbs, NM; or outside of the United States. The story is always the same as people from 2,000 to 75,000 gather for a photograph, autograph, hello or a musical variety show from these special ladies.

The 1977 squad completed two major television shows on national networks in the Spring of 1978 — the NBC Rock N' Roll Sports Classic and the Osmond Brothers Special on ABC. In August of 1978, the '78 squad completed a television commercial for Faberge shampoo and in September, they kicked off the season for Monday Night Football by hosting their own one-hour special on ABC entitled "The 36 Most Beautiful Girls in Texas." A two-hour made for television movie was filmed in November on location in Dallas and aired January 14, 1979. Taking a 48% share of the audience, this movie became the second highest viewed movie made for TV in the history of television. A sequel was aired on January 13, 1980. The DCC have performed for three years on the Academy of Country and Western Music Awards Show, sailed twice on The Love Boat, and battled the Cowboy players on the Family Feud Show in June 1980.

College concerts and half-times have been performed at Fort Haynes State University (KN); Wake Forest University (NC); Fresno State University (CA); Wichita State University (KN); Delta State University (MS); Kent State University (OH); Montana State University; Eastern Michigan University; Utah State University and in December 1981 during half-time of the Tangerine Bowl in Orlando (FL). More performances are planned for the 1985/86 season.

For the past eight years, the DCC have appeared in state and county fairs across the country — Portland (OR); Springfield (IL); Chattanooga (TN); Springfield (MA); Clearfield (PA); Grey (TN); Pensacola (FL); Knoxville (TN); Duquoin (IL); Memphis (TN); Salt Lake City (UT), etc.

A very successful 10-day tour of Japan with the entire squad was made in December 1978. Millions of Japanese people saw the DCC perform in theaters, parades, on national TV and at the Mirage Bowl football game. They also completed several television commercials for Mitsubishi Motor Corporation.

In December 1979, the US Department of Defense (DOD) requested the DCC for a USO tour of Korea where the ladies visited with and performed for thousands of American troops. With the first DOD/USO tour, an ongoing tradition was established. Since 1979, the DCC have spent every Christmas and New Years in Korea, the Philippines, Diego Garcia and the Indian Ocean. A tour was planned each spring

thereafter where they have visited military personnel in W. Germany, Turkey (three times), the Sinai Peninsula, the Azores (Portugal), Greece and Crete (twice), Sicily, and Beirut (twice).

The purpose of the tours is to boost morale and bring a touch of home to our American men and women serving their country so very far from home. The DCC perform one-hour variety shows that bring standing ovations and tears to the eyes of both the audiences and the entertainers. The ladies have meals with the soldiers in the mess halls and share close conversations about the Cowboys, happenings in the U.S. and loved ones at home, whether on board an aircraft carrier or a guardpost on the DMZ in Korea, the message is always the same — these fine Americans are not forgotten. The Cowboys organization is extremely proud of the high regard this nation has for the Dallas Cowboys Cheerleaders.

The DCC have performed their musical variety show at the Pentagon in Washington, DC, as well as at such national conventions as Whirlpool, National Utilities Contractors Association, the Kirchman Corporation, Delta Air Lines, Toastmistress International, RepublicBank Corporation, etc.

These young ladies are bright, energetic and intelligent contributors to society. They represent almost every phase of the American woman: they are secretaries, company executives, homemakers, mothers, students, medical technicians, fashion coordinators, accountants, sales persons, file clerks, receptionists, advertising reps, cashiers, dental hygienists, flight attendants, etc. Some are single, some are married and several have children.

You really have to want to be a DCC before you'll subject yourself to the rigorous physical conditioning and exhaustive practice schedule that govern their part-time life. This elite corps rehearses almost every evening for three hours or more under the trained eye of their choreographer, former four-year veteran Shannon Baker Werthmann. The 1984/85 season added four-year veteran Cheerleader Judy Trammell to the staff as an associate choreographer. The entire operation is directed by Suzanne Mitchell, assisted by Debbie Bond.

Rehearsals of the 50 plus song and dance numbers in each season's repertoire are mandatory. If a Cheerleader misses a rehearsal prior to a home game, she will not perform. Anyone missing two rehearsals prior to a home game without an acceptable reason will be dropped from the squad. The DCC do not travel with the Cowboys team. They

only perform at home games and at the Super Bowl.

The DCC organization has complete control over all of its own activities. All requests for interviews, photographs and appearances are carefully screened. Hundreds of requests are rejected for a variety of factors deemed unsuitable by DCC standards. All appearances are arranged by contract, and if the stipulations are not met, the DCC do not appear. The client regulation list is long and demanding. When they are on overnight trips, at least one member of the administrative staff accompanies them. They travel in a group, return as a group and are not permitted to tour individually.

All the precautions are to protect the image of the Dallas Cowboys as a whole and the Cheerleaders as individuals. The Cowboys are a first class organization and the DCC are a reflection of that image.

For appearances where a fee is involved, the girls share the profit. However, most of their non-game activities are for charitable events. Appearances have included the Jerry Lewis Labor Day Telethon, The George Lindsey Celebrity Golf Tournament for Special Olympics, the Association for Hearing Impaired Children, Veterans Administration Hospitals across the country, nursing homes in the metroplex area, March of Dimes, American Heart Association, Arthritis Foundations, Cancer Society, United Way and a seven year association with the Variety Club Telethons in St. Louis, Los Angeles, Chicago and Winnipeg, Canada for handicapped children. For the past three years, the DCC have appeared on the Osmond family's Children's Miracle Network Telethon.

While serving as disciplinarian, mediator, consultant and administrator in all areas to the squad for 10 years, Director Suzanne Mitchell has probably come to know the mystique of the Dallas Cowboys Cheerleaders better than anyone else. "What we look for in our cheerleading squad is simply something for everyone," says Suzanne. "We want everyday ladies with that something special. They must be givers who understand that they have been given a gift and now have the opportunity to give to others. The organization offers them a chance to broaden their lives as they travel through the U.S. and around the world. They are able to put things in proper perspective and learn what is really important in life."

This unique group of young women has a deep responsibility as they assume a corporate identity without losing sight of themselves and strive to help make the world a little better through their commitment.

1985/86 Dallas Cowboys Cheerleaders

Keri Baird

Rhonda Borth

Deanna Childers

Cindee Doughty

Deborah Duffey

Beth Elias

Laci Folks

Vicki Foster

Tamara Fulton

Susan Goldi

Julee Graham

Eydie Guevara

Leslie Haynes

Peggy Kinn

Becky Kuhn

Debbie Lewis

Judy London

Barbara May

Lori Mock

Rena Morelli

Karen McCaghren

Natasha McCarley

Kelli McGonagill

Tiffany Pate

Gina Piazza

Mary Reynolds

Courtney Riggs

Sonja Samuel

Sheri Scholz

Kim Stevens

Kim Wiman

Kelly Zaloudek

ChaChis Ortiz

Cowboys Club Directory

General Partner: H. R. "Bum" Bright
President and General Manager: Texas E. Schramm
Vice President-Personnel Development: Gil Brandt
Vice President-Treasurer: Don Wilson
Vice President-Administration: Joe Bailey

Coaching:
Tom Landry — Head Coach
Jim Myers — Assistant Head Coach/Offensive Line
Neill Armstrong — Research & Development
Al Lavan — Running Backs
Alan Lowry — Special Teams
Dick Nolan — Receivers
Jim Shofner — Quarterbacks
Gene Stallings — Defensive Backs
Ernie Stautner — Defensive Coordinator/Defensive Line
Jerry Tubbs — Linebackers
Bob Ward — Conditioning
Marge Anderson — Secretary
Barbara Goodman — Secretary
Tula Johnapelus — Secretary

Scouting:
Bob Ferguson — Scout
Bob Griffin — Scout
Mike Hagen — Scout
Charlie Mackey — Scout
Dick Mansperger — Scout
Ron Marciniak — Scout
Jeff Smith — Scout
John Wooten — Scout
Walt Yowarsky — Scout
Lily McNally — Secretary
Hazel Nichols — Secretary

Medical:
Don Cochren — Trainer
Ken Locker — Assistant Trainer
Dr. Marvin P. Knight
Dr. J. Pat Evans
Dr. J. R. Zamorano

Counseling Services:
Larry Wansley — Director

Photography:
Bob Friedman — Director
Robert Blackwell — Assistant

Equipment:
Buck Buchanan — Manager
Jerry Fowler — Assistant
Otis Jackson — Assistant

Public Relations:
Doug Todd — Director
Greg Aiello — Media Services Marketing
Dave Pelletier — Assistant
Jerri Mote — Secretary

Administration:
Dan Werner — Business Manager
Jill Buckley — Secretary
Kathy Coleman — Accounting
Pat Miller — Accounting
Deana Patterson — Administrative Asst.

Ticket Office:
Steve Orsini — Ticket Manager
Ann Lloyd — Assistant Manager
Mary Reed — Assistant

Cheerleaders:
Suzanne Mitchell — Director
Shannon Werthmann — Choreographer
Judy Trammell — Choreographer
Debbie Bond — Asst. Director

Entertainment:
Jim Skinner — Halftime Director
Bill Lively — Band Director

Cowboys Weekly:
Steve Perkins — Editor
Carlton Stavers — Associate Editor
Peggie Bullock — Advertising Director
Sharon Carnahan — Circulation Manager
Cindy Brine — Advertising Sales

PLAYERS

Vince Albritton 36

Ht: 6-2, Wt: 209
Born: 7/23/62

Safety ★ Washington
2nd Year ★ FA for '84

One of the six '84 Dallas defensive backs who wasn't drafted out of college. Appeared in all 16 games on special teams and as a valuable contributor to the club's 4-0 defense. "He's big and strong, and there's a possibility he could become a linebacker," says Tom Landry. "He has the size and could put on some weight." Albritton played safety, linebacker and cornerback for the Washington Huskies. Games: '84 (16). Total: 16.

Dowe Aughtman 76

Ht: 6-3, Wt: 258
Born: 1/28/61

Guard ★ Auburn
2nd Year ★ D-11 for '84

Joined the Cowboys as a longshot defensive tackle candidate after being drafted in the 11th round in '84. That he made the team, finishing the season as a bright, young offensive guard prospect is a testament to his greatest quality — his competitive nature. Switched to offense in September of his rookie year after injuries decimated the offensive line. Highly aggressive. Two-time All-Southeastern Conference nose tackle at Auburn. Games: '84 (7). Total: 7.

Bill Bates 40

Ht: 6-1, Wt: 201
Born: 6/6/61

Safety ★ Tennessee
2nd Year ★ FA for '83

As a rookie free agent in '83, he made an immediate impact with his reckless style and earned a spot on the team. In his only start at strong safety last season vs. Indianapolis (10/28), he had a team-high 7 tackles, 1 interception, 1 sack, recovered a fumble and knocked down a pass. Saw more playing time final two games of '85 in Cowboys' 4-0 defense. In '84, was first NFC player to be named to Pro Bowl in newly created spot as non-returner on special teams. Games: '83 (16), '84 (12). Total: 28.

Jim Cooper 61

Ht: 6-5, Wt: 267
Born: 9/28/55

Tackle ★ Temple
9th Year ★ D-6 for '77

Cooper, perhaps the Cowboys' most consistently solid offensive lineman, probably would just as soon forget the '84 season. The night after the Cowboys lost their second straight to fall to 4-3, Cooper was at a Dallas restaurant with teammate Tom Rafferty and their wives. Cooper got up to leave the table, slipped on the hardwood floor and broke his ankle, causing him to miss the rest of the season. After surgery, Cooper had a good off-season conditioning program and should be ready for the '85 season. Games: '77 (14), '78 (14), '79 (15), '80 (15), '81 (16), '82 (9), '83 (16), '84 (7). Total: 106.

Brian Baldinger 62

Ht: 6-4, Wt: 258
Born: 1/7/59

Guard-Tackle ★ Duke
4th Year ★ FA for '82

Baldinger was a pleasant surprise in '84. All of his previous playing experience was at guard or center, when he suddenly became a tackle after Phil Pozderac was injured against Buffalo. Baldinger started at tackle the next two weeks and more than held his own. Earlier in the season, he started against St. Louis and Washington at guard for the injured Kurt Petersen. "Brian is a big asset to us because he can play tackle, guard or center," Tom Landry says. "He'll probably line up at tackle because he looked pretty good there last year." Games: '82 (4), '83 (16), '84 (16). Total: 36.

Dextor Clinkscale 47

Ht: 5-11, Wt: 189
Born: 4/13/58

Safety ★ South Carolina State
5th Year ★ FA for '80

Intelligent and instinctive football player. Earned starting strong safety position in '83 after two seasons as pass-defense specialist and one on injured reserve. Finished third on team in tackles and interceptions in '84 and tied for club lead in fumbles recovered. In '83, led the club in fumbles recovered, finished fifth in tackles and scored crucial TD in victory over the Giants (9/18). Games: '80 (16), '81 (IR), '82 (9), '83 (15), '84 (15). Total: 55.

Fred Cornwell 85

Ht: 6-6, Wt: 237
Born: 8/7/61

Tight End ★ Southern Cal
2nd Year ★ D-3 for '84

Billy Joe Dupree's retirement prior to last season left need for good backup tight end. Cornwell filled the void well, developing into a consistent second tight end for blocking purposes and dependable backup for Doug Cosbie. Although known mainly as a blocker, he stepped in for an injured Cosbie in second half against St. Louis (10/7) and caught his first NFL pass and first NFL TD. Saw most of his playing time on short yardage and goal line offenses. Games: '84 (14). Total: 14.

Doug Cosbie 84

Ht: 6-6, Wt: 235
Born: 2/27/56

Tight End ★ Santa Clara
7th Year ★ D-3 for '79

Big target, excellent hands. Broke his own club record for receptions by tight end in '85 with 60 catches, good enough for second in the NFC. In 1983, he broke by four Billy Joe Dupree's 1976 team record of 42 catches by a tight end, earning him a spot on his first Pro Bowl team. Took over starting position from Dupree in '82 and that year led NFC tight ends with 30 catches. Games: '79 (16), '80 (16), '81 (16), '82 (9), '83 (16), '84 (16). Total: 89.

John Dutton 78

Ht: 6-7, Wt: 267

Defensive Tackle ★ Nebraska
12th Year ★ Trade, Balt., '79

After six seasons as an All-Pro defensive end with the Baltimore Colts, Dutton has settled in and given a steady performance as the starting left tackle with the Cowboys. Reported to '84 training camp at 258 pounds — his lowest playing weight in 11 years. Had his best game of the season against Green Bay (9/23), when he recorded 7 tackles, 1½ sacks and knocked down a pass. Games: '74, (14 Balt.), '75 (14 Balt.), '76 (14 Balt.), '77 (12 Balt.), '78 (14 Balt.), '79 (8), '80 (16), '81 (16), '82 (9), '83 (16), '84 (16). Total: 149.

Steve DeOssie 55

Ht: 6-2, Wt: 248
Born: 11/22/62

2nd Year ★ D-4 for '84

"DeOssie improved as the season went on in 1984," Tom Landry said. "He's very bright, and as he plays in our system, he'll become better and better because he'll know where to be all the time. This is a quality that could make him a top linebacker." Appeared in all 16 games as a rookie, DeOssie contributed on special teams and earned a game ball for his efforts against Washington in December. Nicknamed "Barney Rubble" by his teammates, DeOssie is a rough-and-tumble player whose enthusiasm is contagious. He is the Cowboys' snapper on deep punts. Games: '84 (16). Total: 16.

Tony Dorsett 33

Ht: 5-11, Wt: 185
Born: 4/7/54

Running Back ★ Pittsburgh
9th Year ★ D-1 for '77

His place in NFL history already is assured, but Dorsett gives no indication his show is ready to close. Dorsett entered the '85 season 475 yards shy of becoming the sixth NFL rusher to gain 10,000 yards. In '84, he became the 15th NFL player to surpass 12,000 combined net yards gained. He has scored 69 TDs, seven short of Bob Hayes' club record of 76. He has rushed for 1,000 yards in seven of eight NFL seasons and in 13 of the 14 years he has played running back dating back to his junior year of high school. Games: '77 (14), '78 (16), '79 (14), '80 (15), '81 (16), '82 (9), '83 (16), '84 (16). Total: 116.

Michael Downs 26

Ht: 6-3, Wt: 195
Born: 6/9/59

Safety ★ Rice
5th Year ★ FA for '81

Enjoyed his finest season as a pro in '84, earning All-Pro and All-NFC honors, and, according to Tom Landry, "Everybody thought he should have gone to the Pro Bowl." For the fourth time in four years as a Cowboy, Downs started every game at free safety and led the secondary in tackles. For the third time in four years, Downs led the entire team in tackles, and for good measure, was the Cowboys' top pass interceptor with seven. He also had 3½ quarterback traps, knocked down 13 passes, forced three fumbles and recovered two. Games: '81 (15), '82 (9), '83 (16), '84 (16). Total: 56.

Ron Fellows 27

Ht: 6-0, Wt: 174
Born: 11/7/58

Cornerback ★ Missouri
5th Year ★ D-7A for '81

Won the starting right cornerback position in '84 after Dennis Thurman moved back to safety. Previously, he had been a regular on passing downs at right corner since the 11th game of his rookie year of '81. Has become recognized as one of the top "extra" defensive backs in the NFL. Considered a "heady" player with tremendous quickness. Had three interceptions in '84. Games: '81 (16), '82 (9), '83 (16), '84 (16). Total: 57.

Mike Hegman 58

Linebacker ★ Tennessee State
10th Year ★ D-7 for '75

Unheralded though he may be, Hegman has given the Cowboys solid outside linebacking for the past five years. Last season was his best, including career highs of three interceptions and 3½ quarterback traps and 71 tackles. Received game balls from coaching staff following victory over the Eagles and Colts. "Mike had a pretty solid year," Tom Landry says. "He played consistently and performed well. We feel pretty good about that." Games: '76 (14), '77 (14), '78 (16), '79 (16), '80 (16), '81 (11), '82 (9), '83 (16), '84 (16). Total: 128.

Ht: 6-1, Wt: 231
Born: 1/17/53

Tony Hill 80

Wide Receiver ★ Stanford
9th Year ★ D-3A for '77

Since becoming a starter in '78, Hill has established himself as one of the top receivers in the NFL. Despite missing five games due to injury in '84, Hill caught 58 passes — two short of his career high — and led team in receiving yardage for seventh straight season with 864 yards. Only injuries and players' strike have kept Hill from consecutive 1,000-yard receiving seasons. In '84, Hill injured shoulder in season opener against Rams and missed next five games. Games: '77 (14), '78 (16), '79 (16), '80 (16), '81 (16), '82 (9), '83 (12), '84 (11). Total: 110.

Ht: 6-2, Wt: 198
Born: 6/23/56

Gary Hogeboom 14

Quarterback ★ Central Michigan
6th Year ★ D-5 for '80

A focal point for the past two years of one of the NFL's hottest stories, the battle with Danny White for the starting QB job. After 4-year apprenticeship, he received his first chance last year when Tom Landry named him to open the season as a starter. Cowboys posted a 6-4 record in his 10 starts. In his debut against the Rams, he completed a club-record 33 passes in 47 attempts for 343 yards and a TD in a 20-13 come-from-behind victory. Games: '80 (2), '81 (1), '82 (4), '83 (6), '84 (10). Total: 29.

Ht: 6-4, Wt: 202
Born: 8/21/58

Jim Jeffcoat 77

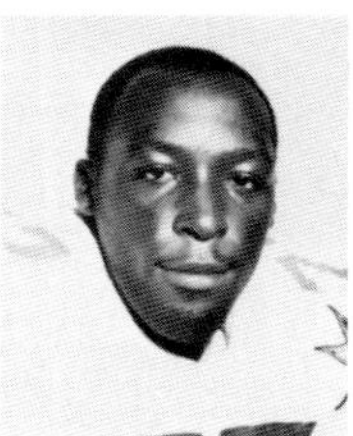

Defensive End ★ Arizona
3rd Year ★ D-1 for '83

Took over for retired Harvey Martin and appears to be settling in for a long stay. By the end of the '84 season, Jeffcoat ranked second on team with 11½ sacks. Biggest single play of '84 season for Jeffcoat was when he recovered a fumble in the endzone for the TD that tied the score at 27 with 2:52 to play, and eventually gave the Cowboys the chance to win in overtime, 30-27. "The thing that encouraged us a great deal in the defensive line last year was the progress of Jim Jeffcoat," Landry said. "He seemed to get better as the year went on. I see a bright future for him." Games: '83 (16), '84 (16). Total: 32.

Ht: 6-5, Wt: 257
Born: 4/1/61

Ed Jones 72

Defensive End ★ Tennessee State
11th Year ★ D-1A for '74

When opposing quarterbacks go back to pass, chances are they won't be throwing in the direction of "Too Tall." Batted down career-high 16 passes in '84, giving him 51 over the past five seasons (12 in '83, 2 in '82, 10 in '81, 11 in '80). Also had career-high 86 tackles last year to go along with eight traps and team-high five forced fumbles. Three-time Pro Bowler ('81-83), Jones was named All-Pro by NEA in '81 and AP in '82. In '83 he was AP and NEA second-team All-Pro and UPI and Pro Football Weekly All-NFC. Games: '74 (14), '75 (14), '76 (14), '77 (14), '78 (16), '79 (DNP), '80 (16), '81 (16), '82 (9), '83 (16), '84 (16). Total: 145.

Ht: 6-9, Wt: 287
Born: 2/23/51

James Jones

Running Back/Wide Receiver ★ Mississippi
5th Year ★ D-3B for '80

Most heartwarming story of the '84 season was Jones' comeback after being sidelined for nearly 2½ years by a knee injury. Activated for eighth game last year to replace injured tackle Jim Cooper. Used mostly as a receiver out of the backfield in passing situation. Caught 8-yard TD pass from Gary Hogeboom in victory at St. Louis (11/11), the first scoring reception of his career. In '81, Jones averaged a team-leading 5.3 yards per carry in his role as Tony Dorsett's backup. Games: '80 (16), '81 (16), '82 (5), '83 (IR), '84 (9). Total: 46.

Ht: 5-10, Wt: 189
Born: 12/6/58

Eugene Lockhart 56

Linebacker ★ Houston
2nd Year ★ D-6A for '84

Eugene "The Hitting Machine" proved invaluable in his rookie season, first filling in for and later taking over for injured middle linebacker Bob Breunig. Received his first pro start against Philadelphia, a game in which he led team in tackles and was voted defensive MVP by media. Started seven more games, averaging 10 tackles per start and led Cowboys linebackers in tackles. Named to All-Rookie team by UPI, Pro Football Writers Association, Pro Football Weekly and Football Digest. Games: '84 (15). Total: 15.

Ht: 6-2, Wt: 233
Born: 4/2/61

Timmy Newsome 30

Ht: 6-1, Wt: 232
Born: 5/17/58

Running Back ★ Winston-Salem State
6th Year ★ D-6 for '80

Took over as starting fullback with four games to go in '84 season. Against Washington, Newsome led the team in rushing with six carries for 48 yards and caught two passes for 22 yards. "With Newsome, we have a power runner who has a lot of ability that is really untapped," Landry said. "He has size and speed to go with his explosiveness. With that kind of talent, we could use the fullback more this year as a runner." Pound for pound the strongest man on the team (bench press 430 pounds). Good speed, excellent receiving hands. Games: '80 (16), '81 (15), '82 (9), '83 (16), '84 (15). Total: 71.

Steve Pelluer 16

Ht: 6-4, Wt: 210
Born: 7/29/62

2nd Year ★ D-5A for '84

A competent third-string quarterback who could develop into a future star. Didn't see any playing time during the '84 regular season, but when he was given his chance in preseason, he impressed the coaches. In fourth quarter vs. San Diego (8/11), Pelluer led the team 77 yards on 13 plays to a TD. Finished preseason nine of 15 (60 percent), for 69 yards, one TD and one interception. Drafted with a pick obtained from Tampa Bay for Danny Spradlin, who had beat out Steve's brother Scott, a Cowboys draft choice in '81. Games: '84 (1). Total: 1.

Kurt Petersen 65

Ht: 6-4, Wt: 267
Born: 6/17/57

Guard ★ Missouri
6th Year ★ D-4 for '80

Despite being a defensive lineman in college, Petersen has started at offensive guard four of his five seasons with the Cowboys. Past two years, he was bothered by injuries that forced him to miss a handful of games. Called the Cowboys' "blue-ribbon workhorse" by a Dallas newspaper, Petersen combines size, quickness, intelligence and unusual strength. Considered the strongest player overall on the team by conditioning coach Bob Ward. Spent his rookie year making the difficult switch from defense to offense. Games: '80 (16), '81 (16), '82 (9), '83 (14), '84 (13). Total: 68.

Phil Pozderac 75

Ht: 6-9, Wt: 276
Born: 12/19/59

Tackle ★ Notre Dame
4th Year ★ D-5 for '82

Pozderac's career has followed a steady ascent since he joined the team. In '84, Poz was named the starting left tackle before the opener after earning the position in training camp. Started the first seven games at left tackle before moving to right tackle for injured Jim Cooper. "Pozderac has come along very well," says Tom Landry. "He shows the potential we hoped he had." In '82, Poz started three of four preseason games and two regular-season games. Games: '82 (9), '83 (16), '84 (15). Total: 38.

Tom Rafferty 64

Ht: 6-3, Wt: 254
Born: 8/2/54

Center ★ Penn State
10th Year ★ D-4 for '76

Versatile and durable. Has started 60 of the Cowboys' 61 games at center since taking over job in '81. Starter at right guard for four years ('77-80), Rafferty was pressed into service at center when Robert Shaw went down with a knee injury in the second game of '81. Last season, Rafferty was the only offensive lineman to start every game. Has played in 124 straight games and has missed only one game in his career. Games: '76 (13), '77 (14), '78 (16), '79 (16), '80 (16), '81 (16), '82 (9), '83 (16), '84 (16). Total: 132.

Mike Renfro 82

Ht: 6-0, Wt: 188
Born: 6/19/55

Wide Receiver ★ Texas Christian
8th Year ★ Trade, Houston, '84

Acquired from Houston for Butch Johnson in spring of '84. Expected to play role as "possession" receiver in special situations for Cowboys. Performed beyond expectations, starting 11 games, catching 35 passes for 583 yards (16.7-yard average) and two TDs. Also threw a 49-yard TD pass to Doug Donley in 23-17 victory over Philadelphia. "No one could have asked for more than Mike Renfro gave us last year," Landry says. "He learned our system in a hurry, worked very hard and made a lot of key catches for us." Games: '78 (14 — Hou.), '79 (15 — Hous.), '80 (16 — Hou.), '81 (12 — Hou.), '82 (9 — Hou.), '83 (9 — Hou.), '84 (16 — Dallas). Total: 91.

Howard Richards 70

Ht: 6-6, Wt: 260
Born: 8/7/59

Guard-Tackle ★ Missouri
5th Year ★ D-1 for '81

Last year was supposed to be the year Richards took over starting position and became the newest star in the Cowboys' offensive line. But injuries turned '84 into a year of frustration for the talented lineman. Battled a groin injury throughout training camp and found himself in a backup role when the season began. Took over starting left tackle spot for the New Orleans game (10/21) after Phil Pozderac moved to right tackle for injured Jim Cooper. After four games, he injured his leg and missed the rest of the season. Games: '81 (16), '82 (8), '83 (16), '84 (11). Total: 51.

Jeff Rohrer 50

Ht: 6-3, Wt: 225
Born: 12/25/58

Linebacker ★ Yale
4th Year ★ D-2 for '82

One of the Cowboys' best special teams players. Also plays linebacker in short-yardage and goal-line situations. Began '85 season hoping to win starting job. Primarily an outside linebacker, although he has worked in the middle. After outside linebacker Billy Cannon suffered a career-ending injury in the season's eighth game, Rohrer moved back outside to provide depth. "Jeff needs to move forward and challenge the outside linebackers and become a starter," Tom Landry says. Games: '82 (8), '83 (16), '84 (16). Total: 40.

Brian Salonen 89

Ht: 6-2, Wt: 227
Born: 7/29/61

Tight End ★ Montana
2nd Year ★ D-10 for '84

Appeared in all 16 games in '84, mostly on special teams. Won a game ball for his performance against New England. In training camp '85, was expected to battle fellow second-year man Fred Cornwell and possibly USFL newcomer Todd Fowler for the backup tight end position behind Pro Bowler Doug Cosbie. "Of the two youngsters, Cornwell and Salonen, Brian might be the better receiver because he has a little more quickness and movement," Landry says. "Both show promise, and both can play in our system and play well." Games: '84 (16). Total: 16.

Victor Scott 22

Ht: 5-11, Wt: 196
Born: 6/1/62

Cornerback ★ Colorado
2nd Year ★ D-2 for '84

A talented young athlete who gives the Cowboys depth at cornerback and safety. The 40th player selected in the '84 draft, Scott saw action in 16 games last year on specialty teams and as an extra defensive back on passing downs. His diving, fourth-quarter interception of a deflected pass at St. Louis (11/11) marked his first interception of his career and set up the winning TD in one of the Cowboys' biggest victories of the season. Games: '84 (16). Total: 16.

Rafael Septien 1

Ht: 5-10, Wt: 180
Born: 12/12/53

Kicker ★ Southwest Louisiana
9th Year ★ FA for '78

Entering his 9th season in the NFL, Septien had established himself as one of the most productive and consistent kickers in the game's history. The '84 campaign was typical for Septien — 102 points on 23-of-29 field goal kicking (79.3 percent) and 33-of-34 extra points. He kicked the second longest field goal of his career, a 52-yarder at Los Angeles in the season-opening victory over the Rams. Inside the 40, Septien is amazing. His career totals from 39 yards and closer are 110-of-123 for 89.4 percent. Games: '77 (14 — L.A.), '78 (16 — Dallas), '79 (16 — Dallas), '80 (16 — Dallas), '81 (16 — Dallas), '82 (9 — Dallas), '83 (16), '84 (16). Total: 120 (106 — Dallas).

Don Smerek  60

Ht: 6-7, Wt: 255
Born: 12/20/57

Defensive Tackle ★ Nevada-Reno
4th Year ★ FA for '80

Entering '84 training camp, Smerek was heir apparent to retired Harvey Martin's right end position. But due to Randy White's holdout, Smerek was moved to White's right tackle position, where he started all four preseason games. After White's return before the season opener, Smerek was never able to catch up at right end. Spent the rest of '84 season playing left tackle in passing situations for John Dutton. "Don Smerek's season was hurt last year somewhat by circumstances," Landry says. "He never got a chance to compete at right end, and I think this was a mental setback for him." Games: '81 (2), '82 (7), '83 (15), '84 (16). Total: 40.

Glen Titensor 63

Ht: 6-4, Wt: 264
Born: 2/21/58

Guard ★ Brigham Young
5th Year ★ D-3 for '81

Quietly moved into the starting left guard position last year and performed consistently well the rest of the season. After starting the last three preseason games in place of injured Herb Scott at left guard, Glen started the first regular-season game of his pro career in the opener against the Rams (9/3). Claimed starting left guard position before the St. Louis game (11/7) and stayed there the remaining 11 games. "Glen came along extremely well last season in his first year as a starter," Landry says. "He was a bright spot on the offensive line last year. He shows great promise." Games: '81 (16), '82 (3), '83 (15), '84 (15). Total: 49.

Dennis Thurman 32

Ht: 5-11, Wt: 175
Born: 4/13/56

Safety ★ Southern Cal
8th Year ★ D-11 for '78

Key man in the Cowboys' go-for-broke attacking secondary. After starting at cornerback for three seasons, Thurman was listed behind All-Pro Michael Downs at free safety on the 84 depth chart. But with Cowboys using six and seven defensive backs most of the season, Thurman logged almost as much playing time as he ever had. He is a big-play man in the secondary. He ranks No. 5 on the team's all-time list of interceptors and is third-leading pass interceptor in NFL playoff history. Never missed a game in his seven years as a pro. Games: '78 (16), '79 (16), '80 (16), '81 (16), '82 (9), '83 (16), '84 (16). Total: 105.

Mark Tuinei 71

Ht: 6-5, Wt: 274
Born: 3/31/60

Center ★ Hawaii
3rd Year ★ FA for '83

With a strong need to develop offensive line depth, Cowboys decided in the off-season to move Tuinei from defensive lineman to offensive center. Cowboys hope with Tuinei they will be able to duplicate the past success they have had in making such conversions. One of the team's strongest players and possesses the quick feet and overall athletic ability necessary to succeed as an offensive lineman. Spent first two seasons backing up the defensive end and tackle positions plus contributing on special teams and short-yardage defenses. Games: '83 (10), '84 (16). Total: 26.

Everson Walls 24

Cornerback ★ Grambling
5th Year ★ FA for '81

Ht: 6-1, Wt: 190
Born: 12/28/59

Four years ago, Walls was struggling to make the team. Now, he's a certified star, with All-Pro and Pro Bowl credentials to bolster the claim. Improbable perhaps, but Walls has shown a knack for defying the odds. Named to the Pro Bowl his first three seasons, and owns the Pro Bowl career record of four interceptions, two in each of his first two appearances. All-Rookie choice in '81, consensus All-Pro in '82, AP All-Pro in '83 and UPI All-NFC selection in '84. Only player to lead league in interceptions twice and only second player to lead NFL two years in a row. Games: '81 (16), '82 (9), '83 (16), '84 (16). Total: 57.

Danny White 11

Quarterback ★ Arizona State
10th Year ★ D-3A for '74

Ht: 6-2, Wt: 197
Born: 2/9/52

After four years as the starting quarterback, White found himself backing up Gary Hogeboom for almost two-thirds of the '84 season. Moved back into No. 1 spot for the final four games. "If you finish the season as a starter, you go into training camp as the starter," Landry says. "That's been our policy, and we'll just have to see how it goes from there." Through '84, the Cowboys were 48-21 (69.6 percent) when White started at quarterback. Owns or shares 10 club passing records. Games: '76 (14), '77 (14), '78 (16), '79 (16), '80 (16), '81 (16), '82 (9), '83 (16), '84 (14). Total: 131.

Randy White 54

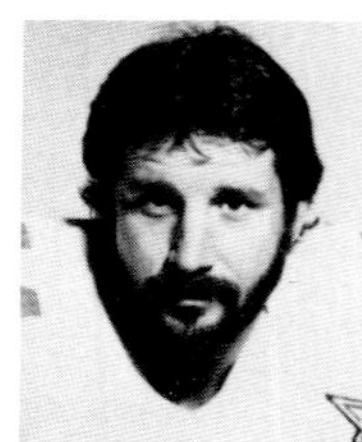

Defensive Tackle ★ Maryland
11th Year ★ D-1A for '84

Ht: 6-4, Wt: 260
Born: 1/15/53

Much to the dismay of opposing coaches and linemen, this Pro Bowler is improving with age. Coming off best two years since becoming starter in '77. Led team in '84 for second straight year with 12½ sacks and was second on team with 108 tackles. All-Pro for club-record seven straight years, breaking record held with Hall of Famer Bob Lilly. "Randy is the premiere defensive tackle in the business," says Tom Landry. Games: '75 (14), '76 (14), '77 (14), '78 (16), '79 (15), '80 (16), '81 (16), '82 (9), '83 (16), '84 (16). Total: 146.

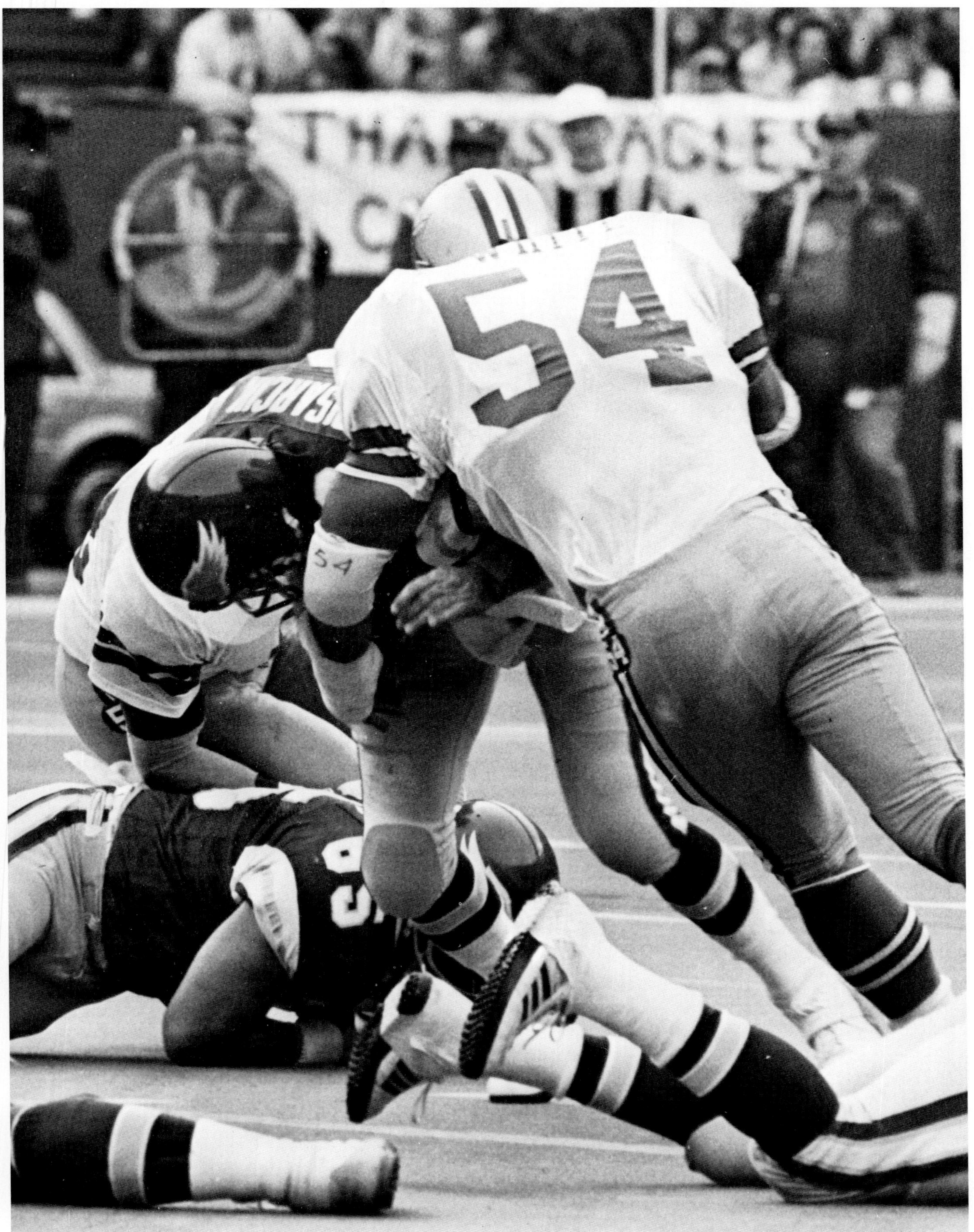
54
54

The Player Lottery

1985 DRAFT

Eternal optimists among Dallas Cowboys fans will — before examining the 1985 rookie crop — think back to the last time the ball club did not make the playoffs, and then recall what followed immediately: The Dirty Dozen, and a return to the Super Bowl war.

Indeed, the way the NFL draft was designed to work, there is supposed to be a reward for teams resting on the lower rungs of the ladder. So an 8-6 record as in 1974, and a 9-7 record 10 years later, it says here, enables you to pick a better crop of athletes.

There were 15 draftees in the Cowboys' 12 rounds this time, and with another 80 or more free agents expected, as usual, at Thousand Oaks, California training camp, it is not beyond the realm of hope that another dozen, dirty or not, will make the final roster. (A Baker's Dozen made it last year.)

Due to the aborted effort to trade upward in the draft to select wide receiver Eddie Brown of Miami, a trade which surely would have meant surrender of the club's second-round choice, approximately 20 of those free agents will be prospective pass catchers along the outer limits. The good news about the Mission Eddie Brown failure is that Dallas was able to draft defensive end Kevin Brooks of Michigan and linebacker Jesse Penn of Virginia Tech. (See "blessing in disguise," the Tex Schramm interview.)

The first thing that had to be settled about Brooks was his height, which, so it seems, is not likely to be settled at all. Michigan's press brochure listed him at 6-5 for the 1984 season, and so did ESPN's draft-day reports. But the Cowboys are sticklers about height, weight and speed in the 40, and they "knew" he was 6-6½″ when they drafted him. So Brooks shows up at his first press conference and labels himself 6-7. Don't hold your breath. Real Dallas trivia buffs know that Calvin Hill gained an inch in height *after* his Cowboys rookie year.

Aside from that point of confusion, there are several things about Brooks that are very clear. He is a polished and poised fellow, and at Michigan he was disciplined both on the football field and in the classroom. He could have played another season for the Wolverines due to a redshirt year, but he was strong enough academically to choose taking his communications degree this June on a four-year schedule.

And if Ed Jones retires to his music booking business in a year or so, Brooks might be the Cowboys' next too-tall pass rusher.

All of the amateur or semi-amateur gurus of the college draft, including *Sports Illustrated*, had Brooks tabbed to be selected in the first 10 choices. Gil Brandt, the Dallas vice-president of personnel, knows why Brooks was held in such high regard.

"He's an outstanding pass rusher," says Brandt, "and that's the hardest thing there is to find today, somebody who can rush the passer. Because the rules permit extension of arms by offensive linemen, the guy who can rush the passer now is not usually a big guy, because a big guy wouldn't be quick or agile enough. So the guys that are doing a good job rushing the passer are the Richard Dents (Chicago) and people like that who weigh 235 pounds. But Brooks looks as though he has the athletic ability to play the run and also be very good against the pass.

And if Ed Jones retires to his music booking business in a year or so, Brooks might be the Cowboys' next too-tall pass rusher.

"I think, for example, he has more athletic ability than Jim Jeffcoat. Jim Jeffcoat has great desire. I think if you could test Jim Jeffcoat's desire, he would rate up there with Roger Staubach.

"But this guy has the athletic ability to rush the passer, and at that size, he's pretty imposing."

There is a dimension to these men other than their physical qualities, however, as Cowboys people recall from the rookie-camp days of Harvey Martin. Martin was just naturally too good-natured for his own good until he had a heart-to-heart talk with Coach Ernie Stautner and then at practice that afternoon punched out an offensive lineman. Brooks, too, seems a gentle sort of fellow.

"There is some of that about him," Brandt admits. "But he gets after people, too. He played well against Ohio State and he played well against Brigham Young (Brooks was also defensive player of the game against both Washington and Iowa), but I tell you what happens to a lot of young guys. As they mature and get older, then they start to get a tougher personality. Growing up they are so much bigger than anybody else — when Kevin's classmates were 5-6 and 5-7, he was 6-2.

"Incidentally, (Don) Shula called me the week after the draft and told me he tried to trade up to get Kevin Brooks. Shula also said he had Jesse Penn as the best linebacker in the draft. So did Forrest (Gregg)."

Having cited two head coaches who do not flap their lips merely to create a breeze, let us let it be known that Cowboys linebacker coach Jerry Tubbs had Penn rated at least the best outside linebacker in the draft.

Tom Landry even waxed uncharacteristically enthusiastic over the selection of Penn: "He plays like a linebacker is supposed to play. On film you see him drop back into pass coverage, he gets in the face of the tight end, he pursues, he goes for the ball, he tackles."

Penn further endeared himself to the Cowboys by being both the first draftee to sign a contract and the first to move to Dallas and begin working out with the veterans in early May.

"Jesse Penn," says Brandt, "has got the ability to shed the blocker and to cover the pass. Lots of times players are strong enough to get rid of the

blocker on a run play but aren't fast enough to cover the pass. I think Penn has got a chance to play a lot for us this year. For two reasons — he was down in Dallas early and working, which was a good sign, and the other thing is, when you play as much a passing situation now as you do, that's easiest for him to do, so I think he may play a lot."

The Cowboys' third-round selection was something of an anomaly. Only a week before the draft, Landry told a Dallas newspaperman that "we don't pick a lot of huge offensive linemen, because we don't run those kind of plays."

And yet, the Cowboys' third pick was 290-pound Crawford Ker of Florida, advertised at 6-3. (Closer to 6-4, says Brandt.)

"Coming out of high school," says Brandt, who has probably checked this kid all the way to the cradle, "he was only a 200-pound offensive lineman, so Florida didn't recruit him. But he really liked Florida, and he got his dad to pay his way out to Arizona to go to junior college. In effect, his dad gave him a one-way bus ticket and said, 'Don't come back without a scholarship.' And, of course, he went out there and got big and Florida finally took him. He's strong, and he's not fat. He's got a huge frame. He was what Florida calls their 'power champion' in lifting weights."

In response to that description, offensive line coach Jim Myers said, "I want to see him bench-press 515. The only guy around here who bench-pressed 500 was Randy White and he was struggling."

A few sidelights also embellish the fourth-round selection, the 6-0, 195-pound running back Robert Lavette out of Georgia Tech. He has been the most productive player in the long and storied history of Georgia Tech football, a program that has not exactly been starting chopped liver at running back the last 65 years. Lavette gained 4,006 yards at Tech, to rank 17th on the all-time NCAA list, and was also the school's best career receiver and scorer.

"And," says Brandt, "he's productive in big games. I mean, he gains 175 yards against North Carolina and he gains it against Georgia. You know, a lot of times

runners will gain 700 hundred yards against real poor teams in their conference, and then when they play the good teams they gain 38 yards, 55 yards. But this guy is really an excellent competitor. The other thing about him is he's a guy who really loves the Cowboys. Signing with us is kind of his dream."

The seemingly last burst in the Roman candle of draft choices was a big starburst, the selection of Herschel Walker, against the day the United States Football League is no longer in business. The Cowboys now own the NFL rights to Walker for the next four years. After that, should another NFL team try to sign him, Dallas has the right to match the offer and sign him.

The rest of the story — in truth, probably almost all of it — is a lottery. And only the weeks in Thousand Oaks, and perhaps the games of the pre-season, will fill in the numbers, lucky or not.

1985 DRAFT

ROUND	PLAYER	POS.	HT.	WT.	COLLEGE
1 (17)	Kevin Brooks	DE	6-7	262	Michigan
2 (44)	Jesse Penn	LB	6-2	222	Virginia Tech
3 (76)	Crawford Ker	G	6-4	293	Florida
4 (103)	Robert Lavette	RB	5-11	192	Georgia Tech
5A (114)	Herschel Walker	RB	6-1	224	Georgia
5B (119)	Matt Darwin	C-G	6-4	260	Texas A&M
6A (144)	Kurt Ploeger	DT	6-5	265	Gustavus Adolphus
6B (157)	Matt Moran	G	6-4	265	Stanford
7A (178)	Karl Powe	WR	6-2	177	Alabama State
7B (184)	Jim Herrman	DE	6-5	255	BYU
8 (216)	Leon Gonzales	WR	5-10	158	Bethune-Cookman
9 (243)	Scott Strasburger	LB	6-2	204	Nebraska
10 (270)	Joe Jones	TE	6-4	247	Virginia Tech
11 (297)	Neal Dellocono	LB	6-0	219	UCLA
12 (324)	Karl Jordan	LB	6-1	244	Vanderbilt

Robert Lavette

Running Back ★ Georgia Tech ★ D-4

Finished his career as Georgia Tech's all-time leading rusher, receiver and scorer. In setting 19 school records in four seasons, Lavette rushed for 4,066 yards, No. 17 on the NCAA's all-time list. Caught 114 career passes for 862 yards and scored 46 TDs for 276 points. Had 18 100-yard games and accounted for 5,393 total yards, an average of 125.5 per game. A big-play performer.

Ht: 5-11, Wt: 192
Born: 9/8/63

Kevin Brooks

Defensive End ★ Michigan ★ D-1

Began his career at Michigan as a 6-4, 215-pound linebacker before maturing into a defensive lineman with a rare combination of size and speed. After spending his freshman year at outside linebacker, Brooks was switched to defensive tackle and became a 3-year starter at that position. The Cowboys will try him first at defensive end. Observers agree that he could be better in the pros than he was in college because he is still filling out and maturing. He is not expected to be an impact player, but has the potential to become a regular at defensive end.

Ht: 6-7, Wt: 262
Born: 2/9/63

Herschel Walker

Running Back ★ Georgia ★ D-5A

One of the greatest college running backs of all time. Led Georgia to the national championship his freshman year. Under contract through the 1989 season with the New Jersey Generals of the United States football League. Cowboys for four years hold the NFL right to sign Walker, plus a right of first refusal thereafter.

Ht: 6-1, Wt: 224
Born: 3/3/62

Jesse Penn

Linebacker ★ Virginia Tech ★ D-2

An exceptional athlete who roamed the Virginia Tech defense from the line of scrimmage to the secondary, making sacks, tackles and interceptions. A 2-year starter at standup defensive end, Penn excelled at pass coverage, finishing his career with eight interceptions, a school record for linemen. Exciting performer who is capable of making the big plays. Started every game the last two seasons. Had 65 tackles his senior year to go with five interceptions, eight passes broken up, two sacks and two fumble recoveries.

Ht: 6-2, Wt: 222
Born: 9/6/62

Matt Darwin

Center-Guard ★ Texas A&M ★ D-5B

Versatile offensive lineman for the Aggies, playing center, guard and tackle during his college career. A freshman All-America at tackle in '81, then moved to center, but also saw action at guard. A&M's top offensive lineman last year. Cowboys' offensive line coach Jim Myers coached Matt's father, Bill, in 1958-59 when Myers was head coach at A&M.

Ht: 6-4, Wt: 260
Born: 3/11/63

Crawford Ker

Offensive Guard ★ Florida ★ D-3

The trend today is toward mammoth offensive linemen, and Ker definitely fits the bill. A Western Arizona Junior College All-America, Ker transferred to Florida and started 13 games at tackle, earning second-team All-Southeastern Conference and honorable mention All-America honors from Associated Press in 1984. Strong, holds the Florida bench press record of 515 pounds. He also has leg-pressed 1,090 pounds. Has incredible speed (5.0 in the 40) for his size. Very hard worker.

Ht: 6-4, Wt: 293
Born: 5/5/62

Kurt Ploeger

Defensive Tackle ★ Gustavus Adolphus ★ D-6A

Dominant player on the small college level. Hurdler on the track team in college before deciding to concentrate on football. Two-time small college All-America. Led team with 113 tackles (45 solos), 11 sacks and blocked four passes.

Ht: 6-5, Wt: 265
Born: 12/1/62

Matt Moran

Guard ★ Stanford ★ D-6B

Two-time All-Pac 10 honorable mention choice. Finished his college career with 35 consecutive starts, so durability is a plus. Started 43 out of possible 44 games in college. Played left tackle his freshman year.

Ht: 6-4, Wt: 265
Born: 5/14/62

Scott Strasburger

Linebacker ★ Nebraska ★ D-9

Walkon as a freshman. Played standup defensive end at Nebraska, but is projected as an outside linebacker with the Cowboys. Two-time Academic All-America and also won a National Football Hall of Fame scholarship for post-graduate studies in medicine. All-Big Eight in '84.

Ht: 6-2, Wt: 204
Born: 2/14/63

Karl Powe

Wide Receiver ★ Alabama State ★ D-7A

Something of a mystery man. Ran track in college in the sprints and never participated in spring football workouts. As a result, he played backup most of his career. He has 4.4 speed in the 40. Caught 16 passes last season for 314 yards and two TDs. Returned 11 kickoffs for 300 yards.

Ht: 6-2, Wt: 177
Born: 1/17/62

Joe Jones

Tight End ★ Virginia Tech ★ D-10

Improved his draft position with solid performance in the Senior Bowl. Good receiver who rarely drops a catchable pass. Runs a 4.8 40. Led Virginia Tech with 39 catches in '84.

Ht: 6-4, Wt: 247
Born: 6/26/62

Jim Herrmann

Defensive End ★Brigham Young ★ D-7B

Sprouted from a 195-pound freshman into a 255-pound senior co-captain who helped lead BYU to its first national championship. Voted first team All-Western Athletic Conference and honorable mention All-America. Grandfather was John Smith, a Grantland Rice All-America lineman for University of Pennsylvania in 1927.

Ht: 6-5, Wt: 255
Born: 10/20/62

Neal Dellocono

Linebacker ★ UCLA ★ D-11

Three-year starter at outside linebacker, senior co-captain and one of UCLA's most honored players. Earned third-team All-America honors in '84. Led Bruins with nine quarterback traps and caused three fumbles. Started the final 35 games of his career.

Ht: 6-0, Wt: 219
Born: 6/1/63

Leon Gonzales

Wide Receiver ★ Bethune-Cookman ★ D-8

Despite his diminutive size, "Speedy" posted impressive numbers the past two seasons, catching 99 passes for 1,659 yards and 15 TDs. Earned All-Mideastern Athletic Conference honors both years. Last year, he led the MEAC in receiving with 56 receptions for 941 yards and nine TDs.

Ht: 5-10, Wt: 158
Born: 9/21/63

Karl Jordan

Linebacker ★ Vanderbilt ★ D-12

Starter at five different positions during college career. Projected as a middle linebacker prospect by the Cowboys. Earned second-team All-Southeastern Conference honors at defensive tackle last year after leading Vanderbilt in quarterback traps with 4½ and tackles for losses with 10 for 50 yards. Exceptionally strong.

Ht: 6-1, Wt: 244
Born: 1/12/63

COACHES

The Landry Years

The longest-running show in professional sports — "Tom Landry Presents the Dallas Cowboys" — entered its 26th season in 1985.

Landry has been known to point out that he never has received a promotion during those 26 years, but it is an arrangement that has worked out well for all concerned.

The first 25 years gave Landry and the Cowboys a combined record of 243 victories, 141 losses and six ties. Those numbers placed the 61-year-old native Texan second only to George Halas among the National Football League's all-time winningest coaches.

Along the way, Landry has led the Cowboys to a record 19 consecutive winning seasons, the longest such active streak in pro sports and the third longest ever behind the New York Yankees' 39 straight from 1926 through 1964 and the Montreal Canadiens' 32 in a row (1952-83).

The Cowboys have made 17 trips to the NFL playoffs, including a league-record nine straight from 1975 through 1983. They've won 12 division championships and five NFC titles for a record five Super Bowl appearances.

Landry's team won world championships with victories over Miami in Super Bowl VI and Denver in Super Bowl XII.

The Cowboys haven't had a season in which they lost more games than they won since 1964, when the record was 5-8-1. On Feb. 5 of that year, Landry had signed a 10-year contract, establishing himself as a master of good timing.

He also is recognized as an innovator. He introduced the "flex" defense and the multiple offense in the 1960s, revived and restructured the shotgun offense (or "spread" in Dallas terminology) in the 1970s and is in the forefront of "situation substitutions" on both offense and defense in the 1980s.

For Landry, a bomber pilot in World War II, the most important quality a coach must possess is leadership.

"Leadership is a matter of having people look at you and gain confidence," he says. "If you're in control, they're in control."

YEAR	W	L	T	YEAR	W	L	T
1960	0	11	1	*1972	10	4	0
1961	4	9	1	*1973	10	4	0
1962	5	8	1	1974	8	6	0
1963	4	10	0	*1975	10	4	0
1964	5	8	1	*1976	11	3	0
1965	7	7	0	*1977	12	2	0
*1966	10	3	1	*1978	12	4	0
*1967	9	5	0	*1979	11	5	0
*1968	12	2	0	*1980	12	4	0
*1969	11	2	1	*1981	12	4	0
*1970	10	4	0	*1982	6	3	0
*1971	11	3	0	*1983	12	4	0
				*1984	9	7	0
				TOTALS	223	126	6

*Qualified for Playoffs (Won Super Bowl VI on Jan. 16, 1972; won Super Bowl XII on Jan. 15, 1978). Landry is 20-15 in playoff games.

THE TOP 20 WINNINGEST COACHES

(At the start of the 1985 season)

		CAREER			
Coach	Teams	Won	Lost	Tied	Pct.
1. **George Halas**	Bears	326	150	30	.674
2. **Tom Landry**	Cowboys	243	141	6	.631
3. **Don Shula**	Colts, Dolphins	242	94	6	.716
4. **Curly Lambeau**	Packers, Cardinals, Redskins	234	135	23	.626
5. **Paul Brown**	Browns (AAFC and NFL), Bengals	222	112	9	.660
6. **Bud Grant**	Vikings	161	99	5	.617
7. **Chuck Noll**	Steelers	157	95	1	.623
8. **Steve Owen**	Giants	154	108	17	.582
9. **Hank Stram**	Chiefs, Saints	136	100	10	.573
10. **Weeb Ewbank**	Colts, Jets	134	130	7	.507
11. **Sid Gillman**	Rams, Chargers, Oilers	123	104	7	.541
12. **Chuck Knox**	Rams, Bills, Seahawks	119	71	1	.626
13. **George Allen**	Rams, Redskins	118	54	5	.681
14. **John Madden**	Raiders	112	39	7	.731
15. **Buddy Parker**	Cardinals, Lions, Steelers	107	76	9	.581
16. **Don Coryell**	Cardinals, Chargers	105	74	1	.586
17. **Vince Lombardi**	Packers, Redskins	105	35	6	.740
18. **Lou Saban**	Patriots, Bills, Broncos	97	100	7	.493
19. **Jimmy Conzelman**	Independents, Badgers, Panthers, Steam Roller, Cardinals	89	68	17	.560
20. **Bum Phillips**	Oilers, Saints	82	72	0	.532

71

Neill Armstrong

Research and Development

Joined the Cowboys in '82, bringing 27 years of coaching experience, including 10 as a head coach. Studies and evaluates all players and teams in the league. His reports provide the basis for the formulation of the Cowboys' game plans. Compiled 30-34 record in four seasons as head coach of the Chicago Bears (1978-81). Directed the Bears to the playoffs in '79 with a 10-6 finish. Assistant coach with the Minnesota Vikings for nine years before joining Bears.

Dick Nolan

Receivers

Returned to the Cowboys, where he was a player-coach in '62 and defensive coach from 1963-67, as receivers coach in '82. Served as head coach of San Francisco 49ers from 1968-1975, where his teams won NFC West championship in '70, '71 and '72. NFC coach of the year in '70. Joined New Orleans as linebackers coach in '77 and was head coach of the Saints from 1978-80. Worked as linebackers coach for Houston Oilers in '81. Teammates with Landry in New York Giants defensive backfield in 1954-55.

Al Lavan

Running Backs

Spent eight years coaching in college and pros before joining Cowboys in '80. Helped Cowboys' running game remain one of the most feared in the NFL. Tony Dorsett, Ron Springs and Timmy Newsome have matured under his tutelage. Coached running backs at Stanford in '79 after two years at Georgia Tech handling receivers and running backs. Coached defensive backs and special teams for Atlanta Falcons in 1975-76. Played defensive back for Philadelphia Eagles in '68 and Atlanta in 1969-70.

Alan Lowry

Special Teams

Named to Cowboys staff in '82 after five seasons as defensive backfield coach at his alma mater, the University of Texas. One of the few football players in Southwest Conference history to earn All-Conference honors on defense, as defensive back in 1970-71, and offense, as quarterback in '72. Served as assistant coach at Virginia Tech before moving to the University of Wyoming. Spent one year in Cowboys' scouting department before joining UT staff.

Jim Myers

Assistant Head Coach * Offensive Line

Has consistently produced impressive offensive lines for Cowboys with numerous All-Pro and Pro Bowl players to his credit, including Ralph Neely, John Niland, Rayfield Wright, Blaine Nye, Herb Scott and Pat Donovan. Has a talent for converting college defensive linemen into top NFL offensive linemen. Joined Cowboys in '62 after serving as head coach at Iowa State in '57 and Texas A&M, where he also was athletic director. His 24 years with Cowboys gives him longest tenure on coaching staff besides Landry.

Jim Shofner

Quarterbacks

Former NFL assistant coach with Houston, Cleveland and San Francisco, as well as head coach at TCU, his alma mater. Joined the Cowboys in '83. Outstanding all-around athlete. Turned down pro baseball offer to play defensive back for Cleveland Browns (1958-63). Defensive backfield coach at San Francisco in '67, but switched to coaching receivers and quarterbacks in 1968 when Nolan became head coach. Coached quarterbacks for Browns from 1977-79. Houston Oilers' offensive coordinator 1981-82.

Gene Stallings

Defensive Backfield

Has turned Cowboys' secondary into an effective unit despite working primarily with free agents and low-round draft choices. Joined Cowboys in '72 after seven seasons (1965-72) as head coach of his alma mater, Texas A&M. Presided over development of three All-Pros — Charlie Waters, Cliff Harris, Everson Walls, and Michael Downs. All-Southwest Conference receiver under Bear Bryant. Served as assistant to Bryant at Alabama until returning to A&M as head coach.

Bob Ward

Conditioning

Has Cowboys players participating in innovative conditioning programs, which include aerobic conditioning, weightlifting, flexibility training and nutrition. Directs Cowboys' voluntary off-season conditioning program by working with computers and emphasizing futuristic concepts, using biomechanics to devise individual programs for each player. Coached track for 11 years at Fullerton College before joining Cowboys in '75. Trained in martial arts and applied those concepts to football.

Ernie Stautner

Defensive Coordinator * Defensive Line

Builds consistently excellent defenses and All-Pro linemen like Bob Lilly, George Andrie, Harvey Martin, Randy White, Ed Jones and John Dutton. Joined Cowboys in '66. Fabled "Doomsday Defense" began to emerge shortly after. Fashioned "Doomsday II," which carried Cowboys to second Super Bowl title in '77. All-Pro defensive end and tackle with Pittsburgh Steelers (1950-64). Veteran of nine Pro Bowls and elected to Hall of Fame in '69, his first year of eligibility.

Don Cochren

Trainer

Joined Cowboys in '65 after experience in college, military and Canadian Football League training. The Purdue graduate earned physical therapy certificate at Pennsylvania. Trainer at Case Institute (now Case-Western Reserve) in Cleveland for two years, with Toronto Argonauts of the CFL for four years and at University of New Hampshire for one year before coming to Dallas. One of 28 trainers selected to serve the U.S. team at '80 Winter Olympics.

Ken Locker

Assistant Trainer

Works with Cochren and supervises Cowboys' medical rehabilitation program. Came to Cowboys in '73 after four years as assistant trainer and interim head trainer at North Texas State University. Received master's degree in physical education from Texas Woman's University. Served two years as trainer of World Championship Tennis, making the men's tour in '75 and '76. In '82 served as trainer for NBC's "Survival of the Fittest" competition in New Zealand.

Jerry Tubbs

Linebackers

Only original Cowboys player still with the club. Came to Dallas in '60 expansion from San Francisco 49ers and became Cowboys' first starting middle linebacker and only one of four in club history. Cowboys' first All-Pro and Pro Bowl linebacker ('62). Coached four Pro Bowl linebackers in Dallas — Breunig, Jordan, Chuck Howley and Thomas Henderson. All-America center-linebacker for Bud Wilkinson's unbeaten Oklahoma teams (1954-56). Walter Camp Award winner in '56 as nation's outstanding player.

Buck Buchanan

Equipment Manager

Joined the Cowboys in '73 after supervising athletic programs in the Air Force for 20 years. Served as noncommissioned officer in charge of athletics and programs at U.S. Air Force Academy Prep School in Colorado Springs for four years. Awarded Bronze Star for performance during 1968-69 tour of duty in Thailand.

T. RANDALL
63
DALLAS
COWBOYS

The All-Time

DALLAS COWBOYS Records & Statistics

Historical Highlights

1960

NFL FRANCHISE — Clint Murchison, Jr., and Bedford Wynne were awarded an expansion franchise in the NFL at the annual league meeting in Miami Beach, Fla. The Cowboys were to play as a "swing" team, playing every other team one time during the first season, although listed in the Western Conference standings (January 28).

COWBOYS STOCKED — A player pool was set up in a league meeting at L.A., with each of 12 NFL teams freezing 25 names on its roster and the Cowboys allowed to pick three from each team for a total of 36 veterans. Dallas, once given the list, had to select its 36 players within 24 hours (March 13).

TRAINING STARTS — Rookies report to first Cowboys camp at Pacific U., in Forest Grove, Oregon (July 9).

FIRST PRE-SEASON GAME — The Cowboys, less than six months in existence, get their first test and drop a 10-16 pre-season game to San Francisco in Seattle (August 6).

FIRST HOME GAME — In their Dallas debut, in the Salesmanship Club pre-season game, the Cowboys led the World Champion Baltimore Colts into the final minute before a 62-yard pass from Johnny Unitas to Lenny Moore gave the Colts a 14-10 victory (August 19).

FIRST VICTORY — In a pre-season game at Louisville, Ky., the Cowboys beat New York's Giants, 14-3, with Frank Clarke catching touchdown passes of 73 yards (Eddie LeBaron) and 74 yards (Don Meredith) (August 27).

FIRST LEAGUE GAME — In their first league game, Dallas fell to Pittsburgh, 35-28, with Bobby Layne leading a fourth period Steeler rally (Sept. 24, Saturday night).

STREAK SNAPPED — Dallas snaps a 10-game loss streak by tying New York, 31-31, at Yankee Stadium (Dec. 4).

1961

TRAINING STARTS — Rookies launch training at new campsite — St. Olaf College in Northfield, Minn. (July 9).

FIRST LEAGUE WIN — Scoring ten points in the final 56 seconds, the Cowboys score their first NFL victory, 27-24, over Pittsburgh in the '61 league opener in the Cotton Bowl. Allen Green's 27-yard field goal on the game's final play won it before 23,500 (Sept. 17).

1962

TRAINING STARTS — Team begins training at new campsite — Northern Michigan College in Marquette, Mich. (July 13).

PENALTY HISTORY — For the first time in anyone's memory in an NFL game, points were awarded for a penalty. The Cowboys were detected holding in the end zone on a 99-TD pass from LeBaron to Clarke, and Pittsburgh was awarded a safety. The Steelers eventually won, 30-28 (Sept. 23).

100-YARD FIRSTS — Cowboys Amos Marsh returned a kickoff 101 yards and Mike Gaechter returned a pass interception 100 yards, both plays for fourth quarter TDs in a 41-19 win over Philadelphia in Dallas. It was the first time in NFL history that two 100-yard runs had been made in the same game, much less by the same team in the same quarter (Oct. 14).

1963

SHIFT TO KANSAS CITY — The rival Dallas Texans of the AFL announce they are moving the franchise to Kansas City (Feb. 8).

CALIFORNIA TRAINING SITE — The Cowboys open training at California Lutheran College in Thousand Oaks, Calif. (July 12).

HOWTON SETS RECORD — Bill Howton broke Don Hutson's all-time receiving mark with a 14-yard catch against Washington (there). Hutson's record was 7,991 yards and the catch gave Howton an even 8,000 yards (Sept. 29).

1964

LANDRY CONTRACT — With one year to go on his original contract, Tom Landry is signed to a ten-year extension, in effect giving him an 11-year pact, possibly the longest in major pro sports history (Feb. 5).

1965

FIRST SELLOUT — An overflow crowd of 76,251 jams the Cotton Bowl for the Cleveland game, notching the team's first home sellout. Cleveland won, 24-17 (Nov. 21).

1966

PLAYOFF BOWL — After defeating New York, 38-20, in the season finale (and winning five of their last seven games) to get into the Playoff Bowl at Miami, the Cowboys fall to Baltimore, 35-3 (Jan. 15).

MERGER — Peace comes to pro football with Cowboys GM Tex Schramm completing two months of negotiations with AFL's Lamar Hunt, merging the two leagues under the NFL banner (June 8).

SCHRAMM ELEVATED — Texas E. Schramm, Vice-President and General Manager of the Cowboys from the beginning, was named President of the club by owner Clint Murchison, Jr., who retained the title of Chairman of the Board.

NEELY CASE SOLVED — Dallas and Houston reached agreement in the Ralph Neely case. Neely remained with Dallas with Houston receiving the Cowboys' Nos. 1, 2 and two fifth place picks in the 1967 draft (Nov. 17).

THE CHAMPIONSHIP — The Cowboys won their first championship, capturing the Eastern Conference title with a 10-3-1 record, but lost the NFL Championship Game to Green Bay, 34-27.

1967

TEXAS STADIUM — On Dec. 23, owner Clint Murchison, Jr., formally announced plans to build Texas Stadium in suburban Irving. The stadium, to be financed through a bond-option plan, would be ready for the 1970 season. The stadium would seat a maximum of 58,000.

SECOND CHAMPIONSHIP — Under the NFL's new format, the Cowboys easily won the Capitol Division and defeated Cleveland, Century Division winner, 52-14, in the Cotton Bowl for the Eastern conference championship. However, on Dec. 31 in Green Bay, the Cowboys lost their second bid for an NFL title, falling to the Packers, 21-17, in the 13 degree below weather.

1968

WIN CAPITOL — For the second straight year the Cowboys won the Capitol Division, but for the first time in three years the Cowboys did not win the Eastern Championship, being upset at Cleveland, 31-20, on December 21st. Dallas won the Runner-Up Bowl over Minnesota, 17-13.

1969

TEXAS STADIUM — Ground was broken for Texas Stadium in suburban Irving on January 25, and on June 29 Bert Rose was named general manager of the stadium.

ORIGINALS RETIRE — An era ended for the Cowboys in July. On July 5th at a press conference in Dallas, quarterback Don Meredith, the last of the original Cowboys, announced his retirement. Then, on July 18th, the day the veterans were to report to training camp, all-time rushing great Don Perkins officially retired.

REPEAT CAPITOL WINS — Once again the Cowboys rolled to the Capitol Division Championship with an 11-2-1 season. However, the Cowboys failed to win the Eastern Championship when on Dec. 28, the Cowboys lost to Cleveland, 38-14, in the Cotton Bowl.

1970

FIVE STRAIGHT PLAYOFFS — The Cowboys won their last five games to finish 10-4, claim the Eastern Division championship and make the playoffs, for the fifth year in a row. They defeated Detroit, 5-0, in the opening round to get a shot at the National Conference championship.

FIRST NFC TITLE — The Cowboys captured the biggest prize of their 11-year history on Jan. 3 when they downed San Francisco, 17-10, for the NFC crown. A 16-13 loss to Baltimore in the Super Bowl Jan. 17 left Dallas with one major goal still unrealized.

1971

TEXAS STADIUM — The Cowboys opened a new era in their sparkling Irving, Tex., home with a 44-21 victory over the New England Patriots on October 24. Duane Thomas scored the first touchdown in the new stadium, a 56-yard run just two minutes and 16 seconds after the opening kickoff. Attendance was 65,708.

SIX STRAIGHT PLAYOFFS — The Cowboys won their last seven games to finish 11-3, claim the Eastern Division championship and make the playoffs for the sixth year in a row. They defeated Minnesota 20-12 in the opening round.

SECOND NFC TITLE — For the second consecutive year, the Cowboys met the San Francisco 49ers in the National Conference showdown. This time Dallas won, 14-3, to qualify for its second straight Super Bowl.

FIRST WORLD CHAMPIONSHIP — The Cowboys downed the Miami Dolphins, 24-3, to win Super Bowl VI in New Orleans on Jan. 16. It was the 10th victory in a row for Dallas as Roger Staubach passed for two touchdowns and was named the game's Most Valuable Player.

1972

FIRST 1,000-YARD BACK — Calvin Hill became the first Dallas player to rush for 1,000 yards when he gained 111 on Dec. 9 against the Washington Redskins in Texas Stadium. Hill wound up with 1,036 yards for the season on a record 245 carries.

SEVEN STRAIGHT PLAYOFFS — The Cowboys qualified for the NFL playoffs a record seventh consecutive year, their 10-4 record earning them the National Conference Wild Card berth. Roger Staubach passed for two touchdowns in the last 1½ minutes to give the Cowboys a 30-28 victory at San Francisco in the first round. Then, at Washington on New Year's Eve, Dallas was foiled in its bid for a third straight NFL title when the Redskins won, 26-3.

1973

100 VICTORIES — The Cowboys and Coach Tom Landry recorded their 100th victory with a 40-3 Texas Stadium win over the New Orleans Saints on Sept. 24. Landry, the only head coach the Cowboys have had, ended the season with a career mark of 108-80-6 to rank ninth on the list of the NFL's all-time winningest coaches.

EIGHT STRAIGHT PLAYOFFS — The Cowboys regained the NFC Eastern Division title with a 10-4 record and broke their own NFL record by reaching the playoffs for the eighth year in a row. Dallas defeated Western Division champion Los Angeles in the first round, 27-16, but fell to Central Division winner Minnesota in the NFC Championship Game, 27-10.

1974

FIRST TOP DRAFT CHOICE — For the first time in their history, the Cowboys had the very first choice in the NFL college draft. The No. 1 pick came to Dallas from Houston in exchange for Tody Smith and Billy Parks. The Cowboys selected Ed "Too Tall" Jones, a 6-9, 260-pound defensive end from Tennessee State.

PLAYOFFS MISSED — The Cowboys record-breaking string of eight straight years in the NFL playoffs was broken when the club's 8-6 record failed to qualify.

1975

LILLY HONORED — "Mr. Cowboy" was honored on Bob Lilly Day at Texas Stadium at halftime of the Philadelphia game on Nov. 23. It was the first such recognition ever given to a Dallas player. Lilly never missed a game in 14 years with the Cowboys, earning All-Pro honors seven times at defensive tackle before retiring prior to the '75 season.

TEN STRAIGHT WINNING SEASONS — The Cowboys' 10-4 record earned them the NFC Wild Card berth in the playoffs. The composite record over 10 straight winning seasons was 101-37-2.

THIRD NFC TITLE — After shocking Minnesota in the first round, 17-14 on Roger Staubach's 50-yard "Hail Mary" pass to Drew Pearson, the Cowboys traveled to Los Angeles for the NFC showdown. Staubach threw four touchdown passes, three to Preston Pearson, and Dallas won, 37-7. Pittsburgh won Super Bowl X on Jan. 18 in Miami, 21-17.

1976

ELEVEN STRAIGHT WINNING SEASONS — The Cowboys won the NFC Eastern Division title after their 11-3 record, giving them their 11th straight winning season and 10th playoff berth in that period. A 14-12 first round loss to Los Angeles — the first time Dallas had lost in the first round under the current playoff setup — ended the season.

MEREDITH, PERKINS HONORED — Former Cowboys greats Don Meredith and Don Perkins joined Bob Lilly in the "Ring of Honor" at Texas Stadium during halftime ceremonies at the New York Giants game on Nov. 7.

1977

HOWLEY HONORED — Former All-Pro linebacker Chuck Howley, a Cowboy from 1961 through 1973, became the fourth member of the Ring of Honor. Howley was honored during ceremonies at halftime of the Detroit Lions game on Oct. 30.

TWELVE STRAIGHT WINNING SEASONS — Getting off to an 8-0 start, their best ever, the Cowboys rolled to a 12-2 record, the championship of the NFC East, and their 12th consecutive winning season. They opened their 11th visit to the playoffs in those 12 years with a 37-7 first-round victory over the Chicago Bears at Texas Stadium.

FOURTH NFC TITLE — Dallas crushed the Minnesota Vikings at Texas Stadium, 23-6, for National Conference crown No. 4 and the right to meet the Denver Broncos in Super Bowl XII.

SECOND WORLD CHAMPIONSHIP — The Cowboys stopped the Denver Broncos, 27-10, to win Super Bowl XII in New Orleans on January 15, 1978. In the process, Dallas tied Minnesota for most Super Bowl appearances (four) and Green Bay, Miami and Pittsburgh for most Super Bowl victories (two). Defensive linemen Harvey Martin and Randy White were named co-Most Valuable Players in the game.

1978

THIRTEEN STRAIGHT WINNING SEASONS — After a mediocre 6-4 start, the Cowboys won six straight games to finish the expanded regular season with a 12-4 record and their 10th Division crown. It marked the Cowboys' 13th consecutive winning season and 12th trip to the playoffs in that span. Dallas rallied to beat Atlanta 27-20 in a divisional playoff at Texas Stadium, sending the Cowboys to their seventh NFC championship game in the last nine years.

FIFTH NFC TITLE — Dallas shut out the Rams in Los Angeles 28-0 in the National Conference title game to advance to the Super Bowl a record fifth time, including three of the last four. In the first Super Bowl rematch, Pittsburgh edged the Cowboys 35-31 for the NFL championship on Jan. 21 in Miami's Orange Bowl.

1979

TWENTIETH ANNIVERSARY — The Cowboys celebrated their 20th anniversary season at halftime of the St. Louis Cardinals game at Texas Stadium on Oct. 21. Stars from each of those 20 seasons plus Coach Tom Landry were introduced during the halftime ceremonies.

FOURTH STRAIGHT NFC EAST TITLE — Rallying from a mid-season slump, the Cowboys won their final three games to finish with an 11-5 record, their 11th division championship, including the past four NFC East titles, and 14th consecutive winning season. The Cowboys made their 13th trip to the playoffs in those 14 years, but were eliminated by Los Angeles 21-19 in a divisional playoff at Texas Stadium.

1980

LILLY ENTERS HALL OF FAME — Bob Lilly, a seven-time all-pro defensive tackle in his 14-year career with the Cowboys from 1961-74, became the first Cowboys-only player to be inducted into the Pro Football Hall of Fame. Enshrined along with Lilly on Aug. 2 at Canton, Ohio, were Herb Adderley, who played for the Cowboys from 1970-72, Jim Otto and Deacon Jones.

STAUBACH RETIRES — At a press conference at Texas Stadium on March 31, Roger Staubach announced his retirement after 11 record-breaking years as the Cowboys' quarterback. Staubach held all major Cowboys passing records and was the all-time leading NFL passer.

FIFTEEN STRAIGHT WINNING SEASONS

— Behind new starting quarterback Danny White, the Cowboys rolled to their 15th consecutive winning season with a surprising 12-4 record, tied for best in the league with Philadelphia and Atlanta. The Cowboys lost the NFC East title to Philadelphia on a tie-breaker, but entered the playoffs for the 14th time in 15 years, this time as a wild card team. The Cowboys beat Los Angeles 34-13 at Texas Stadium in the NFC wild card playoff and rallied past the Falcons at Atlanta 30-27 to advance to the NFC Championship Game at Philadelphia. But the Cowboys lost 20-7 in their bid for a sixth Super Bowl appearance.

LANDRY'S 200th VICTORY — Tom Landry joined George Halas and Curly Lambeau as the only coaches with 200 NFL victories when the Cowboys beat Los Angeles 34-13 on Dec. 28 at Texas Stadium in the NFC wild card playoff, raising Landry's record to 200-119-6, counting regular-season and playoff games.

1981

RENFRO HONORED — Former All-Pro defensive back Mel Renfro, the Cowboys' all-time leading pass interceptor, became the fifth member of the Cowboys' Ring of Honor. Renfro, who played for Dallas from 1964 through 1977, was honored during halftime ceremonies of the Cowboys-Miami Dolphins game at Texas Stadium Oct. 25.

TWELFTH DIVISION CHAMPIONSHIP — The Cowboys regained the NFC Eastern Division Championship, their 12th division title since 1966, with a 12-4 record and tied Oakland's NFL mark of 16 consecutive winning seasons. Entering the playoffs for the 15th time in that span, the Cowboys advanced to the NFC Championship Game for the ninth time in 12 years by routing Tampa Bay 38-0 at Texas Stadium. But for the second year in a row Dallas lost the conference title game. San Francisco scored a last minute touchdown at Candlestick Park to edge the Cowboys 28-27 for a berth in Super Bowl XVI.

1982

200th REGULAR-SEASON VICTORY — The Cowboys beat Washington 24-10 at RFK Stadium on Dec. 5 for the club's and Coach Tom Landry's 200th regular-season victory.

SEVENTEEN STRAIGHT WINNING SEASONS — The Cowboys finish the strike-shortened regular season with a 6-3 record to establish an NFL record of 17 consecutive winning seasons. Entering the playoffs for a record-tying eighth straight year and for the 16th time in 17 years, the Cowboys beat Tampa Bay 30-17 and Green Bay 37-26, both at Texas Stadium, to advance to the NFC Championship Game for the third year in a row. But again the Cowboys come up short, losing 31-17 at Washington.

1983

STAUBACH HONORED — Former quarterback Roger Staubach, who led the Cowboys to four Super Bowls, became the sixth member of the club's Ring of Honor during halftime ceremonies of the Cowboys' 27-24 overtime victory over Tampa Bay at Texas Stadium Oct. 9.

VALLEY RANCH AND COWBOYS CENTER — Formal ground-breaking ceremonies took place on Nov. 29 for the Cowboys' new headquarters and training facility at Valley Ranch in northwest Dallas County. On March 27, 1984 the Cowboys and Triland International announced plans for Cowboys Center, an innovative joint venture that will develop business opportunities in a conference center, visitors center, athletic club and retail and restaurant outlets at Valley Ranch.

COWBOYS SOLD — During halftime of the Cowboys-San Diego Chargers game at San Diego, Cowboys President and General Manager Tex Schramm confirms that the club is for sale. On March 19, 1984 the NFL approved the sale of the Cowboys by Clint Murchison, Jr., and the estate of John Murchison to a group headed by Dallas businessman H. R. "Bum" Bright at the annual NFL meeting in Honolulu.

LANDRY TIES LAMBEAU — At the Kingdome in Seattle, the Cowboys defeated the Seahawks 36-10 to give coach Tom Landry his 234th career victory, including playoffs, tying him for second place on the NFL's career list with Curly Lambeau (234-135-23). Landry's record is 234-134-6.

EIGHTEEN STRAIGHT WINNING SEASONS — The Cowboys' 12-4 regular-season record extended their NFL record of 18 consecutive winning seasons. The Los Angeles Rams cut short the Cowboys' NFL record ninth straight playoff appearance by defeating Dallas 24-17 at Texas Stadium in the NFC Wild Card Game.

1984

RETIREMENTS — The Cowboys were hit hard offensively and defensively with the retirements of former Pro Bowlers Billy Joe DuPree, Pat Donovan, Harvey Martin, Drew Pearson and veteran fullback Robert Newhouse. DuPree never missed playing in a Cowboys game during his 11 years, a streak of 160 games. Donovan earned four consecutive trips to the Pro Bowl at left tackle. Martin led the club in quarterback traps 10 of the 11 years he was with the team. Pearson, retiring because of injuries sustained in an auto accident, left as the Cowboys all-time leading receiver.

25th ANNIVERSARY TEAM — The Cowboys introduced their 25th anniversary, all-time team at halftime of their game against the New York Giants at Texas Stadium on Nov. 4. The team was selected by fans in voting sponsored by The Southland Corporation and KRLD Radio.

NINETEEN STRAIGHT WINNING SEASONS — At Veterans Stadium in Philadelphia, the Cowboys defeat the Eagles 26-10 to extend their NFL record to 19 consecutive winning seasons. However, Dallas failed to make the playoffs for the first time since 1974 ending the Cowboys' NFL record string of nine straight years in postseason play.

1985

STAUBACH ENTERS HALL OF FAME — Former quarterback Roger Staubach, who led the Cowboys to four Super Bowls during his 11-year career, is named to the Pro Football Hall of Fame on Jan. 22. Staubach joins Bob Lilly as the only players who spent their entire careers with the Cowboys to be elected to the Hall of Fame.

1984 Awards

Bill Bates/S . . . . All-Pro (John Madden, College and Pro Football Newsweekly-2nd team)
All-NFC (Pro Football Weekly)
NFL Special Teams Player of the Year (NFL Alumni Association)
NFC Special Teams Player of the Year (NFLPA, USA Today/Player Poll)
Pro Bowl

Doug Cosbie/TE . . . . All-NFC (UPI-2nd team)
Pro Bowl

Michael Downs/S . . . . All-Pro (PFWA, Sports Illustrated, Football Digest, AP-2nd team)
All-NFC (UPI)

Eugene Lockhart/LB . . . . All-Rookie (UPI, PFWA, Pro Football Weekly, Football Digest)

Everson Walls/CB . . . . All-NFC (UPI)

Randy White/DT . . . . All-Pro (AP, NEA, PFWA, Pro Football Weekly, NFL Films, Sports Illustrated, College and Pro Football Newsweekly, Football Digest, Seagrams Sports Award)
All-NFC (UPI, Pro Football Weekly)
Pro Bowl

Dallas Cowboys
1985 Veterans Roster

NO	NAME	POS	HT	WT	BIRTHDATE	COLLEGE	NFL EXP.
36	Albritton, Vince	S	6-2	209	7/23/62	Washington	2
31	Allen, Gary	WR	5-10	179	4/23/60	Hawaii	4
76	Aughtman, Dowe	G	6-3	258	1/28/61	Auburn	2
62	Baldinger, Brian	G	6-4	258	1/7/59	Duke	4
40	Bates, Bill	S	6-1	201	6/6/61	Tennessee	3
47	Clinkscale, Dextor	S	5-11	189	4/13/58	South Carolina State	5
61	Cooper, Jim	T	6-5	267	9/28/55	Temple	9
85	Cornwell, Fred	TE	6-6	237	8/7/61	Southern Cal.	2
84	Cosbie, Doug	TE	6-6	235	2/27/56	Santa Clara	7
55	DeOssie, Steve	LB	6-2	248	11/22/62	Boston College	2
51	Dickerson, Anthony	LB	6-2	222	6/9/57	SMU	6
33	Dorsett, Tony	RB	5-11	185	4/7/54	Pittsburgh	9
26	Downs, Michael	S	6-3	195	6/9/59	Rice	5
78	Dutton, John	DT	6-7	267	2/6/51	Nebraska	12
27	Fellows, Ron	CB	6-0	174	11/7/58	Missouri	5
28	Granger, Norm	RB	5-9	220	9/14/61	Iowa	2
86	Harris, Duriel	WR	5-11	176	11/27/54	New Mexico State	10
58	Hegman, Mike	LB	6-1	231	1/17/53	Tennessee State	10
15	Hewko, Bob	QB	6-3	195	6/8/60	Florida	2
80	Hill, Tony	WR	6-2	198	6/23/56	Stanford	9
14	Hogeboom, Gary	QB	6-4	200	8/21/58	Central Michigan	6
97	Hopkins, Thomas	T	6-6	260	1/13/60	Alabama A&M	2
21	Howard, Carl	CB	6-2	188	9/20/61	Rutgers	2
79	Hunt, John	G	6-4	253	11/6/62	Florida	2
77	Jeffcoat, Jim	DE	6-5	257	4/1/61	Arizona State	3
72	Jones, Ed	DE	6-9	282	2/23/51	Tennessee State	11
23	Jones, James	RB	5-10	189	12/6/58	Mississippi State	5
73	Kitson, Syd	G	6-4	262	9/27/58	Wake Forest	5
56	Lockhart, Eugene	LB	6-2	233	3/8/61	Houston	2
35	McSwain, Chuck	RB	6-0	190	2/21/61	Clemson	3
30	Newsome, Timmy	RB	6-1	232	5/17/58	Winston-Salem State	6
16	Pelluer, Steve	QB	6-4	210	7/29/62	Washington	2
65	Petersen, Kurt	G	6-4	267	6/17/57	Missouri	6
81	Phillips, Kirk	WR	6-1	202	7/31/60	Tulsa	2
75	Pozderac, Phil	T	6-9	276	12/19/59	Notre Dame	4
64	Rafferty, Tom	C	6-3	254	8/2/54	Penn State	10
82	Renfro, Mike	WR	6-0	188	6/19/55	TCU	8
70	Richards, Howard	G	6-6	260	8/7/59	Missouri	5
50	Rohrer, Jeff	LB	6-3	225	12/25/58	Yale	4
89	Salonen, Brian	TE	6-2	227	7/29/61	Montana	2
66	Schultz, Chris	T	6-8	265	2/16/60	Arizona	2
22	Scott, Victor	CB	5-11	196	6/1/62	Colorado	2
1	Septien, Rafael	K	5-10	180	12/12/53	SW Louisiana	9
60	Smerek, Don	DT	6-7	255	12/20/57	Nevada-Reno	5
20	Springs, Ron	RB	6-1	224	11/1/56	Ohio State	7
32	Thurman, Dennis	S	5-11	175	4/13/56	USC	8
63	Titensor, Glen	G	6-4	264	2/21/58	Brigham Young	5
71	Tuinei, Mark	C	6-5	274	3/31/60	Hawaii	3
57	Turner, Jimmie	LB	6-2	220	2/16/62	Presbyterian	2
24	Walls, Everson	CB	6-1	190	12/28/59	Grambling	5
5	Warren, John	P	6-0	207	11/8/60	Tennessee	3
11	White, Danny	QB	6-2	197	2/9/52	Arizona State	10
54	White, Randy	DT	6-4	260	1/15/53	Maryland	11

How the Cowboys Were Built

There were 57 players active with the Cowboys in 1984. Here's a look at how they came to Dallas:

FROM THE DRAFT:

1974 — Ed Jones (1st, Tennessee State); Danny White (3rd, Arizona State).
1975 — Randy White (1st, Maryland); Bob Breunig (3rd, Arizona State); Mike Hegman (7th, Tennessee State); Herbert Scott (13th, Virginia Union).
1976 — Tom Rafferty (4th, Penn State).
1977 — Tony Dorsett (1st, Pittsburgh); Tony Hill (3rd, Stanford); Jim Cooper (6th, Temple).
1978 — Dennis Thurman (11th, Southern California).
1979 — Doug Cosbie (3rd, Santa Clara); Ron Springs (5th, Ohio State).
1980 — James Jones (3rd, Mississippi State); Kurt Petersen (4th, Missouri); Gary Hogeboom (5th, Central Michigan); Timmy Newsome (6th, Winston-Salem State).
1981 — Howard Richards (1st, Missouri); Doug Donley (2nd, Ohio State); Glen Titensor (3rd, Brigham Young); Ron Fellows (7th, Missouri).
1982 — Jeff Rohrer (2nd, Yale); Phil Pozderac (5th, Notre Dame).
1983 — Jim Jeffcoat (1st, Arizona State); Chuck McSwain (5th, Clemson).
1984 — Billy Cannon (1st, Texas A&M); Victor Scott (2nd, Colorado); Fred Cornwell (3rd, Southern California); Steve DeOssie (4th, Boston College); Steve Pelluer (5th, Washington); Norm Granger (5th, Iowa); Eugene Lockhart (6th, Houston); John Hunt (8th, Florida); Brian Salonen (10th, Montana); Dowe Aughtman (11th, Auburn).

CLAIMED ON WAIVERS:

1984 — Duriel Harris (New Mexico State, from Cleveland Browns).

SIGNED AS FREE AGENTS:

1978 — Rafael Septien (SW Louisiana, after preseason release by Los Angeles Rams).
1980 — Anthony Dickerson (Southern Methodist); Don Smerek (Nevada-Reno); Dextor Clinkscale (South Carolina State).
1981 — Michael Downs (Rice); Everson Walls (Grambling).
1982 — Brian Baldinger (Duke).
1983 — Gary Allen (Hawaii, after preseason release by Houston Oilers); Bill Bates (Tennessee); Jim Miller (Mississippi, after release by San Francisco 49ers); Kirk Phillips (Tulsa); Mark Tuinei (Hawaii).
1984 — Vince Albritton (Washington); Harold Carmichael (Southern, after release by N.Y. Jets); Carl Howard (Rutgers); Syd Kitson (Wake Forest, after release by Green Bay Packers); Waddell Smith (Kansas, after release by L.A. Raiders); Jimmie Turner (Presbyterian, re-signed after preseason release); John Warren (Tennessee, re-signed after midseason release).

OBTAINED IN TRADES:

1979 — John Dutton (Nebraska, from Baltimore for Cowboys' 1st and 2nd round draft choices in 1980).
1984 — Mike Renfro (TCU, from Houston along with 5th round choice in 1985 for Butch Johnson. Also switched 5th round choices in 1984).

Cowboys All-Time Roster

ASSISTANT COACHES
Allen, Ermal, 1962-83
Armstrong, Neill, 1982-84
Berry, Raymond, 1968
Dahms, Tom, 1960-62
Dimancheff, Babe, 1960-62
Ditka, Mike, 1973-81
Ecklund, Brad, 1960-63
Franklin, Bobby, 1968-72
Gillman, Sid, 1972
Hickey, Red, 1964
Hughes, Ed, 1973-76
Lavan, Al, 1980-84
Lowry, Alan, 1982-84
Mackovic, John, 1981-82
Myers, Jim, 1962-84
Nolan, Dick, 1962-67, 1982-84
Reeves, Dan, 1970-80
Renfro, Ray, 1968-72
Roy, Alvin, 1973-75
Shofner, Jim, 1983-84
Stallings, Gene, 1972-84
Stautner, Ernie, 1966-84
Tubbs, Jerry, 1966-84
Ward, Bob, 1976-84

PLAYERS
Adderley, Herb, CB, Mich. St., 1970-72
Adkins, Margene, WR, Henderson J.C., 1970-71
Albritton, Vince, S, Washington, 1984
Allen, Gary, RB, Hawaii, 1983-84
Alworth, Lance, WR, Arkansas, 1971-72
Andrie, George, DE, Marquette, 1962-72
Arneson, Jim, G-C, Arizona, 1973-74
Asher, Bob, T, Vanderbilt, 1970
Aughtman, Dowe, OL, Auburn, 1984
Babb, Gene, LB-RB, Austin College, 1960-61
Babinecz, John, LB, Villanova, 1972-73
Baker, Sam, P-K, Oregon State, 1962-63
Baldinger, Brian, C, Duke 1982-84
Barnes, Benny, CB, Stanford, 1972-82
Barnes, Gary, WR, Clemson, 1963
Barnes, Rodrigo, LB, Rice, 1973-74
Bateman, Marv, P, Utah, 1972-74
Bates, Bill, S, Tennessee, 1983-84
Baynham, Craig, RB, Georgia Tech, 1967-69
Belden, Bob, QB, Notre Dame, 1969-70
Bercich, Bob, S, Michigan State, 1960-61
Bethea, Larry, DE, Michigan St., 1978-83
Bielski, Dick, TE, Maryland, 1960-61
Bishop, Don, CB, CCLA, 1960-65
Blackwell, Alois, RB, Houston, 1978-79
Boeke, Jim, T, Heidelberg, 1964-67
Borden, Nate, DE, Indiana, 1960-61
Braatz, Tom, LB, Marquette, 1960
Bradfute, Byron, T, So. Miss., 1960-61
Breunig, Bob, LB, Arizona State, 1975-84
Brinson, Larry, RB, Florida, 1977-79
Brock, Clyde, DT, Utah State, 1962-63
Brown, Guy, LB, Houston, 1977-82
Brown, Otto, CB-S, Prairie View, 1969
Bullocks, Amos, RB, So. Ill., 1962-64
Burkett, Jackie, LB, Auburn, 1968-69
Butler, Bill, S, Chattanooga, 1960
Caffey, Lee Roy, LB, Texas A&M, 1971
Cannon, Billy, LB, Texas A&M, 1984
Capone, Warren, LB, Louisiana State, 1975
Carano, Glenn, QB, Nevada-Las Vegas, 1977-83
Carmichael, Harold, WR, Southern, 1984
Carroll, Duane, P, Florida State, 1974
Clark, Mike, K, Texas A&M, 1968-71, 1973
Clark, Monte, T, Southern California, 1962
Clark, Phil, CB-S, Northwestern, 1967-69
Clarke, Frank, TE-WR, Colorado, 1960-67
Clinkscale, Dextor, S, South Carolina St., 1980, 1982-84
Cole, Larry, DE-DT, Hawaii, 1968-80
Coleman, Ralph, LB, N. Car., A&T, 1972
Colvin, Jim, DT, Houston, 1964-66
Cone, Fred, K, Clemson, 1960
Connelly, Mike, C, Utah State, 1960-67
Conrad, Bobby Joe, WR, Texas A&M, 1969
Cooper, Jim, C-G, Temple, 1977-84
Cornwell, Fred, TE, Southern Cal, 1984
Cosbie, Doug, TE, Santa Clara, 1979-84
Cronin, Gene, DE, Pacific, 1960
Cvercko, Andy, G, Northwestern, 1961-62
Daniels, Dick, S, Pacific (Ore.), 1966-68
Davis, Donnie, WR, Southern, 1962
Davis, Kyle, C, Oklahoma, 1975
Davis, Sonny, LB, Baylor, 1961
DeOssie, Steve, LB, Boston College, 1984
Dennison, Doug, RB, Kutztown State, 1974-78
Deters, Harold, K, North Carolina St., 1967
Dial, Buddy, WR, Rice, 1964-66
Dickerson, Anthony, LB, SMU, 1980-84
Dickson, Paul, T, Baylor, 1960
Diehl, John, DT, Virginia, 1965
Ditka, Mike, TE, Pittsburgh, 1969-72
Doelling, Fred, S, Pennsylvania, 1960
Donley, Doug, WR, Ohio State, 1981-84
Donohue, Leon, G, San Jose State, 1965-67
Donovan, Pat, T, Stanford, 1975-83
Doran, Jim, WR, Iowa State, 1960-61
Dorsett, Tony, RB, Pittsburgh, 1977-84
Douglas, Merrill, RB, Utah, 1961
Dowdle, Mike, RB-LB, Texas, 1960-62
Downs, Michael, S, Rice, 1981-84
Dugan, Fred, WR, Dayton, 1960
Dunn, Perry Lee, RB, Mississippi, 1964-65
Dupre, L. G., RB, Baylor, 1960-61
DuPree, Billy Joe, TE, Michigan St., 1973-83
Dutton, John, DE, Nebraska, 1979-84
East, Ron, DT, Montana State, 1967-70
Edwards, Dave, LB, Auburn, 1963-75
Eidson, Jim, G-C, Miss. State, 1976
Falls, Mike, G, Minnesota, 1960-61
Fellows, Ron, CB, Missouri, 1981-84
Fisher, Ray, T, Eastern Illinois, 1960
Fitzgerald, John, G-C, Bost. Coll., 1971-80
Flowers, Richmond, S, Tennessee 1969-71
Folkins, Lee, TE, Washington, 1962-64
Franckhauser, Tom, CB, Purdue, 1960-61
Frank, Bill, T, Colorado, 1964
Frederick, Andy, T, New Mexico, 1977-81
Fritsch, Toni, K, Vienna, Austria, 1971-73, 1975
Frost, Ken, DT, Tennessee, 1961-62
Fry, Bob, T, Kentucky, 1960-64
Fugett, Jean, TE, Amherst, 1972-75
Gaechter, Mike, S, Oregon, 1962-69
Garrison, Walt, RB, Okla. St. 1966-74
Gent, Pete, WR-TE, Mich. St., 1964-68
Gibbs, Sonny, QB, Texas Christian, 1963
Gonzaga, John, DE, no college, 1960
Granger, Charlie, T, Southern, 1961
Granger, Norm, RB, Iowa, 1984
Green, Allen, P-K, Mississippi, 1961
Green, Cornell, CB-S, Utah State, 1962-74
Gregg, Forrest, G-T, SMU, 1971
Gregory, Bill, DT-DE, Wisconsin, 1971-77
Gregory, Glynn, WR-CB-S, SMU, 1961-62
Grottkau, Bob, G, Oregon, 1961
Guy, Buzz, G, Duke, 1960
Hagen, Halvor, C-G, Weber State, 1969-70
Hansen, Wayne, LB, Texas Western, 1960
Harris, Cliff, S, Ouachita, 1970-79
Harris, Duriel, WR, New Mexico State, 1984
Harris, Jim, S, Oklahoma, 1961
Hayes, Bob, WR, Florida A&M, 1965-74
Hayes, Wendell, RB, Humboldt State, 1963
Hays, Harold, LB, So. Miss., 1963-67
Healy, Don, DT, Maryland, 1960-61
Hegman, Mike, LB, Tennessee State, 1976-84
Heinrich, Don, QB, Washington, 1960
Henderson, Thomas, LB, Langston, 1975-79
Herchman, Bill, DT, Texas Tech, 1960-61
Herrera, Efren, K, UCLA, 1974, 1976-77
Hill, Calvin, RB, Yale, 1969-74
Hill, Rod, CB, Kentucky State, 1982-83
Hill, Tony, WR, Stanford, 1977-84
Hogeboom, Gary, QB, Central Michigan, 1980-84
Homan, Dennis, WR, Alabama, 1968-70
Hoopes, Mitch, P, Arizona, 1975
Houser, John, C-G, Redlands, 1960-61
Houston, Bill, WR, Jackson State, 1974
Howard, Carl, DB, Rutgers, 1984
Howard, Percy, WR, Austin Peay, 1975
Howard, Ron, TE, Seattle, 1974-75
Howley, Chuck, LB, West Virginia, 1961-73
Howton, Bill, WR, Rice, 1960-63
Hoyem, Lynn, C-G, Long Beach, 1962-63
Hughes, Randy, S, Oklahoma, 1975-80
Humphrey, Buddy, QB, Baylor, 1961
Hunt, John, OL, Florida, 1984
Hunter, Monty, S, Salem, 1982
Hurt, Eric, CB, San Jose St., 1980
Husmann, Ed, DT, Nebraska, 1960
Hutcherson, Ken, LB, Livingston State, 1974
Huther, Bruce, LB, New Hampshire, 1977-80, 1983
Isbell, Joe Bob, G, Houston, 1962-65
Jeffcoat, Jim, DE, Arizona State, 1983-84
Jensen, Jim, RB, Iowa, 1976
Johnson, Butch, WR, Cal-Riverside, 1976-83
Johnson, Mike, CB, Kansas, 1966-69
Johnson, Mitch, G, UCLA, 1965
Jones, Ed, DE, Tennessee State, 1974-78, 1980-84
Jones, James, RB, Miss. State, 1980-82, 1984
Jordan, Lee Roy, LB, Alabama, 1963-76
Keller, Mike, LB, Michigan, 1972
Killian, Gene, G, Tennessee, 1974
Kiner, Steve, LB, Tennessee, 1970
King, Angelo, LB, South Carolina St., 1981-83
Kitson, Syd, OL, Wake Forest, 1984
Klein, Dick, T, Iowa, 1960
Kowalczyk, Walt, RB, Michigan State, 1960
Kupp, Jake, G, Washington, 1964-65
Kyle, Aaron, CB, Wyoming, 1976-79
Laidlaw, Scott, RB, Stanford, 1975-79
Lawless, Burton, G, Florida, 1975-79
LeBaron, Eddie, QB, Pacific, 1960-63
Lewis, D. D., LB, Miss. State, 1968-81
Lewis, Woodley, WR, Oregon, 1960
Lilly, Bob, DE-DT, Texas Christian, 1961-74
Liscio, Tony, T, Tulsa, 1963-64, 1966-71
Livingston, Warren, CB, Arizona, 1961-66
Lockett, J. W., RB, Central Okla., 1961-62
Lockhart, Eugene, LB, Houston, 1984
Logan, Obert, S, Trinity (Tex.), 1965-66
Long, Bob, LB, UCLA, 1962
Longley, Clint, QB, Abilene Christian, 1974-75
Lothridge, Billy, P-QB, Georgia Tech, 1964
Manders, Dave, C, Mich. State, 1964-66, 1968-74
Manning, Wade, CB, Ohio State, 1979
Marsh, Amos, RB, Oregon State, 1961-64
Martin, Harvey, DE, East Texas St., 1973-83
Mathews, Ray, WR, Clemson, 1960
McCreary, Bob, T, Wake Forest, 1961
McDaniels, David, WR, Miss. Val., 1968
McDonald, Tommy, WR, Oklahoma, 1964
McIlhenny, Don, RB, SMU, 1960-61
McLean, Scott, LB, Florida State, 1983
McSwain, Chuck, RB, Clemson, 1983-84
Memmelaar, Dale, G, Wyoming, 1962-63
Meredith, Don, QB, SMU, 1960-68
Meyers, John, DT, Washington, 1962-63
Miller, Jim, P, Mississippi, 1983-84
Mitchell, Aaron, CB, Nevada-Las Vegas, 1979-80
Moegle, Dick, S, Rice, 1961
Montgomery, Mike, RB-WR, Kans. St., 1972-73
Mooty, Jim, CB, Arkansas, 1960
Morgan, Dennis, RB, Western Illinois, 1974
Morton, Craig, QB, California, 1965-74
Murchison, Ola Lee, WR, Pacific, 1961
Neely, Ralph, G-T, Oklahoma, 1965-77
Newhouse, Robert, RB, Houston, 1972-83
Newsome, Timmy, RB, Winston-Salem, 1980-84
Niland, John, G, Iowa, 1966-74
Nolan, Dick, S, Maryland, 1962
Norman, Pettis, TE, J. C. Smith, 1962-70
Norton, Jerry, S, SMU, 1962
Nutting, Ed, T, Georgia Tech, 1963
Nye, Blaine, G, Stanford, 1968-76
Overton, Jerry, S, Utah, 1963
Parks, Billy, WR, Long Beach State, 1972
Patera, Jack, LB, Oregon, 1960-61
Pearson, Drew, WR, Tulsa, 1973-83
Pearson, Preston, RB, Illinois, 1975-80
Pelluer, Steve, QB, Washington, 1984
Peoples, George, RB, Auburn, 1982
Percival, Mac, K, Texas Tech, 1974
Perkins, Don, RB, New Mexico, 1961-68
Petersen, Kurt, G, Missouri, 1980-84
Peterson, Calvin, LB, UCLA, 1974-75
Phillips, Kirk, WR, Tulsa, 1984
Pinder, Cyril, RB, Illinois, 1973
Poimboeuf, Lance, K, SW La., 1963
Porterfield, Garry, DE, Tulsa, 1965
Pozderac, Phil, T, Notre Dame, 1982-84
Pugh, Jethro, DT, Eliz. City St., 1965-78
Putnam, Duane, G, Pacific, 1960
Rafferty, Tom, G-C, Penn State, 1976-84
Randall, Tom, DG, Iowa State, 1978
Randle, Sonny, WR, Virginia, 1968
Reece, Beasley, CB-WR, N. Texas St., 1976
Reese, Guy, DT, SMU, 1962-63
Reeves, Dan, RB-QB, S. Car., 1965-72
Renfro, Mel, CB-RB-S, Oregon, 1964-77
Renfro, Mike, WR, TCU, 1984
Rentzel, Lance, WR, Oklahoma, 1967-70
Rhome, Jerry, QB, Tulsa, 1965-68
Richards, Golden, WR, Hawaii, 1973-78
Richards, Howard, T, Missouri, 1981-84
Richardson, Gloster, WR, Jack. St., 1971
Ridgway, Colin, P-K, Lamar Tech, 1965
Ridlon, Jim, S, Syracuse, 1963-64
Roach, John, QB, SMU, 1964
Robinson, Larry, RB, Tennessee, 1973
Roe, Bill, LB, Colorado, 1980
Rohrer, Jeff, LB, Yale, 1982-84
Rucker, Reggie, WR, Boston U., 1970-71
Saldi, Jay, TE, South Carolina, 1976-82
Salonen, Brian, TE, Montana, 1984
Sandeman, Bill, DT, Pacific, 1966
Schaum, Greg, DE, Michigan State, 1976
Schoenke, Ray, T, SMU, 1963-64
Schultz, Chris, T, Arizona, 1983
Scott, Herbert, G, Virginia Union, 1975-84
Scott, Victor, DB, Colorado, 1984
Sellers, Ron, WR, Florida State, 1972
Septien, Rafael, K, SW Louisiana, 1978-84
Shaw, Robert, C, Tennessee, 1979-81
Sherer, Dave, P, SMU, 1960
Shy, Les, RB, Long Beach State, 1966-69
Simmons, Cleo, TE, Jackson State, 1983
Simmons, Dave, LB, Georgia Tech, 1968
Smerek, Don, DL, Nevada-Reno, 1981, 1982-84
Smith, J. D., RB, N. Car. A&T, 1965-66
Smith, Jackie, TE, NW Louisiana, 1978
Smith, Jim Ray, G-T, Baylor, 1963-64
Smith, Tody, DE-DT, USC, 1971-72
Smith, Waddell, WR, Kansas, 1984
Solomon, Roland, S, Utah, 1980
Spradlin, Danny, LB, Tennessee, 1981-82
Springs, Ron, RB, Ohio State, 1979-84
Stalls, Dave, DE, Northern Colorado, 1977-79
Staubach, Roger, QB, Navy, 1969-79
Steele, Robert, WR, N. Alabama, 1978
Stephens, Larry, DE, Texas, 1963-67
Stiger, Jim, RB, Washington, 1963-65
Stincic, Tom, LB, Michigan, 1969-71
Stokes, Sim, WR, Northern Arizona, 1967
Stowe, Otto, WR, Iowa State, 1973
Strayhorn, Les, RB, East Carolina, 1973-74
Stynchula, Andy, DE, Penn State, 1968
Talbert, Don, DE-T, Texas, 1962, 1965, 1971
Thomas, Bill, RB, Boston College, 1972
Thomas, Duane, RB, W. Texas St., 1970-71
Thomas, Ike, CB, Bishop, 1971
Thornton, Bruce, DE-DT, Illinois, 1979-81
Thurman, Dennis, CB, USC, 1978-84
Titensor, Glen, G, Brigham Young, 1981-84
Toomay, Pat, DE, Vanderbilt, 1970-74
Townes, Willie, DE, Tulsa, 1966-68
Truax, Billy, TE, Louisiana State, 1971-73
Tubbs, Jerry, LB, Oklahoma, 1960-67
Tuinei, Mark, DT, Hawaii, 1983-84
Turner, Jimmie, LB, Presbyterian, 1984
Van Raaphorst, Dick, K, Ohio State, 1964
Villanueva, Danny, P-K, New Mex. St., 1965-67
Walker, Louie, LB, Colorado State, 1974
Walker, Malcolm, C, Rice, 1966-69
Wallace, Rodney, G-T, New Mex., 1971-73
Walls, Everson, CB, Grambling, 1981-84
Walter, Mike, LB, Oregon, 1983
Walton, Bruce, G, UCLA, 1973-75
Warren, John, P, Tennessee, 1983-84
Washington, Mark, CB, Morgan St., 1970-78
Waters, Charlie, S-CB, Clemson, 1970-78, 1980-81
Wayt, Russell, LB, Rice, 1965
Welch, Claxton, RB, Oregon, 1969-71
Wells, Norm, G, Northwestern, 1980
White, Danny, QB-P, Arizona State, 1976-84
White, Randy, LB-DE, Maryland, 1975-84
Whitfield, A. D., RB, N. Texas St., 1965
Whittingham, Fred, LB, Cal. Poly, 1969
Widby, Ron, P, Tennessee, 1968-71
Wilbur, John, T, Stanford, 1966-69
Williams, Joe, RB, Wyoming, 1971
Wilson, Steve, WR, Howard, 1979-81
Wisener, Gary, WR, Baylor, 1960
Woolsey, Rolly, CB-S, Boise State, 1975
Wright, Brad, QB, New Mexico, 1982
Wright, Rayfield, TE-T, Ft. Valley St., 1967-79
Wright, Steve, T, Northern Iowa, 1981-82
Youmans, Maury, DE, Syracuse, 1964-65
Young, Charles, RB, N.C. State, 1974-76

Cowboys All-Time Draft

1961
(Drafted 2nd)

1. **(A) NO CHOICE**
Choice traded along with sixth choice to Washington for EDDIE LeBARON.
1. **(B) BOB LILLY**
T, Texas Christian University, 6-5, 242 — Choice from Cleveland for first round pick in 1962.
2. **E.J. HOLUB**
LB, Texas Tech, 6-4, 218 (went to AFL).
3. **STEW BARBER**
G, Penn State, 6-3, 230 (went to AFL).
4. **SONNY DAVIS**
E, Baylor, 6-2, 210.
5. **NO CHOICE**
Choice traded to San Francisco for GENE BABB.
6. **NO CHOICE**
Choice traded, along with first choice to Washington for LeBARON.
7. **ART GILMORE**
HB, Oregon State, 6-0, 200.
8. **DON TALBERT**
T, Texas, 6-5, 220.
9. **GLENN GREGORY**
HB, SMU, 6-2, 195.
10. **NO CHOICE**
Choice traded to Green Bay for FRED CONE.
11. **NORRIS STEVENSON**
HB, Missouri, 6-1, 205.
12. **LOWNDES SHINGLER**
QB, Clemson, 6-1, 205.
13. **DON GOODMAN**
HB, Florida, 6-0, 200.
14. **BILL SHAW**
T, Georgia Tech, 6-3, 222 (went to AFL).
15. **JULIUS VARNADO**
T, San Francisco State, 6-4, 220 (went to AFL).
16. **JERRY STEFFEN**
HB, Colorado, 6-10, 190.
17. **EVERETT CLOUD**
HB, Maryland, 6-0, 190.
18. **RANDY WILLIAMS**
HB, Indiana, 6-3, 208.
19. **LYNN HOYEM**
C, Long Beach State, 6-4, 225.
20. **JERRY MORGAN**
QB, Iowa State, 6-3, 195.

1962
(Drafted 4th)

1. **NO CHOICE**
Choice traded to Cleveland for first round pick in 1961 when Cowboys picked BOB LILLY.
2. **SONNY GIBBS***
QB, TCU, 6-7, 225.
3. **(A) NO CHOICE**
Choice to Chicago for DON MEREDITH.
3. **(B) BOBBY PLUMMER**
G, TCU, 6-2, 235 — Choice from Cleveland for DUANE PUTNAM.
4. **NO CHOICE**
Choice to San Francisco for BILL HERCHMAN.
5. **NO CHOICE**
Choice to Los Angeles for JIMMY HARRIS.
6. **(A) DONNIE DAVIS**
E, Southern University, 6-2, 235.
6. **(B) GEORGE ANDRIE**
E, Marquette, 6-7, 247 — Choice and ALLEN GREEN from New York for FRED DUGAN.
7. **NO CHOICE**
Choice to Los Angeles for JOHN HOUSER.
8. **KEN TUREAUD**
B, Michigan, 6-1, 198.
9. **NO CHOICE**
Choice to Baltimore for DON PERKINS.
10. **JOHN M. LONGMEYER**
G, Southern Illinois, 6-3, 230.
11. **LARRY HUDAS**
E, Michigan State, 6-4, 208.
12. **NO CHOICE**
Choice to Green Bay for STEVE MEILINGER.
13. **ROBERT MOSES**
E, Texas, 6-3, 211.
14. **HAROLD HAYS***
G, Southern Mississippi, 6-3, 218.
15. **GUY REESE**
T, SMU, 6-5, 238.
16. **ROBERT JOHNSTON**
T, Rice, 6-4, 215.
17. **RAY JACOBS**
T, Howard Payne, 6-3, 265 (went to AFL).
18. **DAVE CLOUTIER***
B, Maine, 6-0, 195 (went to AFL).
19. **PAUL HOLMES**
T, Georgia, 6-5, 220.
20. **AMOS BULLOCKS**
B, Southern Illinois, 6-1, 197.

1963
(Drafted 6th)

1. **LEE ROY JORDAN**
LB, Alabama, 6-2, 210.
2. **NO CHOICE**
Choice traded, along with ninth choice, to Chicago for CHUCK HOWLEY.
3. **JIM PRICE**
LB, Auburn, 6-3, 225.
4. **WHALEY HALL***
G, Mississippi, 6-3, 230.
5. **NO CHOICE**
Choice traded to New York for DICK NOLAN.
6. **NO CHOICE**
Choice traded to Green Bay for JOHN SUTRO.
7. **MARV CLOTHIER**
G, Kansas, 6-4, 220.
8. **NO CHOICE**
Choice traded to Green Bay for LEE FOLKINS.
9. **NO CHOICE**
Choice traded to Chicago.
10. **ROD SCHEYER**
T, Washington, 6-2, 220.
11. **RAY SCHOENKE**
C, SMU, 6-3, 225.
12. **BILL PERKINS**
B, Iowa, 6-2, 218.
13. **PAUL WICKER***
T, Fresno State, 6-5, 248.
14. **LOU CIOCI**
LB, Boston College, 6-2, 225.
15. **JERRY OVERTON**
B, Utah, 6-2, 192.
16. **DENNIS GOLDEN**
T, Holy Cross, 6-4, 235.
17. **ERNEST PARKS***
G, McMurry, 6-4, 230 (went to AFL).
18. **BILL FRANK**
T, Colorado, 6-4, 250.
19. **JIM STIGER**
B, Washington, 5-11, 195.
20. **TOMMY LUCAS**
E, Texas, 6-3, 218.

1964
(Drafted 4th)

1. **NO CHOICE**
Choice traded to Pittsburgh for BUDDY DIAL.
2. **MEL RENFRO**
B, Oregon, 6-0, 195.
3. **NO CHOICE**
Choice traded to Los Angeles for BOB LONG and JOHN MEYERS.
4. **PERRY LEE DUNN**
B, Mississippi, 6-2, 205.
5. **NO CHOICE**
Choice traded to Green Bay for GARY BARNES.
6. **(A) BILLY LOTHRIDGE**
QB, Georgia Tech, 6-1, 188.
6. **(B) JIM CURRY**
E, Cincinnati, 6-4, 215 — Choice from Cleveland for ANDY CVERCKO.
6. **(C) JIMMY EVANS**
E, Texas Western, 6-1, 194 — Choice from Green Bay for JERRY NORTON.
7. **BOB HAYES***
WR, Florida A&M, 5-11, 189.
8. **AL GEVERINK**
B, UCLA, 6-2, 190.
9. **JAKE KUPP**
E, Washington, 6-3, 215.
10. **ROGER STAUBACH***
QB, Navy, 6-2, 190.
11. **BOBBY CRENSHAW**
G, Baylor, 6-3, 230 (went to AFL).
12. **JOHNNY NORMAN**
E, Northwestern Louisiana, 6-1, 185.
13. **JERRY RHOME**
QB, Tulsa, 6-0, 185.
14. **JIM WORDEN**
LB, Wittenberg, 6-1, 230.
15. **BILL VAN BURKLEO**
B, Tulsa, 5-11, 185.
16. **PAUL CERCEL**
C, Pittsburgh, 6-2, 222.
17. **HARRY ABELL**
E, Missouri, 6-3, 212 (went to AFL).
18. **NO SELECTION**
Player chosen not eligible.
19. **H.D. MURPHY**
B, Oregon, 6-0, 190.
20. **JOHN HUGHES**
LB, SMU, 6-2, 220.

1965
(Drafted 5th)

1. **CRAIG MORTON**
QB, California, 6-4, 215.
2. **MALCOLM WALKER**
LB, Rice, 6-4, 245.
3. **NO CHOICE**
Choice traded to Green Bay (who traded it to New York) for JOHN ROACH.
4. **(A) JIM SIDLE**
B, Auburn, 6-2, 215.
4. **(B) BOB SVIHUS**
T, USC, 6-4, 240 (went to AFL) — Choice from Detroit for SONNY GIBBS.
5. **ROGER PETTEE**
LB, Florida, 6-4, 230.
6. **SONNY UTZ**
RB, VPI, 5-11, 215.
7. **BRIG OWENS**
B, Cincinnati, 5-11, 183.
8. **RUSSELL WAYT**
LB, Rice, 6-4, 235.
9. **JIM ZANIOS**
FB, Texas Tech, 6-0, 215.
10. **GAYLON McCOLLOUGH**
C, Alabama, 6-3, 215.
11. **JETHRO PUGH**
T, Elizabeth City State, 6-6, 255.
12. **ERNIE KELLERMAN**
QB, Miami (Ohio), 6-0, 175.
13. **JACK SCHRAUB**
E, California, 6-6, 210.
14. **GARRY PORTERFIELD**
E, Tulsa, 6-3, 235.
15. **GENE FOSTER**
B, Arizona State, 6-0, 195 (went to AFL).
16. **DOUG McDOUGAL**
E, Oregon State, 6-4, 228.
17. **MITCH JOHNSON**
T, UCLA, 6-4, 245.
18. **MARTIN AMSLER**
T, Evansville, 6-5, 250.
19. **MARV RETTENMUND**
HB, Ball State, 5-10, 195.
20. **RON BARLOW***
T, Kansas State, 6-2, 230.

1966
(Drafted 5th)

1. **JOHN NILAND**
G, Iowa, 6-3, 245.
2. **WILLIE TOWNES***
DE, Tulsa, 6-5, 265.
3. **NO CHOICE**
Choice to San Francisco for LEON DONOHUE.
4. **NO CHOICE**
Choice to Baltimore for RALPH NEELY.
5. **(A) NO CHOICE**
Choice to San Francisco for J.D. SMITH.
5. **(B) WALT GARRISON**
RB, Oklahoma State, 6-0, 209 — Choice from Baltimore through Detroit for AMOS MARSH.
6. **BOB DUNLEVY**
E, West Virginia, 6-4, 195.
7. **ART ROBINSON**
E, Florida A&M, 6-0, 208.
8. **DON KUNIT**
RB, Penn State, 6-2, 200.
9. **DARRELL ELAM**
FL, West Virginia Tech, 6-2, 189.
10. **MASON MITCHELL**
RB, Washington, 6-1, 170.
11. **AUSTIN DENNEY***
E, Tennessee, 6-2, 225.
12. **(A) LES SHY**
RB, Long Beach State, 6-1, 200 — Choice from Pittsburgh for LEE FOLKINS.
12. **CRAIG BAYNHAM***
RB, Georgia Tech, 6-1, 200.
13. **RONNIE LAMB**
B, South Carolina, 6-2, 216.
14. **LEWIS TURNER**
RB, Norfolk State, 6-2, 183.
15. **MARK GARTUNG***
DT, Oregon State, 6-4, 255.
16. **TOM PIGGEE**
RB, San Francisco State, 5-11, 200.
17. **GEORGE ALLEN**
T, West Texas State, 6-7, 245 (went to AFL).
18. **STEVE ORR**
DT, Washington, 6-4, 230.
19. **BYRON JOHNSON**
E, Central Washington State, 6-5, 255.
20. **LOU HUDSON**
FL, Minnesota, 6-5, 220.

1967
(Drafted 23rd)

1. **NO CHOICE**
Choice given along with second and two fifths, to Houston for RALPH NEELY.
2. **NO CHOICE**
NEELY trade.
3. **PHIL CLARK**
DB, Northwestern, 6-2, 207.
4. **CURTIS MARKER**
G, Northern Michigan, 6-2, 253.
5. **(A) NO CHOICE**
Choice and JIM STEFFEN from Washington for BRIG OWENS, MITCH JOHNSON and JAKE KUPP; NEELY trade.
5. **(B) NO CHOICE**
Choice from Cleveland for JOE BOB ISBELL; NEELY trade.
5. **(C) NO CHOICE**
Choice to Green Bay for HENRY GREMMINGER.
6. **SIMS STOKES**
E, Northern Arizona, 6-1, 198.
7. **RAYFIELD WRIGHT**
T, Ft. Valley State, 6-7, 235.
8. **STEVE LAUB**
QB, Illinois Wesleyan, 6-1, 190.
9. **BYRON MORGAN**
DB, Findlay (Ohio), 6-3, 212.
10. **EUGENE BOWEN**
RB, Tennessee A&I, 5-8, 210.
11. **PAT RILEY**
E, Kentucky, 6-2, 205.
12. **HAROLD DETERS**
K, North Carolina State, 6-0, 200.
13. **AL KERKIAN**
DE, Akron, 6-6, 235.
14. **TOM BOYD**
G, Tarleton State, 6-3, 250.
15. **LEAVIE DAVIS**
DB, Edward Waters College (Florida), 6-4, 210.
16. **PAUL BROTHERS**
HB, Oregon State, 6-1, 195.
17. **GEORGE ADAMS**
LB, Morehead State (Kentucky), 6-2, 218.

1968
(Drafted Alternately 20th, 19th, 21st)

1. **DENNIS HOMAN**
FL, Alabama, 6-1, 181.
2. **DAVID McDANIELS**
E, Mississippi Valley, 6-4, 200.
3. **(A) NO CHOICE**
Choice to Minnesota for LANCE RENTZEL.
3. **(B) ED HARMON**
LB, Louisville, 6-4, 246 — Choice from Chicago for AUSTIN DENNEY and MAC PERCIVAL.
4. **(A) NO CHOICE**
Choice to New Orleans for LARRY STEPHENS.
4. **(B) JOHN DOUGLAS**
LB, Missouri, 6-2, 215 — Choice from New York for JIM COLVIN.
5. **BLAINE NYE**
G, Stanford, 6-4, 255.
6. **D.D. LEWIS**
LB, Mississippi State, 6-1, 210.
7. **BOB TAUCHER**
T, Nebraska, 6-4, 251.
8. **FRANK BROWN**
DE, Albany (Ga.) State, 6-3, 249.
9. **KEN KMIEC**
DB, Illinois, 6-2, 187.
10. **BEN OLISON**
FL, Kansas, 6-1, 170.

11. **RON SHOTTS**
RB, Oklahoma, 6-0, 206.
12. **WILSON WHITTY**
LB, Boston University, 6-3, 224.
13. **CARTER LORD**
TE, Harvard, 6-2, 214.
14. **RON WILLIAMS**
DB, West Virginia, 6-2, 190.
15. **TOMMY LUNCEFORD**
P, Auburn, 6-2, 202.
16. **LARRY COLE**
DE, Hawaii, 6-5, 250.
17. **GEORGE NORDGREN**
RB, Houston, 6-0, 200.

1969
(Drafted Alternately 24th, 23rd, 22nd)

1. **CALVIN HILL**
RB, Yale, 6-3, 230.
2. **RICHMOND FLOWERS**
WR, Tennessee, 6-0, 183.
3. **(A) TOM STINCIC**
LB, Michigan, 6-2, 226.
3. **(B) HALVOR HAGEN**
DE, Weber State, 6-5, 250 — Choice from San Francisco for HAROLD HAYS.
4. **NO CHOICE**
Choice to New Orleans for DAVE SIMMONS.
5. **(A) NO CHOICE**
Choice to Baltimore for ANDY STYNCHULA.
5. **(B) CHUCK KYLE**
LB, Purdue, 6-1, 220 — Choice from Los Angeles for COY BACON.
6. **RICH SHAW**
FL, Arizona State, 6-4, 205.
7. **LARRY BALES**
WR, Emory & Henry, 5-11, 185.
8. **ELMER BENHARDT**
LB, Missouri, 6-2, 200.
9. **CLAXTON WELCH**
RB, Oregon, 5-11, 200.
10. **STUART GOTTLIEB**
G, Weber State, 6-5, 250.
11. **CLARENCE WILLIAMS**
DT, Prairie View A&M, 6-5, 250.
12. **BOB BELDEN**
QB, Notre Dame, 6-2, 210.
13. **RENE MATISON**
WR, New Mexico, 6-0, 185.
14. **GERALD LUTRI**
T, Northern Michigan, 6-4, 256.
15. **BILL JUSTUS**
DB, Tennessee, 6-1, 180.
16. **FLOYD KERR**
DB, Colorado State, 6-3, 195.
17. **BILL BAILEY**
DT, Lewis & Clark, 6-4, 260.

1970
(Drafted 23rd)

1. **DUANE THOMAS**
RB, West Texas, 6-1, 220.
2. **(A) BOB ASHER**
T, Vanderbilt, 6-5, 250 — Choice from Chicago for CRAIG BAYNHAM and PHIL CLARK.
2. **(B) MARGENE ADKINS**
WR, Henderson, J.C., 5-10, 183.
3. **(A) CHARLIE WATERS**
CB, Clemson, 6-1, 193 — Choice from Houston through Cleveland for JERRY RHOME.
3. **(B) STEVE KINER**
LB, Tennessee, 6-1, 220 — Choice from Cleveland for JERRY RHOME.
3. **(C) DENTON FOX**
S, Texas Tech, 6-2, 205.
4. **JOHN FITZGERALD**
T, Boston College, 6-4, 265.
5. **NO CHOICE**
Choice to St. Louis for BOBBY JOE CONRAD.
6. **PAT TOOMAY**
DE, Vanderbilt, 6-5, 230.
7. **DON ABBEY**
LB, Penn State, 6-2, 252.
8. **JERRY DOSSEY**
G, Arkansas, 6-4, 244.
9. **ZENON ANDRUSYSHYN**
K, UCLA, 6-2, 212.
10. **PETE ATHAS**
S, Dade J.C., 6-0, 186.
11. **IVAN SOUTHERLAND**
DT, Clemson, 6-4, 246.
12. **JOE WILLIAMS**
RB, Wyoming, 6-1, 193.
13. **MARK WASHINGTON**
CB, Morgan State, 5-11, 183.
14. **JULIAN MARTIN**
WR, North Carolina Central, 6-3, 190.
15. **KEN DeLONG**
TE, Tennessee, 6-2, 223.
16. **SEABERN HILL**
CB, Arizona State, 6-2, 195.
17. **GLENN PATTERSON**
C, Nebraska, 6-3, 220.

1971
(Drafted 25th)

1. **TOBY SMITH**
DE, Southern California, 6-5, 250.
2. **ISAAC THOMAS**
CB, Bishop, 6-2, 190.
3. **(A) SAM SCARBER**
RB, New Mexico, 6-2, 235 — Choice from St. Louis for JOHN WILBUR.
3. **(B) BILL GREGORY**
DE, Wisconsin, 6-5, 240.
4. **(A) JOE CARTER**
TE, Grambling, 6-3, 219 — Choice from New Orleans for WILLIE TOWNES.
4. **(B) BUDDY MITCHELL**
T, Mississippi, 6-5, 232.
5. **RON KADZIEL**
LB, Stanford, 6-3, 215.
6. **STEVE MAIER**
WR, Northern Arizona, 6-3, 192.
7. **BILL GRIFFIN**
T-G, Catawba, 6-5, 250.
8. **RON JESSIE**
WR, Kansas, 6-0, 183.
9. **HONOR JACKSON**
WR, Pacific, 6-2, 190.
10. **RODNEY WALLACE**
DT, New Mexico, 6-5, 260.
11. **ERNEST BONWELL**
LB, Lane College, 6-4, 225.
12. **STEVE GOEPEL**
QB, Colgate, 6-1½, 200.
13. **JAMES FORD**
RB, Texas Southern, 6-0, 200.
14. **TYRONE COUEY**
DB, Utah State, 6-1½, 194.
15. **BOB YOUNG**
TE, Delaware, 6-5, 250.
16. **JOHN BRENNAN**
T, Boston College, 6-2½, 260.
17. **JOHN BOMER**
C, Memphis State, 6-3, 230.

1972
(Drafted 26th)

1. **BILL THOMAS**
RB, Boston College, 6-2, 225.
2. **(A) ROBERT NEWHOUSE**
RB, Houston, 5-10, 202 — Choice from New England for HALVOR HAGEN and HONOR JACKSON.
2. **(B) JOHN BABINECZ**
LB, Villanova, 6-1, 222 — Choice from New Orleans for MARGENE ADKINS.
2. **(C) CHARLES McKEE**
WR, Arizona, 6-2, 199.
3. **(A) MIKE KELLER**
LB, Michigan, 6-4, 221 — Choice from New England for HALVOR HAGEN and HONOR JACKSON.
3. **(B) MARV BATEMAN**
P-K, Utah, 6-4, 213.
4. **(A) TIM KEARNEY**
LB, Northern Michigan, 6-2, 225 — Choice from New Orleans for JOE WILLIAMS.
4. **(B) ROBERT WEST**
WR, San Diego State, 6-4, 218 — Choice from New England for STEVE KINER.
4. **(C) CHARLES ZAPIEC**
LB, Penn State, 6-2, 222 — Choice from Detroit for RON JESSIE.
4. **(D) NO CHOICE**
Choice to New Orleans for DON TALBERT.
5. **NO CHOICE**
Choice to San Diego for TONY LISCIO.
6. **CHARLES BOLDEN**
DB, Iowa, 6-3, 195.
7. **NO CHOICE**
Choice to Chicago for LEE ROY CAFFEY.
8. **RALPH COLEMAN**
LB, North Carolina A&T, 6-4, 216.
9. **ROY BELL**
RB, Oklahoma, 5-10, 208.
10. **RICHARD AMMAN**
DE, Florida State, 6-5, 234.
11. **LONNIE LEONARD**
T-G, North Carolina A&T, 6-4, 244.
12. **JIMMY HARRIS**
WR, Ohio State, 5-10, 180.
13. **JEAN FUGETT**
TE, Amherst, 6-3, 219.
14. **ALAN THOMPSON**
RB, Wisconsin, 6-0, 225.
15. **CARLOS ALVAREZ**
WR, Florida 5-10, 184.
16. **GORDON LONGMIRE**
QB, Utah, 6-1, 205.
17. **ALFONSO CAIN**
DT, Bethune-Cookman, 6-3, 271.

1973
(Drafted Alternately 20th, 22nd and 21st)

1. **BILLY JOE DuPREE**
TE, Michigan State, 6-4, 225.
2. **(A) GOLDEN RICHARDS**
WR, Hawaii, 6-0, 172 — Choice from Green Bay for RON WIDBY and IKE THOMAS.
2. **(B) NO CHOICE**
Choice to Chicago as compensation for signing JACK CONCANNON.
3. **(A) HARVEY MARTIN**
DT, East Texas State, 6-5, 262 — Choice from Houston through New Orleans for TOM STINCIC.
3. **(B) NO CHOICE**
Choice to New England for RON SELLERS.
4. **DRANE SCRIVENER**
DB, Tulsa, 6-0, 176.
5. **BRUCE WALTON**
T, UCLA, 6-6, 251.
6. **BOB LEYEN**
G, Yale, 6-4, 256.
7. **RODRIGO BARNES**
LA, Rice, 6-1, 215.
8. **DAN WERNER**
QB, Michigan State, 6-4, 195.
9. **MIKE WHITE**
CB, Minnesota, 6-0, 196.
10. **CARL JOHNSON**
LB, Tennessee, 6-1, 225.
11. **GERALD CASWELL**
G, Colorado State, 6-4, 250.
12. **JIM ARNESON**
G, Arizona, 6-3, 236.
13. **JOHN SMITH**
WR, UCLA, 6-1, 187.
14. **BOB THORNTON**
G-C, North Carolina, 6-3, 234.
15. **WALT BAISY**
LB, Grambling, 6-2, 222.
16. **JOHN CONLEY**
TE, Hawaii, 6-2, 228.
17. **LES STRAYHORN**
RB, East Carolina, 5-10, 205.

1974
(Drafted Alternately 22nd, 21st, 20th and 23rd)

1. **(A) ED JONES**
DE, Tennessee State, 6-8, 260 — Choice from Houston for TODY SMITH and BILLY PARKS.
1. **(B) CHARLES YOUNG**
RB, North Carolina State, 6-1, 215.
2. **NO CHOICE**
Choice and RON SELLERS to Miami for OTTO STOWE.
3. **(A) DANNY WHITE**
QB, Arizona State, 6-2, 180 — Choice from Houston for TODY SMITH and BILLY PARKS.
3. **(B) CALVIN PETERSON**
LB, UCLA, 6-3, 218.
4. **(A) KEN HUTCHERSON**
LB, Livingston State, 6-1, 214 — Choice from Oakland for GLOSTER RICHARDSON.
4. **(B) ANDY ANDRADE**
RB-DB, Northern Michigan, 5-11, 193.
5. **JOHN KELSEY**
T, Missouri, 6-6, 226.
6. **JIM BRIGHT**
DB, UCLA, 6-1, 210.
7. **RAYMOND NESTER**
LB, Michigan State, 6-2, 224.
8. **MIKE HOLT**
DB, Michigan State, 5-11, 176.

9. **BILL DULIN**
T, Johnson C. Smith, 6-6, 244.
10. **DENNIS MORGAN**
DB, Western Illinois, 5-11, 203.
11. **HARVEY McGEE**
WR, Southern Mississippi, 6-2, 209.
12. **KEITH BOBO**
QB, Southern Methodist, 6-3, 196.
13. **FRED LIMA**
K, Colorado, 5-9, 202.
14. **DOUG RICHARDS**
DB, Brigham Young, 6-4, 185.
15. **BRUCE CRAFT**
DT, Geneva, Pa., 6-4, 232.
16. **GENE KILLIAN**
T, Tennessee, 6-4, 225.
17. **LAWRIE SKOLROOD**
T, North Dakota, 6-5, 230.

1975
(Drafted 18th)

1. **(A) RANDY WHITE**
DE, Maryland, 6-4, 250 — Choice from N.Y. Giants for CRAIG MORTON.
1. **(B) THOMAS HENDERSON**
LB, Langston, 6-2, 214.
2. **BURTON LAWLESS**
G, Florida, 6-4, 253.
3. **BOB BREUNIG**
LB, Arizona State, 6-2, 236.
4. **(A) PAT DONOVAN**
DE, Stanford, 6-5, 240 — Choice from Houston for MIKE MONTGOMERY.
4. **(B) RANDY HUGHES**
DB, Oklahoma, 6-4, 209.
5. **(A) KYLE DAVIS**
C, Oklahoma, 6-3, 240 — Choice from Green Bay for JACK CONCANNON.
5. **(B) NO CHOICE**
Choice to Cincinnati for CLINT LONGLEY.
6. **ROLLY WOOLSEY**
DB, Boise State, 6-1, 175.
7. **MICHAEL HEGMAN**
LB, Tennessee State, 6-4, 220.
8. **MITCH HOOPES**
P, Arizona, 6-0, 210.
9. **ED JONES**
DB, Rutgers, 6-0, 193.
10. **DENNIS BOOKER**
RB, Millersville State, 6-1, 235.
11. **GREG KRPALEK**
C, Oregon State, 6-5, 242.
12. **CHUCK BLAND**
DB, Cincinnati, 5-11, 188.
13. **HERBERT SCOTT**
G, Virginia Union, 6-2, 248.
14. **SCOTT LAIDLAW**
RB, Stanford, 6-0, 206.
15. **WILLIE HAMILTON**
RB, Arizona, 5-11, 182.
16. **PETE CLARK**
TE, Colorado State, 6-4, 234.
17. **JIM TESTERMAN**
TE, Dayton, 6-5, 225.

1976
(Drafted 27th)

1. **AARON KYLE**
DB, Wyoming, 5-11, 183.
2. **(A) JIM JENSEN**
RB, Iowa, 6-4, 226 — Choice from N.Y. Giants for CRAIG MORTON.
2. **(B) JIM EIDSON**
G, Mississippi St., 6-4, 253.
3. **(A) DUKE FERGERSON**
WR, San Diego St., 6-1, 186 — Choice from San Francisco for BOB HAYES.
3. **(B) JOHN SMITH**
RB, Boise State, 6-0, 191 — Choice from Denver for OTTO STOWE.
3. **(C) BUTCH JOHNSON**
WR, UC-Riverside, 6-1, 175.
4. **TOM RAFFERTY**
G, Penn State, 6-3, 248.
5. **WALLY PESUIT**
T, Kentucky, 6-4, 260.
6. **RUSS McGUIRE**
T, Indiana, 6-3, 265.
7. **(A) GREG SCHAUM**
DT, Michigan State, 6-4, 246 — Choice from San Diego for KEN HUTCHERSON.
7. **(B) DAVID WILLIAMS**
RB, Colorado, 6-2, 210.
8. **HENRY LAWS**
DB, South Carolina, 5-10, 171.
9. **BEASLEY REECE**
DB, North Texas, 6-1, 193.
10. **LEROY COOK**
DE, Alabama, 6-4, 212.
11. **CORNELIUS GREEN**
QB, Ohio, 5-11, 170.
12. **CHARLES McSHANE**
LB, Cal Lutheran, 6-2, 211.
13. **MARK DRISCOLL**
QB, Colorado St., 6-1, 184.
14. **LARRY MUSHINSKIE**
TE, Nebraska, 6-3, 217.
15. **DALE CURRY**
LB, UCLA, 6-2, 222.
16. **RICH COSTANZO**
T, Nebraska, 6-4, 260.
17. **STAN WOODFILL**
K, Oregon, 6-0, 190.

1977
(Drafted Alternately 24th, 25th and 26th)

1. **TONY DORSETT**
RB, Pittsburgh, 5-11, 192 — Choice from Seattle for Cowboys' first-round choice and three second-round choices.
2. **GLENN CARANO**
QB, Nevada-Las Vegas, 6-3, 195 — Choice from Seattle for DUKE FERGERSON.
3. **(A) TONY HILL**
WR, Stanford, 6-2, 196 — Choice from Philadelphia for JOHN NILAND.
3. **(B) VAL BELCHER**
G, Houston, 6-3, 250.
4. **GUY BROWN**
LB, Houston, 6-4, 215.
5. **ANDY FREDERICK**
OL, New Mexico, 6-6, 241.
6. **JIM COOPER**
T, Temple, 6-5, 252.
7. **DAVID STALLS**
DT, Northern Colorado, 6-4, 236.
8. **(A) AL CLEVELAND**
DL, Pacific, 6-4, 246 — Choice from San Diego for MITCH HOOPES.
8. **(B) FRED WILLIAMS**
RB, Arizona State, 5-10, 189.
9. **MARK CANTRELL**
C, North Carolina, 6-3, 252.
10. **STEVE DeBERG**
QB, San Jose State, 6-2, 205.
11. **DON WARDLOW**
TE, Washington, 6-6, 230.
12. **GREG PETERS**
OL, California, 6-5, 257.

1978
(Drafted 28th)

1. **LARRY BETHEA**
DL, Michigan State, 6-5, 258.
2. **TODD CHRISTENSEN**
RB-TE, Brigham Young, 6-3, 224.
3. **DAVID HUDGENS**
OL, Oklahoma, 6-5, 245.
4. **ALOIS BLACKWELL**
RB, Houston, 5-11, 194.
5. **RICH ROSEN**
G, Syracuse, 6-3, 242.
6. **HAROLD RANDOLPH**
LB, East Carolina, 6-1, 191.
7. **TOM RANDALL**
DT, Iowa State, 6-5, 248.
8. **HOMER BUTLER**
WR, UCLA, 6-1, 184.
9. **RUSS WILLIAMS**
DB, Tennessee, 6-1, 197.
10. **BARRY TOMASETTI**
OL, Iowa, 6-3, 249.
11. **DENNIS THURMAN**
S, Southern Cal, 5-11, 172.
12. **LEE WASHBURN**
OL, Montana State, 6-6, 253.

1979
(Drafted 27th)

1. **ROBERT SHAW**
C, Tennessee, 6-4, 252.
2. **AARON MITCHELL**
CB, Nevada-Las Vegas, 6-1, 196.
3. **DOUG COSBIE**
TE, Santa Clara, 6-6, 230, Swapped choices with Seattle in BILL GREGORY trade.
4. **RALPH DeLOACH**
DE, California, 6-5, 254.
5. **(A) BOB HUKILL**
OL, North Carolina, 6-5, 250. Choice from Chicago for GOLDEN RICHARDS.
5. **(B) CURTIS ANDERSON**
DE, Central State (O), 6-6, 240. Choice from Seattle for EFREN HERRERA.
5. **(C) RON SPRINGS**
RB, Ohio State, 6-0, 197.
6. **(A) TIM LAVENDER**
CB, So. California, 6-3, 187. Choice from Seattle for BILL GREGORY.
6. **(B) MIKE SALZANO**
OL, North Carolina, 6-3, 242. Choice from Denver for JIM JENSEN.
6. **(C) CHRIS DeFRANCE**
WR, Arizona St., 6-1, 205.
7. **GREG FITZPATRICK**
LB, Youngstown, 6-2, 227.
8. **BRUCE THORNTON**
DT, Illinois, 6-5, 266.
9. **GARRY COBB**
LB, So. California, 6-2, 209.
10. **MIKE CALHOUN**
DT, Notre Dame, 6-4, 228.
11. **NO CHOICE**
Choice to Detroit for SKIP BUTLER.
12. **QUENTIN LOWRY**
LB, Youngstown, 6-2, 225.

1980
(Drafted Alternately 23rd, 24th and 25th)

1. **NO CHOICE**
Choice given along with second-round choice to Baltimore for JOHN DUTTON.
2. **NO CHOICE**
Choice given along with first-round choice to Baltimore for JOHN DUTTON.
3. **(A) BILL ROE**
LB, Colorado, 6-3, 220 — Choice from Chicago for GOLDEN RICHARDS.
3. **(B) JAMES JONES**
RB, Mississippi State, 5-10, 200.
4. **KURT PETERSEN**
DL, Missouri, 6-5, 255.
5. **GARY HOGEBOOM**
QB, Central Michigan, 6-4, 195.
6. **TIMMY NEWSOME**
RB, Winston-Salem St., 6-1, 228.
7. **LESTER BROWN**
CB, Clemson, 5-11, 176.
8. **LARRY SAVAGE**
LB, Michigan State, 6-3, 225.
9. **JACKIE FLOWERS**
WR, Florida State, 6-0, 194.
10. **MATTHEW TEAGUE**
DE, Prairie View A&M, 6-4, 238.
11. **GARY PADJEN**
LB, Arizona State, 6-1, 238.
12. **NORM WELLS**
DT, Northwestern, 6-5, 249.

1981
(Drafted Alternately 25th, 26th)

1. **HOWARD RICHARDS**
OT, Missouri, 6-5, 255.
2. **DOUG DONLEY**
WR, Ohio St., 6-0, 180.
3. **GLEN TITENSOR**
DL, Brigham Young, 6-4, 250.
4. **(A) SCOTT PELLUER**
LB, Wash. St., 6-1, 213 — Choice from San Francisco for THOMAS HENDERSON.
4. **(B) DERRIE NELSON**
LB, Nebraska, 6-2, 217.
5. **DANNY SPRADLIN**
LB, Tennessee, 6-1, 229.
6. **VINCE SKILLINGS**
DB, Ohio St., 5-11, 176.
7. **(A) RON FELLOWS**
DB, Missouri, 5-11, 165 — Choice from Tampa Bay for DAVE STALLS.
7. **(B) KEN MILLER**
DB, East Michigan, 5-11, 180.
8. **PAUL PIUROWSKI**
LB, Florida St., 6-2, 219.
9. **MIKE WILSON**
WR, Wash. St., 6-3, 202.
10. **PAT GRAHAM**
DT, California, 6-3, 257.
11. **TIM MORRISON**
OG, Georgia, 6-3, 258.
12. **NATE LUNDY**
WR, Indiana, 6-0, 169.

1982
(Drafted 26th)

1. **ROD HILL**
CB, Kentucky State, 6-0, 182.
2. **JEFF ROHRER**
LB, Yale, 6-3, 228.
3. **JIM ELIOPULOS**
LB, Wyoming, 6-2, 224.
4. **(A) BRIAN CARPENTER**
CB, Michigan, 5-11, 166 — Choice from Tampa Bay for DAVE STALLS.
4. **(B) MONTY HUNTER**
S, Salem College, 6-0, 201.
5. **PHIL POZDERAC**
T, Notre Dame, 6-8, 264.
6. **(A) KEN HAMMOND**
G, Vanderbilt, 6-3, 270 — Choice from Cleveland for BRUCE HUTHER.
6. **(B) CHARLES DAUM**
DL, Cal Poly-SLO, 6-6, 229.
7. **BILL PURIFOY**
DL, Tulsa, 6-8, 248.
8. **(A) GEORGE PEOPLES**
RB, Auburn, 6-0, 202 — Choice from Denver through Buffalo for WADE MANNING.
8. **(B) DWIGHT SULLIVAN**
RB, North Carolina State, 5-9, 204.
9. **JOE GARY**
DL, UCLA, 6-4, 262.
10. **TODD ECKERSON**
T, North Carolina State, 6-4, 268.
11. **(A) GEORGE THOMPSON**
WR, Albany State (Ga.), 6-3, 211 — Choice from Tampa Bay for AARON MITCHELL.
11. **(B) MICHAEL WHITING**
RB, Florida State, 6-0, 214.
12. **RICH BURTNESS**
G, Montana, 6-4, 235.

1983
(Drafted 23rd)

1. **JIM JEFFCOAT**
DE, Arizona State, 6-5, 260.
2. **MIKE WALTER**
LB, Oregon, 6-3, 230.
3. **BRYAN CALDWELL**
DE, Arizona State, 6-4, 248.
4. **CHRIS FAULKNER**
TE, Florida, 6-4, 257.
5. **CHUCK McSWAIN**
RB, Clemson, 6-0, 190.
6. **REGGIE COLLIER**
QB, Southern Mississippi, 6-3, 207.
7. **CHRIS SCHULTZ**
T, Arizona, 6-8, 259.
8. **LAWRENCE RICKS**
RB, Michigan, 5-9, 194.
9. **AL GROSS**
S, Arizona, 6-3, 186.
10. **ERIC MORAN**
T, Washington, 6-5, 282.
11. **DAN TAYLOR**
T, Idaho State, 6-3, 258.
12. **LORENZO BOUIER**

1984
(Drafted 25th)

1. **CANNON, BILLY**
LB, Texas A&M, 6-4, 235.
2. **SCOTT, VICTOR**
DB, Colorado, 5-10, 182 — Choice from Minnesota through Houston for BUTCH JOHNSON.
3. **CORNWELL, FRED**
TE, Southern Cal, 6-5, 236.
4. **DeOSSIE, STEVE**
LB, Boston College, 6-2, 250.
5. **(A) PELLUER, STEVE**
QB, Washington, 6-4, 204 — Choice from Tampa Bay for DANNY SPRADLIN.
5. **(B) GRANGER, NORM**
RB, Iowa, 5-9, 217.
6. **(A) LOCKHART, EUGENE**
LB, Houston, 6-2, 228 — Choice from Chicago for JAY SALDI.
6. **(B) LEVELIS, JOE**
OG, Iowa, 6-3, 270.
7. **MARTIN, ED**
LB, Indiana State, 6-3, 218.
8. **REVELL, MIKE**
RB, Bethune Cookman, 5-11, 197.
9. **(A) HUNT, JOHN**
OL, Florida, 6-4, 262 — Choice from Indianapolis for RAUL ALLEGRE.
9. **(B) MAUNE, NEAL**
OL, Notre Dame, 6-4, 249.
10. **SALONEN, BRIAN**
TE, Montana, 6-2, 227.
11. **AUGHTMAN, DOWE**
DL, Auburn, 6-2, 272.
12. **LEWIS, CARL**
WR, Houston, 6-3, 187.

*Drafted as Future

Cowboys vs. NFL Opponents

Atlanta Falcons

(Dallas Leads Series, 7-1)

Year	Site	Winner-Score	Att.
1966	Atlanta	Dallas, 47-14	56,990
1967	Dallas	Dallas, 37-7	54,751
1969	Atlanta	Dallas, 24-17	54,833
1970	Dallas	Dallas, 13-0	53,611
1974	Atlanta	Dallas, 24-0	52,322
1976	Atlanta	Atlanta, 17-10	54,972
1978*	Dallas	Dallas, 27-20	60,338
1981*	Atlanta	Dallas, 30-27	60,022

*NFC Divisional Playoffs

Buffalo Bills

(Dallas Leads Series, 3-1)

Year	Site	Winner-Score	Att.
1971	Buffalo	Dallas, 49-37	46,206
1976	Dallas	Dallas, 17-10	51,779
1981	Dallas	Dallas, 27-14	62,583
1984	Buffalo	Buffalo, 14-3	74,391

Chicago Bears

(Dallas Leads Series, 8-3)

Year	Site	Winner-Score	Att.
1960	Chicago	Chicago, 17-7	39,951
1962	Dallas	Chicago, 34-33	12,692
1964	Chicago	Dallas, 24-10	47,527
1968	Chicago	Dallas, 34-3	46,667
1971	Chicago	Chicago, 23-19	55,049
1973	Chicago	Dallas, 20-17	55,701
1976	Dallas	Dallas, 31-21	61,346
1977*	Dallas	Dallas, 37-7	62,920
1979	Dallas	Dallas, 24-20	64,056
1981	Dallas	Dallas, 10-9	63,499
1984	Chicago	Dallas, 23-14	63,623

*NFC Divisional Playoffs

Cincinnati Bengals

(Dallas Leads Series, 2-0)

Year	Site	Winner-Score	Att.
1973	Dallas	Dallas, 38-10	58,802
1979	Dallas	Dallas, 38-13	63,179

1982 Oct. 24 at Cincinnati

Cleveland Browns

(Cleveland Leads Series, 15-8)

Year	Site	Winner-Score	Att.
1960	Dallas	Cleve., 48-7	28,500
1961	Cleve.	Cleve., 25-7	43,638
1961	Dallas	Cleve., 38-17	23,500
1962	Cleve.	Cleve., 19-10	44,040
1962	Dallas	Dallas, 45-21	24,226
1963	Dallas	Cleve., 41-24	28,710
1963	Cleve.	Cleve., 27-17	55,096
1964	Cleve.	Cleve., 27-6	72,062
1964	Dallas	Cleve., 20-16	37,456
1965	Cleve.	Cleve., 23-17	80,451
1965	Dallas	Cleve., 24-17	76,251
1966	Cleve.	Cleve., 30-21	84,721
1966	Dallas	Dallas, 26-14	80,259
1967	Cleve.	Dallas, 21-14	81,039
1967*	Dallas	Dallas, 52-14	70,786
1968	Dallas	Dallas, 28-7	68,733
1968*	Cleve.	Cleve., 31-20	81,497
1969	Cleve.	Cleve., 42-10	84,850
1969*	Dallas	Cleve., 38-14	69,321
1970	Cleve.	Dallas, 6-2	75,458
1974	Dallas	Dallas, 41-17	48,754
1979	Cleve.	Cleve., 26-7	80,123
1982	Dallas	Dallas, 31-14	48,267

*Eastern Conference Championship Game

Denver Broncos

(Dallas Leads Series, 3-1)

Year	Site	Winner-Score	Att.
1973	Denver	Dallas, 22-10	51,706
1977	Dallas	Dallas, 14-6	63,752
1978*	New O.	Dallas, 27-10	76,400
1980	Denver	Denver, 41-20	74,919

*Super Bowl XII, Jan. 15, 1978

Detroit Lions

(Dallas Leads Series, 6-2)

Year	Site	Winner-Score	Att.
1960	Detroit	Detroit, 23-14	43,272
1963	Dallas	Dallas, 17-14	27,264
1968	Dallas	Dallas, 59-13	61,382
1970*	Dallas	Dallas, 5-0	73,167
1972	Dallas	Dallas, 28-24	65,378
1975	Detroit	Dallas, 36-10	79,784
1977	Dallas	Dallas, 37-0	63,160
1981	Detroit	Detroit, 27-24	79,694

*Divisional Playoff Game

Green Bay Packers

(Green Bay Leads Series, 8-5)

Year	Site	Winner-Score	Att.
1960	Gr. Bay	Gr. Bay, 41-7	32,294
1964	Dallas	Gr. Bay, 45-21	44,975
1965	Milw.	Gr. Bay, 13-3	48,311
1966*	Dallas	Gr. Bay, 34-27	75,504
1967*	Gr. Bay	Gr. Bay, 21-17	50,861
1968	Dallas	Gr. Bay, 28-17	74,604
1970	Dallas	Dallas, 16-3	67,182
1972	Milw.	Gr. Bay, 16-14	47,103
1975	Dallas	Gr. Bay, 19-17	64,934
1978	Milw.	Dallas, 42-14	55,256
1980	Milw.	Dallas, 28-7	54,776
1982†	Dallas	Dallas, 37-26	63,972
1984	Dallas	Dallas, 20-6	64,222

†Super Bowl Tournament

Houston Oilers

(Dallas Leads Series, 3-1)

Year	Site	Winner-Score	Att.
1970	Dallas	Dallas, 52-10	50,504
1974	Houston	Dallas, 10-0	49,775
1979	Dallas	Houston, 30-24	63,897
1982	Houston	Dallas, 37-7	51,808

Indianapolis Colts

(Dallas Leads Series, 6-3)

Year	Site	Winner-Score	Att.
1960	Dallas	Balt., 45-7	25,500
1967	Balt.	Balt., 23-17	60,238
1969	Dallas	Dallas, 27-10	63,191
1970†	Miami	Balt., 16-13	80,055
1972	Balt.	Dallas, 21-0	58,992
1976	Dallas	Dallas, 30-27	64,237
1978	Dallas	Dallas, 38-0	64,224

1981	Balt.	Dallas, 37-13	54,871
1984	Dallas	Dallas, 22-3	58,724

†Super Bowl Jan. 17, 1971

Kansas City Chiefs

(Dallas Leads Series, 2-1)

Year	Site	Winner-Score	Att.
1970	Kan. City	Dallas, 27-16	51,158
1975	Dallas	Kan. City, 34-31	63,539
1983	Dallas	Dallas, 41-21	64,103

L.A. Raiders

(L.A. Leads Series, 2-1)

Year	Site	Winner-Score	Att.
1974	Oakland	Oakland, 27-23	45,850
1980	Oakland	Dallas, 19-13	53,194
1983	Dallas	L.A., 40-38	64,991

Los Angeles Rams

(Dallas Leads Series, 10-9)

Year	Site	Winner-Score	Att.
1960	Dallas	L.A., 38-13	16,000
1962	L.A.	Dallas, 27-17	26,907
1967	Dallas	L.A., 35-13	75,229
1969	L.A.	L.A., 24-23	79,105
1971	Dallas	Dallas, 28-21	66,595
1973	L.A.	L.A., 37-31	81,428
1973†	Dallas	Dallas, 27-16	64,291
1975	Dallas	Dallas, 18-7	49,091
1975‡	L.A.	Dallas, 37-7	84,483
1976†	Dallas	L.A., 14-12	62,436
1978	L.A.	L.A., 27-14	65,749
1978‡	L.A.	Dallas, 28-0	67,470
1979	Dallas	Dallas, 30-6	64,462
1979†	Dallas	L.A., 21-19	64,792
1980	L.A.	L.A., 38-14	62,548
1980§	Dallas	Dallas, 34-13	64,533
1981	Dallas	Dallas, 29-17	64,649
1983§	Dallas	L.A., 24-17	43,521
1984	L.A.	Dallas, 20-13	65,403

§Wild Card Game
†Divisional Playoff Game
‡NFC Championship Game

Miami Dolphins

(Miami Leads Series, 3-2)

Year	Site	Winner-Score	Att.
1971*	New O.	Dallas, 24-3	81,035
1973	Dallas	Miami, 14-7	64,100
1978	Miami	Miami, 23-16	69,414
1981	Dallas	Dallas, 28-27	64,221
1984	Miami	Miami, 28-21	74,139

*Super Bowl VI, Jan. 16, 1972

Minnesota Vikings

(Dallas Leads Series, 10-5)

Year	Site	Winner-Score	Att.
1961	Dallas	Dallas, 21-7	20,500
1961	Minn.	Dallas, 28-0	33,070
1966	Dallas	Dallas, 28-17	64,116
1968	Dallas	Dallas, 20-7	47,644
1970	Minn.	Minn., 54-13	47,900
1971*	Minn.	Dallas, 20-12	49,100
1973†	Dallas	Minn., 27-10	64,524
1974	Dallas	Minn., 23-21	57,847
1975*	Minn.	Dallas, 17-14	48,341
1977	Minn.	Dallas, 16-10(OT)	47,678
1977†	Dallas	Dallas, 23-8	61,968
1978	Dallas	Minn., 21-10	61,848
1979	Minn.	Dallas, 36-20	47,572
1982	Minn.	Minn., 31-27	60,007
1983	Minn.	Dallas, 37-24	60,774

*Divisional Playoff Game
†NFC Championship Game

New England Patriots

(Dallas Leads Series, 5-0)

Year	Site	Winner-Score	Att.
1971	Dallas	Dallas, 44-21	65,708
1975	N. Eng.	Dallas, 34-31	60,905
1978	Dallas	Dallas, 17-10	63,263
1981	N. Eng.	Dallas, 35-21	60,311
1984	Dallas	Dallas, 20-17	55,341

New Orleans Saints

(Dallas Leads Series, 11-1)

Year	Site	Winner-Score	Att.
1967	Dallas	Dallas, 14-10	52,582
1967	N.O.	Dallas, 27-10	83,437
1968	N.O.	Dallas, 17-3	84,728
1969	N.O.	Dallas, 21-17	79,567
1969	Dallas	Dallas, 33-17	68,282
1971	N.O.	N.O., 24-14	83,088
1973	Dallas	Dallas, 40-3	53,972
1976	N.O.	Dallas, 24-6	61,413
1978	Dallas	Dallas, 27-7	57,920
1982	Dallas	Dallas, 21-7	64,506
1983	Dallas	Dallas, 21-20	62,136
1984	Dallas	Dallas, 30-27	50,966

New York Giants

(Dallas Leads Series, 30-13-2)

Year	Site	Winner-Score	Att.
1960	N.Y.	Tie, 31-31	55,033
1961	Dallas	N.Y., 31-10	41,500
1961	N.Y.	Dallas, 17-16	60,254
1962	Dallas	N.Y., 41-10	45,668
1962	N.Y.	N.Y., 41-31	62,694
1963	N.Y.	N.Y., 37-21	62,889
1963	Dallas	N.Y., 34-27	29,635
1964	Dallas	Tie, 13-13	33,225
1964	N.Y.	Dallas, 31-21	63,031
1965	Dallas	Dallas, 31-2	59,366
1965	N.Y.	Dallas, 38-20	62,871
1966	Dallas	Dallas, 52-7	60,010
1966	N.Y.	Dallas, 17-7	62,735
1967	Dallas	Dallas, 38-24	66,209
1968	Dallas	N.Y., 27-21	72,163
1968	N.Y.	Dallas, 28-10	62,617
1969	Dallas	Dallas, 25-3	58,964
1970	Dallas	Dallas, 28-10	57,236
1970	N.Y.	N.Y., 23-20	62,938
1971	Dallas	Dallas, 20-13	68,378
1971	N.Y.	Dallas, 42-14	62,815
1972	N.Y.	Dallas, 23-14	62,725
1972	Dallas	N.Y., 23-3	64,602
1973	Dallas	Dallas, 45-28	64,898
1973	N. Haven	Dallas, 23-10	70,128
1974	Dallas	N.Y., 14-6	46,353
1974	N. Haven	Dallas, 21-7	61,191
1975	N.Y.	Dallas, 13-7	56,511
1975	Dallas	Dallas, 14-3	53,329
1976	N.Y.	Dallas, 24-14	76,042
1976	Dallas	Dallas, 9-3	58,870
1977	Dallas	Dallas, 41-21	64,215
1977	N.Y.	Dallas, 24-10	74,532
1978	N.Y.	Dallas, 34-24	73,265
1978	Dallas	Dallas, 24-3	64,869
1979	N.Y.	Dallas, 16-14	76,490
1979	Dallas	Dallas, 28-7	63,787
1980	Dallas	Dallas, 24-3	59,126
1980	N.Y.	N.Y., 38-35	68,343
1981	Dallas	Dallas, 18-10	63,449
1981	N.Y.	N.Y., 13-10(OT)	73,009
1983	Dallas	Dallas, 28-13	62,347
1983	N.Y.	Dallas, 38-20	76,142
1984	N.Y.	N.Y., 28-7	75,921
1984	Dallas	N.Y., 19-7	60,235

New York Jets

(Dallas Leads Series, 3-0)

Year	Site	Winner-Score	Att.
1971	Dallas	Dallas, 52-10	66,689
1975	N.Y.	Dallas, 31-21	37,279
1978	N.Y.	Dallas, 30-7	52,532

Philadelphia Eagles

(Dallas Leads Series, 33-16)

Year	Site	Winner-Score	Att.
1960	Dallas	Phil., 27-25	18,500
1961	Dallas	Phil., 43-7	25,000
1961	Phil.	Phil., 35-13	60,127
1962	Dallas	Dallas, 41-19	18,645
1962	Phil.	Phil., 28-14	58,070
1963	Phil.	Phil., 24-21	60,671
1963	Dallas	Dallas, 27-20	23,694
1964	Dallas	Phil., 17-14	55,972
1964	Phil.	Phil., 24-14	60,671
1965	Dallas	Phil., 35-24	56,249
1965	Phil.	Dallas, 21-19	54,714
1966	Dallas	Dallas, 56-7	69,372
1966	Phil.	Phil., 24-23	60,658

Cowboys — FG Septien 35
Cardinals — Love 1 pass from Lomax (O'Donoghue kick)
Cardinals — FG O'Donoghue 30
Cowboys — Springs 26 pass from Hogeboom (Septien kick)
Attendance — 48,721

	Cowboys	Cardinals
First Downs	16	25
Total Net Yards	250	435
Net Yards Rushing	116	78
Net Yards Passing	134	357
Passes	12-33	27-52
Passes Intercepted by	2	2
Punts-Average	7-35.6	4-32.8
Fumbles-Lost	2-0	5-4
Penalties-Yards	5-53	9-85

Rushing

Cowboys — Dorsett, 19 for 84; Springs, 8 for 29, 1 touchdown; Hogeboom, 3 for 3.
Cardinals — Anderson, 16 for 69; Ferrell, 3 for 5; Mitchell, 2 for 4; Love, 1 for 2; Lomax, 1 for -2.

Passing

Cowboys — Hogeboom, 12 of 33 for 147 yards, 2 touchdowns, 2 interceptions.
Cardinals — Lomax, 27 of 52 for 388 yards, 2 touchdowns, 2 interceptions.

Receiving

Cowboys — Springs, 4 for 44, 1 touchdown; Cosbie, 3 for 38; Hill, 3 for 36; Dorsett, 1 for 21; J. Jones, 1 for 8, 1 touchdown.
Cardinals — Green, 8 for 99; Tilley, 5 for 76, 1 touchdown; Anderson, 4 for 55; Marsh, 3 for 80; LaFleur, 2 for 30; Harrel, 2 for 20; Ferrell, 1 for 21; Mitchell, 1 for 6; Love, 1 for 1, 1 touchdown.

Buffalo 14, Cowboys 3

At Buffalo, November 18, 1984

DALLAS	0	3	0	0	—	3
BUFFALO	7	0	0	7	—	14

Bills — Bell 85 run (Nelson kick)
Cowboys — FG Septien 20
Bills — Bell 3 pass from Ferguson (Nelson kick)
Attendance — 74,391

	Cowboys	Bills
First Downs	19	14
Total Net Yards	297	307
Net Yards Rushing	78	203
Net Yards Passing	219	104
Passes	22-46	13-30
Passes Intercepted by	2	2
Punts-Average	6-32.5	8-43.5
Fumbles-Lost	2-1	1-0
Penalties-Yards	5-55	4-58

Rushing

Cowboys — Dorsett, 17 for 70; Newsome, 3 for 10; J. Jones, 1 for 2; Hogeboom, 1 for -1; Springs, 2 for -3.
Bills — Bell, 27 for 206, 1 touchdown; Moore, 3 for 3; Riddick, 1 for -2; Ferguson, 2 for -4.

Passing

Cowboys — Hogeboom, 22 of 45 for 242 yards, 2 interceptions; Renfro, 0 of 1.
Bills — Ferguson, 13 of 29 for 117 yards, 1 touchdown, 2 interceptions; Kofler, 0 of 1.

Receiving

Cowboys — Cosbie, 6 for 92; Dorsett, 5 for 29; Hill, 4 for 35; Newsome, 2 for 34; Renfro, 2 for 28; Springs, 2 for 15; J. Jones, 1 for 9.
Bills — Franklin, 6 for 55; Moore, 2 for 14; Bell, 2 for 12, 1 touchdown; Riddick, 1 for 13; Brammer, 1 for 12; Brookins, 1 for 11.

Cowboys 20, New England 17

At Dallas, November 22, 1984

NEW ENGLAND	3	0	0	14	—	17
DALLAS	7	3	7	3	—	20

Cowboys — Downs 17 interception return (Septien kick)
Patriots — FG Franklin 29
Cowboys — FG Septien 28
Cowboys — Hill 9 pass from D. White (Septien kick)
Patriots — Ramsey 1 pass from Eason (Franklin kick)
Patriots — Eason 1 run (Franklin kick)
Cowboys — FG Septien 23
Attendance — 55,341

	Patriots	Cowboys
First Downs	19	18
Total Net Yards	297	342
Net Yards Rushing	150	67
Net Yards Passing	147	275
Passes	19-38	21-41
Passes Intercepted by	1	1
Punts-Average	11-43.6	10-36.8
Fumbles-Lost	2-0	2-1
Penalties-Yards	4-30	5-25

Rushing

Patriots — C. James, 19 for 112; Tatupu, 2 for 15; Eason, 2 for 14, 1 touchdown; Collins, 2 for 9.
Cowboys — Dorsett, 19 for 49; Newsome, 6 for 18; D. White, 2 for 1; J. Jones, 2 for 0; Springs, 1 for -1.

Passing

Patriots — Eason, 19 of 38 for 204 yards, 1 touchdown, 1 interception.
Cowboys — D. White, 21 of 41 for 288 yards, 1 touchdown, 1 interception.

Receiving

Patriots — Starring, 6 for 61; Ramsey, 5 for 71, 1 touchdown; Dawson, 3 for 32; C. James, 2 for 22; C. Jones, 1 for 7; Weathers, 1 for 6; Morgan, 1 for 5.
Cowboys — Hill, 8 for 125, 1 touchdown; Donley, 4 for 74; Dorsett, 3 for 40; Newsome, 3 for 4; Cosbie, 2 for 36; Harris, 1 for 9.

Cowboys 26, Philadelphia 10

At Philadelphia, December 2, 1984

DALLAS	7	0	16	3	—	26
PHILADELPHIA	0	3	0	7	—	10

Cowboys — Thurman 38 interception return (Septien kick)
Eagles — FG McFadden 23
Cowboys — Springs 57 pass from D. White (Septien kick)
Cowboys — Safety Dutton sacked Pisarcik in endzone

Cowboys — Newsome 8 run (Septien kick)
Eagles — Kab 2 pass from Pisarcik (McFadden kick)
Cowboys — FG Septien 32
Attendance — 66,322

	Cowboys	Eagles
First Downs	16	13
Total Net Yards	286	173
Net Yards Rushing	190	38
Net Yards Passing	96	135
Passes	8-26	23-45
Passes Intercepted by	2	5
Punts-Average	6-32.7	8-46.6
Fumbles-Lost	2-1	2-2
Penalties-Yards	5-61	3-27

Rushing
Cowboys — Dorsett, 22 for 110; Newsome, 8 for 37, 1 touchdown; Springs, 5 for 30; D. White, 1 for 7; J. Jones, 3 for 6.
Eagles — Montgomery, 11 for 29; Oliver, 1 for 6; Haddix, 7 for 3.

Passing
Cowboys — D. White, 8 of 25 for 125 yards, 1 touchdown, 4 interceptions; Dorsett, 0 of 1, 1 interception.
Eagles — Pisarcik, 23 of 44 for 190 yards, 1 touchdown, 2 interceptions; Montgomery, 0 of 1.

Receiving
Cowboys — Hill, 3 for 25; J. Jones, 2 for 30; Springs, 1 for 57, 1 touchdown; Renfro, 1 for 12; Newsome, 1 for 1.
Eagles — Spagnola, 11 for 114; Haddix, 6 for 42; Oliver, 2 for -1; Hoover, 1 for 18; Woodruff, 1 for 10; M. Williams, 1 for 5; Kab, 1 for 2, 1 touchdown.

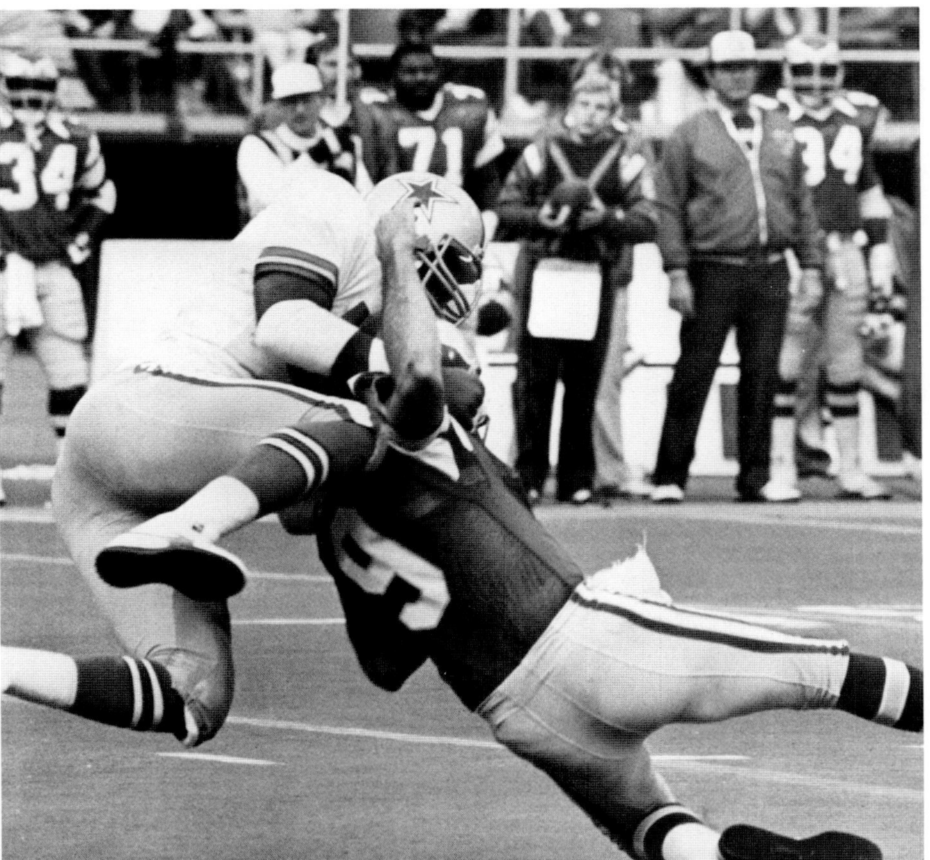

Washington 30, Cowboys 28

At Dallas, December 9, 1984

WASHINGTON	0	6	17	7	—	30
DALLAS	7	14	0	7	—	28

Cowboys — Donley 6 pass from D. White (Septien kick)
Redskins — FG Moseley 31
Cowboys — Cosbie 2 pass from D. White (Septien kick)
Redskins — FG Moseley 34
Cowboys — Renfro 60 pass from D. White (Septien kick)
Redskins — Green 32 interception return (Moseley kick)
Redskins — Muhammad 22 pass from Theismann (Moseley kick)
Redskins —FG Moseley 21
Cowboys — Hill 43 pass from D. White (Septien kick)
Redskins — Riggins 1 run (Moseley kick)
Attendance — 64,286

	Redskins	Cowboys
First Downs	22	25
Total Net Yards	299	387
Net Yards Rushing	151	106
Net Yards Passing	148	281
Passes	17-31	22-42
Passes Intercepted by	2	0
Punts-Average	7-42.7	4-37.3
Fumbles-Lost	3-0	3-2
Penalties-Yards	6-71	6-49

Rushing
Redskins — Riggins, 24 for 111, 1 touchdown; Monk, 1 for 18; Theismann, 6 for 18; Wonsley, 1 for 2; J. Washington, 3 for 2.
Cowboys — Newsome, 6 for 48; Dorsett, 15 for 42; D. White, 1 for 8; Springs, 2 for 8.

Passing
Redskins — Theismann, 17 of 31 for 205 yards, 1 touchdown.
Cowboys — D. White, 22 of 42 for 327 yards, 4 touchdowns, 2 interceptions.

Receiving
Redskins — Monk, 7 for 80; Muhammad, 3 for 43, 1 touchdown; Didier, 3 for 39; Warren, 2 for 27; Brown, 1 for 9; J. Washington, 1 for 7.
Cowboys — Hill, 7 for 119, 1 touchdown; Cosbie, 4 for 39, 1 touchdown; Renfro, 3 for 80, 1 touchdown; Dorsett, 2 for 32; Newsome, 2 for 22; Springs, 2 for 19; J. Jones, 1 for 10; Donley, 1 for 6, 1 touchdown.

Miami 28, Cowboys 21

At Miami, December 17, 1984

DALLAS	0	0	7	14	—	21
MIAMI	0	7	7	14	—	28

Dolphins — Clayton 41 pass from Marino (von Schamann kick)
Dolphins — Hardy 3 pass from Marino (von Schamann kick)
Cowboys — Newsome 1 run (Septien kick)
Cowboys — Newsome 4 run (Septien kick)
Dolphins — Clayton 39 pass from Marino (von Schamann kick)
Cowboys — Hill 66 pass from D. White (Septien kick)
Dolphins — Clayton 63 pass from Marino (von Schamann kick)
Attendance — 75,105

	Cowboys	Dolphins
First Downs	21	17
Total Net Yards	316	389
Net Yards Rushing	90	61
Net Yards Passing	226	328
Passes	20-35	23-40
Passes Intercepted by	2	2
Punts-Average	7-39.9	5-45.4
Fumbles-Lost	2-0	3-1
Penalties-Yards	4-61	3-32

Rushing
Cowboys — Dorsett, 19 for 58; Newsome, 6 for 20, 2 touchdowns; Hill, 1 for 7; Springs, 1 for 5; D. White, 1 for 0.
Dolphins — Nathan, 13 for 39; Bennett, 7 for 14; Carter, 3 for 9; P. Johnson, 2 for 2; Marino, 1 for -3.

Passing
Cowboys — D. White, 20 of 34 for 246 yards, 1 touchdown, 2 interceptions; Springs, 0 of 1.
Dolphins — Marino, 23 of 40 for 340 yards, 4 touchdowns, 2 interceptions.

Receiving
Cowboys — Hill, 6 for 115, 1 touchdown; Dorsett, 6 for 28; Cosbie, 5 for 83; Newsome, 2 for 13; Renfro, 1 for 7.
Dolphins — Nathan, 7 for 46; Clayton, 4 for 150, 3 touchdowns; Duper, 4 for 57; Moore, 3 for 47; Hardy, 3 for 25, 1 touchdown; Cefalo, 1 for 11; Bennett, 1 for 4.

Dallas Cowboys 1984 Statistics

RESULTS AND ATTENDANCE (9-7)

Result	Score	Opponent	Attendance	Opp	
(W)	20	@ Los Angeles	65,403	13	(SO)
(L)	7	@ N.Y. Giants	75,921	28	(SO)
(W)	23	PHILADELPHIA	64,521	17	
(W)	20	GREEN BAY	64,222	6	(SO)
(W)	23	@ Chicago	63,623	14	(SO)
(L)	20	ST. LOUIS	61,438	31	(SO)
(L)	14	@ Washington	55,431	34	(SO)
OT(W)	30	NEW ORLEANS	50,966	27	(SO)
(W)	22	INDIANAPOLIS	58,724	3	
(L)	7	N.Y. GIANTS	60,235	19	(SO)
(W)	24	@ St. Louis	48,721	17	(SO)
(L)	3	@ Buffalo	74,391	14	
(W)	20	NEW ENGLAND	55,341	17	(SO)
(W)	26	@ Philadelphia	66,322	10	(SO)
(L)	28	WASHINGTON	64,286	30	(SO)
(L)	21	@ Miami	74,139	28	(SO)

TEAM STATISTICS	DALLAS	OPP
TOTAL FIRST DOWNS	323	283
Rushing	93	106
Passing	202	155
Penalty	28	22
Third Down-Made/Att	83/238	83/247
Third Down Efficiency	34.9	33.6
Fourth Down-Made/Att	3/7	5/16
TOTAL NET YARDS	5320	5036
Avg. Per Game	332.5	314.8
Total Plays	1121	1094
Avg. Per Play	4.8	4.6
NET YARDS RUSHING	1714	2226
Avg. Per Game	107.1	139.1
Total Rushes	469	510
Avg. Per Rush	3.7	4.4
NET YARDS PASSING	3606	2810
Avg. Per Game	225.4	175.6
Tackled/Yards Lost	48/389	57/390
Gross Yards	3995	3200
Attempts/Completions	*604/322	527/250
Pct. of Completions	53.3	47.4
Had Intercepted	26	28
PUNTS/AVERAGE	*108/38.2	99/42.8
Net Punting Average	34.0	36.3
PUNT RETURNS/ AVERAGE	54/8.3	*55/4.2
KICKOFF RETURNS/ AVERAGE	63/19.0	65/20.2
INTERCEPTIONS/ AVG. RET	28/10.6	26/14.7
PENALTIES/YARDS	100/947	93/854
FUMBLES/BALL LOST	35/17	35/16
TOUCHDOWNS	34	36
Rushing	12	8
Passing	19	23
Returns	3	5

	DALLAS	OPP
EXTRA POINTS/ATTEMPTS	33/34	35/36
FIELD GOALS/ATTEMPTS	23/29	19/28
TOTAL POINTS	308	308
AVG.TIME OF POSSESSION	29:06	31:06

SCORING	TDR	TDP	TDRt	FG	PAT	TP
Septien	0	0	0	23/29	33/34	102
Dorsett	6	1	0	0	0	42
T. Hill	0	5	0	0	0	30
Newsome	5	0	0	0	0	30
Cosbie	0	4	0	0	0	24
Springs	1	3	0	0	0	24
Donley	0	2	0	0	0	12
Renfro	0	2	0	0	0	12
Cornwell	0	1	0	0	0	6
Downs	0	0	1	0	0	6
Jeffcoat	0	0	1	0	0	6
J. Jones	0	1	0	0	0	6
Thurman	0	0	1	0	0	6
Dutton	0	0	0	0	0	2x
COWBOY TOTALS	12	19	y3	23/29	33/34	308
Opp. Totals	8	23	z5	19/28	35/36	308

x Sacked Pisarcik for safety @ Phil (12/2)
y Jeffcoat fum. rec. in EZ vs N.O. (10/21)
Downs 27 int. ret. vs N.E. (11/22)
Thurman 38 int. ret., @ Phil (12/2)
z Headen 81 fum. ret., @ NYG (9/9)
R. Brown 5 int. ret., GBay (9/23)
Coleman 49 int. ret., @ Wash (10/14)
Winston 43 int. ret., N.O.(10/21)
Green 32 int. ret., Wash (12/9)

RUSHING	ATT	YDS	AVG	LG	TD
Dorsett	302	1189	3.9	31t	6
Newsome	66	268	4.1	30	5
Springs	68	197	2.9	16	1
D. White	6	21	3.5	8	0
Hogeboom	15	19	1.3	11	0
J. Jones	8	13	1.6	6	0
T. Hill	1	7	7.0	7	0
Donley	2	5	2.5	6	0
others	1	-5	-5.0	-5	0
COWBOY TOTALS	469	1714	3.7	31t	12
Opp. Totals	510	2226	4.4	85t	8

RECEIVING	NO	YDS	AVG	LG	TD
Cosbie	60	789	13.2	36	4
Hill	58	864	14.9	66t	5
Dorsett	51	459	9.0	68t	1
Springs	46	454	9.9	57t	3
Renfro	35	583	16.7	60t	2
Donley	32	473	14.8	49t	2
Newsome	26	263	10.1	29	0
J. Jones	7	57	8.1	19	1
Cornwell	2	23	11.5	13	1
Harris	1	9	9.0	9	0
Phillips	1	6	6.0	6	0
Pozderac	1	1	1.0	1	0
others	2	14	7.0	7	0
COWBOY TOTALS	322	3995	12.4	68t	19
Opp. Totals	250	3200	12.8	80t	23

INTERCEPTIONS	NO	YDS	AVG	LG	TD
Downs	7	126	18.0	27t	1
Thurman	5	81	16.2	43	1
Clinkscale	3	32	10.7	23	0
Walls	3	12	4.0	12	0
Fellows	3	3	1.0	3	0
Hegman	3	3	1.0	3	0
Lockhart	1	32	32.0	32	0
Scott	1	5	5.0	5	0
Bates	1	3	3.0	3	0
Dickerson	1	0	0.0	0	0
COWBOY TOTALS	28	297	10.6	43	2
Opp. Totals	26	372	14.3	49t	4

PUNTING	NO	YDS	AVG	TB	IN20	LG	BL	NET
D. White	*82	3151	38.4	8	21	54	0	34.6
Warren	21	799	38.1	3	3	48	0	33.0
others	5	173	34.6	0	1	41	0	29.2
COWBOY TOTALS	*108	4123	38.2	11	25	54	0	34.0
Opp. Totals	99	4236	42.8	10	23	59	1	36.3

KO RETURNS	NO	YDS	AVG	LG	TD
Allen	33	666	20.2	34	0
McSwain	20	403	20.2	32	0
Fellows	6	94	15.7	23	0
Salonen	2	30	15.0	22	0
Granger	2	6	3.0	5	0
COWBOY TOTALS	63	1199	19.0	34	0
Opp. Totals	65	1310	20.2	64	0

PUNT RETURNS	NO	FC	YDS	AVG	LG	TD
Allen	#54	15	446	8.3	18	0
COWBOY TOTALS	54	15	446	8.3	18	0
Opp. Totals	*55	19	230	4.2	19	0

SCORE BY QUARTERS	1	2	3	4	OT	TP
COWBOYS	65	89	56	95	3	308
Opponents	64	81	91	72	0	308

FIELD GOALS	11-19	20-29	30-39	40-49	50+
COWBOYS	2-2	6-7	9-9	4-8	2-3
Opponents	0-0	8-8	7-9	2-8	2-3

Septien: (31,52);(-);(28M,47,51,30);(32,42); (44,32,23);(52M,35,36);(-);(36,27,41);(19,19,24); (-); (42M,35,48M,45B);(20,47M);(28,23);(32);(-); (-).

PASSING	ATT	COMP	YDS	PCT	AVG ATT	TD	PCT TD	INT	PCT INT	LG	TRAPS/ YDS	RAT-ING
D. White	233	126	1580	54.1	6.78	11	4.7	11	4.7	66t	22/178	71.5
Hogeboom	367	195	2366	53.1	6.45	7	1.9	14	3.8	68t	26/211	63.7
Renfro	2	1	49	50.0	24.50	1	50.0	0	0.0	49t	0/0	135.4
Springs	1	0	0	0.0	0.00	0	0.0	0	0.0	0	0/0	39.6
Dorsett	1	0	0	0.0	0.00	0	0.0	1	100.0	0	0/0	0.0
COWBOY TOTALS	*604	322	3995	53.3	6.61	19	3.2	26	4.3	68t	48/389	66.6
Opp. Totals	527	250	3200	47.4	6.07	23	4.4	28	5.3	80t	57/390	59.3

*Broke Cowboys Season Record

#Tied Cowboys Season Record

1984 Cowboys Defensive Statistics

(Sixteen Games)
Tackles (Primary-Assists — Combined)

1. **Downs**	96-40 — 136	12. **Bates**	38-14 — 52
2. **R. White**	81-27 — 108	13. **Breunig**	26-26 — 52
3. **Clinkscale**	68-25 — 93	14. **Thurman**	24-10 — 34
4. **E. Jones**	63-23 — 86	15. **Scott**	16- 3 — 19
5. **Lockhart**	49-37 — 86	16. **Cannon**	7- 5 — 12
6. **Jeffcoat**	50-32 — 82	17. **Rohrer**	2- 9 — 11
7. **Walls**	59-22 — 81	18. **Smerek**	6- 4 — 10
8. **Fellows**	54-25 — 79	19. **Albritton**	4- 4 — 8
9. **Dutton**	43-30 — 73	20. **DeOssie**	0- 4 — 4
10. **Dickerson**	44-28 — 72	21. **Howard**	2- 1 — 3
11. **Hegman**	42-29 — 71	22. **Tuinei**	2- 0 — 2

QB Traps (57) — R. White 12½, Jeffcoat 11½, E. Jones 8, Bates 5, Downs 3½, Hegman 3½, Dutton 2½, Lockhart 2½, Dickerson 2, Albritton 1, Clinkscale 1, Smerek 1, Thurman 1, Tuinei 1.

Interceptions (28) — Downs 7, Thurman 5, Walls 3, Clinkscale 3, Fellows 3, Hegman 3, Bates 1, Dickerson 1, Lockhart 1, V. Scott 1.

Passes Defensed (121) — Walls 23, Fellows 19, E. Jones 16, Downs 13, Clinkscale 10, Hegman 7, V. Scott 7, Bates 6, Thurman 6, Albritton 3, Dickerson 2, Dutton 2, Jeffcoat 2, R. White 2, Breunig 1, Smerek 1, Tuinei 1.

Fumbles Recovered (16) — Clinkscale 2, Downs 2, E. Jones 2, Albritton 1, Bates 1, Dickerson 1, Fellows 1, Granger 1, Hegman 1, Jeffcoat 1, Lockhart 1, Rohrer 1, H. Scott 1.

Forced Fumbles (24) — E. Jones 5, R. White 4, Downs 3, Bates 2, Breunig 1, Cannon 1, Clinkscale 1, Dickerson 1, Dutton 1, Hegman 1, Jeffcoat 1, Salonen 1, V. Scott 1, Springs 1.

Cowboys All-Time Leaders

RUSHING

Player	Att.	Yds.	Avg.	Long	TD
1. Dorsett, Tony (1977-84)	2,136	9,525	4.5	99	59
2. Perkins, Don (1961-68)	1,500	6,217	4.1	59	42
3. Hill, Calvin (1969-74)	1,166	5,009	4.3	55	39
4. Newhouse, Robert (1972-83)	1,160	4,784	4.1	54	31
5. Garrison, Walt (1966-74)	899	3,886	4.3	41	30
6. Staubach, Roger (1969-79)	410	2,264	5.5	33	20
7. Springs, Ron (1979-84)	604	2,180	3.6	46	28
8. Marsh, Amos (1961-64)	427	2,065	4.8	71	14
9. Reeves, Dan (1965-72)	535	1,990	3.7	67	25
10. Thomas, Duane (1970-71)	326	1,596	4.9	56	16

PASSING

Player	Att.	Comp.	Pct.	Yds.	TD	Int.	Rating
1. Staubach, R. (1969-79)	2,958	1,685	57.0	22,700	153	109	83.5
2. White, Danny (1976-84)	1,943	1,155	59.4	14,754	109	90	82.7
3. Morton, C. (1965-74)	1,308	685	52.4	10,279	80	73	75.5
4. Meredith, D. (1960-68)	2,308	1,170	50.7	17,199	135	111	74.7
5. LeBaron, E. (1960-63)	692	359	51.9	5,331	45	52	67.8

RECEIVING

Player	No.	Yds.	Avg.	Long	TD
1. Pearson, Drew (1973-83)	489	7,822	16.0	67	48
2. Hayes, Bob (1965-74)	365	7,295	20.0	95	71
3. Hill, Tony (1977-84)	356	6,105	17.2	75	41
4. Dorsett, Tony (1977-84)	292	2,539	8.7	91	9
5. Clarke, Frank (1960-67)	281	5,214	18.6	80	50
6. DuPree, Billy Joe (1973-83)	267	3,565	13.4	42	41
7. Springs, Ron (1979-84)	222	2,029	9.1	80	10
8. Pearson, Preston (1975-80)	189	2,274	12.0	49	11
9. Rentzel, Lance (1967-70)	183	3,521	19.2	86	31
10. Garrison, Walt (1966-74)	182	1,794	9.9	53	9

PUNTING

Player	No.	Avg.	Long	Blk.
1. Baker, Sam (1962-63)	128	45.1	72	0
2. Sherer, Dave (1960)	57	42.5	67	1
3. Widby, Ron (1968-71)	247	41.8	84	2
4. Villanueva, Danny (1965-67)	192	40.3	58	1
5. Lothridge, Billy (1964)	62	40.3	75	1
6. White, Danny (1976-84)	611	40.1	73	4
7. Carrell, Duane (1974)	40	39.8	59	0
8. Hoopes, Mitch (1975)	68	39.4	55	1
9. Bateman, Marv (1972-74)	139	39.3	62	2
10. Warren, John (1983-84)	60	39.2	54	0

INTERCEPTIONS

Player	No.	Yds.	Avg.	Long	TD
1. Renfro, Mel (1964-77)	52	626	12.0	90	3
2.Waters, Charlie (1970-78, 1980-81)	41	584	14.2	56	2
3. Green, Cornell (1962-74)	34	552	16.2	59	2
4. Jordan, Lee Roy (1963-76)	32	472	14.8	49	3
5. Thurman, Dennis (1978-84)	31	541	17.5	96	3
6. Harris, Cliff (1970-79)	29	281	9.7	60	1
7. Walls, Everson (1981-84)	25	276	11.0	37	0
8. Howley, Chuck (1961-73)	24	395	16.5	58	2
9. Bishop, Don (1960-65)	22	364	16.5	57	0
10. Gaechter, Mike (1962-69)	21	420	20.0	100	1

PUNT RETURNS (Min. 40 Returns)

Player	No.	Yds.	Avg.	Long	TD
1. Hayes, Bob (1965-74)	104	1,158	11.1	90	3
2. Allen, Gary (1983-84)	63	599	9.5	68	1
3. Johnson, Butch (1976-83)	146	1,313	9.0	55	0
4. Jones, James (1980-82, 1984)	87	736	8.5	52	0
5. Richards, Golden (1973-78)	62	501	8.1	46	1

KICKOFF RETURNS (Min. 40 Returns)

Player	No.	Yds.	Avg.	Long	TD
1. Renfro, Mel (1964-77)	85	2,246	26.4	100	2
2. Harris, Cliff (1970-79)	63	1,622	25.7	77	0
3. Marsh, Amos (1961-64)	65	1,561	24.0	101	1
4. Johnson, Butch (1976-83)	79	1,832	23.2	74	0
5. Jones, James (1980-82, 1984)	61	1,283	21.0	41	0

SCORING

Player	TD	PAT	FG	Total
1. Septien, Rafael (1978-84)	—	303	128	687
2. Hayes, Bob (1965-74)	76	—	—	456
3. Dorsett, Tony (1977-84)	69	—	—	414
4. Clark, Mike (1968-71, 1973)	—	180	69	387
5. Fritsch, Toni (1971-73, 1975)	—	119	66	317
6. Clarke, Frank (1960-67)	51	—	—	306
7. Pearson, Drew (1973-83)	50	—	—	300
8. Perkins, Don (1961-68)	45	—	—	270
9. Hill, Calvin (1969-74)	45	—	—	270
10. Villanueva, Danny (1965-67)	—	134	42	260

FIELD GOALS

Player	Att.	Made	Pct.	Long
1. Septien, Rafael (1978-84)	177	128	.723	53
2. Clark, Mike (1968-71, 1973)	119	69	.580	50
3. Fritsch, Toni (1971-73, 1975)	107	66	.617	54
4. Herrera, Efren (1974, 1976-77)	65	44	.677	52
5. Villanueva, Danny (1965-67)	81	42	.519	41
6. Baker, Sam (1962-63)	47	23	.489	53
7. Van Raaphorst, Dick (1964)	29	14	.483	43
8. Cone, Fred (1960)	13	6	.462	45
9. Bielski, Dick (1961)	9	6	.667	42
10. Percival, Mac (1974)	8	2	.250	33

Cowboys Leaders By Years

RUSHING

Year	Player	Att.	Yds.	Avg.	Long	TD	NFL/ NFC Rank
1960	Dupre, L. G.	104	362	3.5	18	3	20
1961	*Perkins, Don	200	815	4.1	47	4	6
1962	Perkins, Don	222	945	4.3	35	7	5
1963	Perkins, Don	149	614	4.1	19t	7	10
1964	Perkins, Don	174	768	4.4	59	6	5
1965	Perkins, Don	177	690	3.9	43	0	7
1966	Reeves, Dan	175	757	4.3	67t	8	6
1967	Perkins, Don	201	823	4.1	30	6	6
1968	Perkins, Don	191	836	4.4	28t	4	6
1969	*Hill, Calvin	204	942	4.6	55	8	2
1970	*Thomas, Duane	151	803	5.3	47t	5	8/5
1971	Thomas, Duane	175	793	4.5	56t	11	11/7
1972	Hill, Calvin	245	1,036	4.2	26	6	7/3
1973	Hill, Calvin	273	1,142	4.2	21	6	3/2
1974	Hill, Calvin	185	844	4.6	27	7	8/3
1975	Newhouse, Robert	209	930	4.4	29	2	9/4
1976	Dennison, Doug	153	542	3.5	14	6	35/18
1977	*Dorsett, Tony	208	1,007	4.8	84t	12	9/4
1978	Dorsett, Tony	290	1,325	4.6	63t	7	3/2
1979	Dorsett, Tony	250	1,107	4.4	41	6	11/8
1980	Dorsett, Tony	278	1,185	4.3	56	11	6/6
1981	Dorsett, Tony	342	1,646	4.8	75t	4	2/2
1982	Dorsett, Tony	177	745	4.2	99t	5	2/1
1983	Dorsett, Tony	289	1,321	4.6	77	8	6/5
1984	Dorsett, Tony	302	1,189	3.9	31t	6	7/7

PASSING

Year	Player	Att.	Comp.	Pct.	Yds.	TD	Int.	Rating	NFL/ NFC Rank
1960	LeBaron, E.	225	111	49.3	1,736	12	25	53.4	8
1961	LeBaron, E.	236	120	50.8	1,741	14	16	66.5	9
1962	LeBaron, E.	166	95	57.2	1,436	16	9	95.3	3
1963	Meredith, D.	310	167	53.9	2,381	17	18	73.2	10
1964	Meredith, D.	323	158	48.9	2,143	9	16	67.3	15
1965	Meredith, D.	305	141	46.2	2,415	22	13	79.7	8
1966	Meredith, D.	344	177	51.5	2,805	24	12	87.7	4
1967	Meredith, D.	255	128	50.2	1,834	16	16	68.6	8
1968	Meredith, D.	309	171	55.3	2,500	21	12	88.3	2
1969	Morton, C.	302	162	53.6	2,619	21	15	85.4	5
1970	Morton, C.	207	102	49.3	1,819	15	7	89.7	5/4
1971	Staubach, R.	211	126	59.7	1,882	15	4	104.8	1/1
1972	Morton, C.	339	185	54.6	2,396	15	21	65.9	15/7
1973	Staubach, R.	286	179	62.6	2,428	23	15	94.6	1/1
1974	Staubach, R.	360	190	52.8	2,552	11	15	68.5	14/7
1975	Staubach, R.	348	198	56.9	2,666	17	16	78.6	8/2
1976	Staubach, R.	369	208	56.4	2,715	14	11	79.9	8/5
1977	Staubach, R.	361	210	58.2	2,620	18	9	87.1	2/1
1978	Staubach, R.	413	231	55.9	3,190	25	16	84.9	1/1
1979	Staubach, R.	461	267	57.9	3,586	27	11	92.4	1/1
1980	White, D.	436	260	59.6	3,287	28	25	80.8	9/7
1981	White, D.	391	223	57.0	3,098	22	13	87.5	5/2
1982	White, D.	247	156	63.2	2,079	16	12	91.1	4/2
1983	White, D.	533	334	62.7	3,980	29	23	85.6	9/6
1984	White, D.	233	126	54.1	1,580	11	11	71.5	22/11

RECEIVING

Year	Player	No.	Yds.	Avg.	Long	TD	NFL/ NFC Rank
1960	Doran, Jim	31	554	17.9	75t	3	21
1961	Howton, Billy	56	785	14.0	53	4	6
1962	Howton, Billy	49	706	14.4	69t	6	15
1963	Clarke, Frank	43	833	19.4	75t	10	3
1964	Clarke, Frank	65	973	15.0	49	5	3
1965	*Hayes, Bob	46	1,003	21.8	82t	12	13
1966	Hayes, Bob	64	1,232	19.3	95t	13	4
1967	Rentzel, Lance	58	996	17.2	74t	8	6
1968	Rentzel, Lance	54	1,009	18.7	65t	6	3
1969	Rentzel, Lance	43	960	22.3	75t	12	20
1970	Hayes, Bob	34	889	26.1	89t	10	45/26
1971	Garrison, Walt	40	396	9.9	36	1	23/10
1972	Hill, Calvin	43	364	8.5	33t	3	18/9
1973	Hill, Calvin	32	290	9.1	29	0	36/21
1974	Pearson, Drew	62	1,087	17.9	50t	2	3/2
1975	Pearson, Drew	46	822	17.9	46t	8	16/9
1976	Pearson, Drew	58	806	13.9	54	6	4/1
1977	Pearson, Drew	48	870	18.1	67	2	9/3
1978	Pearson, Preston	47	256	11.2	34	0	26/15
1979	Hill, Tony	60	1,062	17.7	75t	10	12/6
1980	Hill, Tony	60	1,055	17.6	58t	8	16/9
1981	Hill, Tony	46	953	20.7	63t	4	47/26
	Springs, Ron	46	359	7.8	32t	2	
1982	Hill, Tony	35	526	15.0	47	1	22/8
1983	Springs, Ron	73	589	8.1	80t	1	9/4
1984	Cosbie, Doug	60	789	13.2	36	4	28/12

PUNTING

Year	Player	No.	Avg.	Long	Had Blocked	NFL/ NFC Rank
1960	Sherer, Dave	57	42.5	67	1	7
1961	*Green, Allen	61	36.7	53	1	14
1962	Baker, Sam	57	45.4	72	0	3
1963	Baker, Sam	71	44.2	64	0	7
1964	*Lothridge, Billy	62	40.3	75	1	15
1965	Villanueva, Danny	60	41.8	58	0	10
1966	Villanueva, Danny	65	39.2	58	1	13
1967	Villanueva, Danny	67	40.4	57	0	9
1968	Widby, Ron	59	40.9	84	0	5
1969	Widby, Ron	63	43.3	62	0	2
1970	Widby, Ron	69	41.3	59	1	10/2
1971	Widby, Ron	56	41.6	59	1	8/3
1972	*Bateman, Marv	51	38.2	61	0	24/13
1973	Bateman, Marv	55	41.6	62	2	11/7
1974	*Carrell, Duane	40	39.8	59	0	11/5
1975	*Hoopes, Mitch	68	39.4	55	1	16/9
1976	*White, Danny	70	38.4	54	2	20/9
1977	White, Danny	80	39.6	57	1	12/8
1978	White, Danny	76	40.5	56	1	8/5
1979	White, Danny	76	41.7	73	0	4/2
1980	White, Danny	71	40.9	58	0	10/5
1981	White, Danny	81	40.8	60	0	14/8
1982	White, Danny	37	41.7	56	0	8/5
1983	White, Danny	38	40.6	50	1	DNQ
1984	White, Danny	82	38.4	54	0	28/14

SCORING

Year	Player	TD	PAT	FG	Tot.	NFL/ NFC Rank
1960	Cone, Fred	0	21	6	39	27
1961	Clarke, Frank	9	0	0	54	22
1962	Baker, Sam	0	50	14	92	6
1963	Baker, Sam	0	38	9	65	14
1964	*VanRaaphorst, Dick	0	28	14	70	13
1965	Villanueva, Danny	0	37	16	85	10
1966	Villanueva, Danny	0	56	17	107	2
1967	Hayes, Bob	11	0	0	66	16
	Reeves, Dan	11	0	0	66	
1968	Clark, Mike	0	54	17	105	2
1969	Clark, Mike	0	43	20	103	2
1970	Clark, Mike	0	35	18	89	12/8
1971	Clark, Mike	0	47	13	86	13/7
1972	Fritsch, Toni	0	36	21	99	7/3
1973	Fritsch, Toni	0	43	18	97	11/7
1974	*Herrera, Efren	0	33	8	57	26/9
1975	Fritsch, Toni	0	38	22	104	3/2
1976	Herrera, Efren	0	34	18	88	6/4
1977	Herrera, Efren	0	39	18	93	3/2
1978	Septien, Rafael	0	46	16	94	5/2
1979	Septien, Rafael	0	40	19	97	8/3
1980	Septien, Rafael	0	59	11	92	13/6
1981	Septien, Rafael	0	40	27	122	1/1
1982	Septien, Rafael	0	28	10	58	11/5
1983	Septien, Rafael	0	57	22	123	5/5
1984	Septien, Rafael	0	33	23	102	13/6

FIELD GOALS

Year	Player	Att.	Made	Pct.	Long	NFL/ NFC Rank
1960	Cone, Fred	13	6	.462	45	12
1961	Bielski, Dick	9	6	.667	42	13
1962	Baker, Sam	27	14	.519	53	3
1963	Baker, Sam	20	9	.450	53	12
1964	*VanRaaphorst, Dick	29	14	.483	43	8
1965	Villanueva, Danny	27	16	.593	41	7
1966	Villanueva, Danny	31	17	.548	37	8
1967	Villanueva, Danny	23	9	.391	34	14
1968	Clark, Mike	29	17	.586	50	7
1969	Clark, Mike	36	20	.555	47	5
1970	Clark, Mike	27	18	.667	43	7/4
1971	Clark, Mike	25	13	.520	48	19/9
1972	Fritsch, Toni	36	21	.583	54	18/8
1973	Fritsch, Toni	28	18	.643	37	12/4
1974	*Herrera, Efren	13	8	.615	39	11/5
1975	Fritsch, Toni	35	22	.629	43	14/8
1976	Herrera, Efren	23	18	.783	46	1/1
1977	Herrera, Efren	29	18	.621	52	12/1
1978	Septien, Rafael	26	16	.615	48	17/9
1979	Septien, Rafael	29	19	.655	51	9/4
1980	Septien, Rafael	17	11	.647	52	13/7
1981	Septien, Rafael	35	27	.771	47	4/3
1982	Septien, Rafael	14	10	.714	53	13/6
1983	Septien, Rafael	27	22	.815	47	7/3
1984	Septien, Rafael	29	23	.793	52	4/3

KICKOFF RETURNS

Year	Player	No.	Yds.	Avg.	Long	TD	NFL/ NFC Rank
1960	Franckhauser, Tom	26	526	20.2	46	0	19
1961	*Marsh, Amos	26	667	25.7	79	0	13
1962	Marsh, Amos	29	725	25.0	101t	1	10
1963	*Stiger, Jim	18	432	24.0	66	0	12
1964	*Renfro, Mel	40	1,017	25.4	65	0	7
1965	Renfro, Mel	21	630	30.0	100t	1	4
1966	Renfro, Mel	19	487	25.6	87t	1	9
1967	Garrison, Walt	20	366	18.3	36	0	23
1968	Baynham, Craig	23	590	25.7	40	0	7
1969	*Flowers, Richmond	11	283	25.7	30	0	29
1970	*Thomas, Duane	19	416	21.9	33	0	23/10
1971	Harris, Cliff	29	823	28.4	77	0	4/4
1972	Harris, Cliff	26	615	23.7	44	0	23/11
1973	**Montgomery, Mike	6	175	29.2	63	0	DNQ
1974	*Morgan, Dennis	35	823	23.5	43	0	21/11
1975	Pearson, Preston	16	391	24.4	42	0	13/7
1976	*Johnson, Butch	28	693	24.8	74	0	11/5
1977	Johnson, Butch	22	536	24.4	64	0	9/5
1978	Johnson, Butch	29	603	20.8	56	0	27/12
1979	*Springs, Ron	38	780	20.5	70	0	25/12
1980	*Jones, James	32	720	22.5	41	0	11/6
1981	Jones, James	27	517	19.1	33	0	36/17
1982	Fellows, Ron	16	359	22.4	35	0	16/9
1983	Fellows, Ron	43	855	19.9	53	0	26/12
1984	Allen, Gary	33	666	20.2	34	0	24/11

PUNT RETURNS

Year	Player	No.	Yds.	Avg.	Long	TD	NFL/ NFC Rank
1960	Butler, Bill	13	131	10.1	46	0	2
1961	*Marsh, Amos	14	71	5.1	19	0	14
1962	Lockett, J. W.	8	45	5.6	17	0	14
1963	*Stiger, Jim	14	141	10.1	45	0	6
1964	*Renfro, Mel	32	418	13.1	69t	1	3
1965	Renfro, Mel	24	145	6.0	35	0	9
1966	Hayes, Bob	17	106	6.2	18	0	7
1967	Hayes, Bob	24	276	11.5	69t	1	2
1968	Hayes, Bob	15	312	20.8	90t	2	1
1969	Hayes, Bob	18	179	9.9	50	0	3
1970	Hayes, Bob	15	116	7.7	34	0	20/7
1971	Harris, Cliff	17	129	7.6	35	0	11/4
1972	Harris, Cliff	19	78	4.1	21	0	21/11
1973	*Richards, Golden	21	139	6.6	46	0	23/10
1974	*Morgan, Dennis	19	287	15.1	98t	1	3/2
1975	Richards, Golden	28	288	10.3	43t	1	12/5
1976	*Johnson, Butch	45	489	10.9	55	0	8/4
1977	Johnson, Butch	50	423	8.5	38	0	20/7
1978	Johnson, Butch	51	401	7.9	23	0	18/9
1979	*Wilson, Steve	35	236	6.8	13	0	20/7
1980	*Jones, James	54	548	10.1	52	0	5/4
1981	Jones, James	33	188	5.7	17	0	28/14
1982	Fellows, Ron	25	189	7.6	17	0	18/8
1983	Hill, Rod	30	232	7.7	37	0	20/10
1984	Allen, Gary	54	446	8.3	18	0	16/8

INTERCEPTIONS

Year	Player	No.	Yds.	Avg.	Long	TD	NFL/ NFC Rank
1960	Bishop, Don	3	13	4.3	13	0	25
	Franckhauser, Tom	3	11	3.7	9	0	25
1961	Bishop, Don	8	172	21.5	57	0	2
1962	Bishop, Don	6	134	22.3	44	0	9
1963	Green, Cornell	7	211	30.1	55	0	6
1964	*Renfro, Mel	7	110	15.7	39t	1	4
1965	Green, Cornell	3	49	16.3	43	0	27
	Livingston, Warren	3	5	1.7	5	0	27
	*Logan, Obert	3	5	1.7	3	0	27
1966	Green, Cornell	4	88	22.0	41t	1	21
1967	Green,Cornell	7	52	7.4	28	0	7
	Renfro, Mel	7	38	5.4	30	0	9
1968	Howley, Chuck	6	115	19.2	58	1	11
1969	Renfro, Mel	10	118	11.8	41	0	1
1970	*Waters, Charlie	5	45	9.0	20	0	16/9
1971	Adderley, Herb	6	182	30.3	46	0	9/4
1972	Waters,Charlie	6	132	22.0	56	1	7/3
1973	Jordan, Lee Roy	6	78	13.0	31t	1	4/2
1974	Harris, Cliff	3	8	2.7	8	0	42/20
1975	Jordan, Lee Roy	6	80	13.3	38	0	7/4
1976	Washington, Mark	4	49	12.3	22	0	24/11
1977	Harris, Cliff	5	7	1.4	7	0	16/7
1978	Barnes, Benny	5	72	14.4	38	0	25/14
1979	Hughes, Randy	2	91	45.5	68	0	93/45
	Harris,Cliff	2	35	17.5	20	0	
	Barnes, Benny	2	20	10.0	11	0	
	Lewis, D. D.	2	8	4.0	5	0	
	Kyle, Aaron	2	0	0.0	0	0	
1980	Thurman, Dennis	5	114	22.8	78t	1	24/10
	Waters, Charlie	5	78	15.6	29	0	
1981	*Walls, Everson	11	133	12.1	33	0	1/1
1982	Walls, Everson	7	61	8.7	37	0	1/1
1983	Thurman, Dennis	6	49	8.2	34	0	15/8
1984	Downs, Michael	7	126	18.0	27t	1	4/2

*Rookie

**Did Not Qualify (Minimum 14 returns required.)

Cowboys Individual Records

SCORING

TOTAL POINTS

Career
687 Rafael Septien (1978-84), 303 PATs, 128 FGs
456 Bob Hayes (1965-74), 76 TDs
Season
123 Rafael Septien (1983), 57 PATs, 22 FGs
121 Rafael Septien (1981), 40 PATs, 27 FGs
107 Danny Villanueva (1966), 56 PATs, 17 FGs
105 Mike Clark (1968), 54 PATs, 17 FGs
Game
24 Dan Reeves (11/5/67 vs. Atlanta), 4 TDs
24 Bob Hayes (12/20/70 vs. Houston), 4 TDs
24 Calvin Hill (9/19/71 @ Buffalo), 4 TDs
24 Duane Thomas (12/18/71 vs. St. Louis), 4 TDs
Opponent/Game
24 Dick James, @ Washington (12/17/61)
24 Harold Jackson, @ L.A. Rams (10/14/73)

TOUCHDOWNS

Career
76 Bob Hayes (1965-74)
69 Tony Dorsett (1977-84)
51 Frank Clarke (1960-67)
Season
16 Dan Reeves (1966), 8 run, 8 pass
14 Frank Clarke (1962), 14 pass
Game
4 Dan Reeves (11/5/67 vs. Atlanta), 2 run, 2 pass
4 Bob Hayes (12/20/70 vs. Houston), 4 pass
4 Calvin Hill (9/19/71 @ Buffalo), 4 run
4 Duane Thomas (12/18/71 vs. St. Louis), 3 run, 1 pass
Opponent/Game
4 Dick James, @ Washington (12/17/61)
4 Harold Jackson, @ L.A. Rams (10/14/73)

FIELD GOALS MADE

Career
128 Rafael Septien (1978-84), 177 attempts
69 Mike Clark (1968-71, 1973), 119 attempts
66 Toni Fritsch (1971-73,1975), 107 attempts
Season
27 Rafael Septien (1981), 35 attempts
23 Rafael Septien (1984), 29 attempts
22 Rafael Septien (1983), 27 attempts
22 Toni Fritsch (1975), 35 attempts
Game
4 Rafael Septien (9/6/81 @ Washington; 9/21/81 @ New England)
4 Danny Villanueva (11/24/66 vs. Cleveland)
4 Toni Fritsch (11/12/72 vs. St. Louis)
4 Toni Fritsch (9/21/75 vs. L.A. Rams)
Longest Field Goal
54 Toni Fritsch (9/24/72 @ N.Y. Giants)
Opponent/Game
4 Bob Khayat, @ Washington (10/9/60)
4 Tommy Davis, San Francisco (11/20/60)
4 Sam Baker, @ Philadelphia (12/5/65)
4 Fred Cox, @ Minnesota (10/18/70)
4 Jim Bakken, St. Louis (12/18/71)
4 Chris Bahr, L.A. Raiders (10/23/83)
4 Ali Haji-Sheikh, N.Y.Giants (11/4/84)
Opponent/Longest Field Goal
59 Tony Franklin, Philadelphia (11/12/79)

FIELD GOALS ATTEMPTED

Career
177 Rafael Septien (1978-84), 128 FG
119 Mike Clark (1968-71, 1973), 69 FG
107 Toni Fritsch (1971-73,1975), 66 FG
Season
36 Toni Fritsch (1972), 21 FG
36 Mike Clark (1969), 20 FG
Game
7 Mike Clark (11/24/68 @ Chicago), 2 FG
6 Toni Fritsch (9/21/75 vs. L.A. Rams), 4 FG
Opponent/Game
7 Sam Baker, @ Philadelphia (12/5/65), 4 FG

EXTRA POINTS MADE

Career
303 Rafael Septien (1978-84)
180 Mike Clark (1968-71, 1973)
Season
59 Rafael Septien (1980)
57 Rafael Septien (1983)
Game
8 Rafael Septien (10/12/80 vs. San Francisco) Att. 8
8 Mike Clark (9/15/68 vs. Detroit) Att. 8
8 Danny Villanueva (10/9/66 vs. Philadelphia) Att. 8
Opponent/Game
7 Gerry Perry, @ St. Louis (12/9/62) Att. 7

RUSHING

TOTAL YARDS

Career
9,525 Tony Dorsett (1977-84)
6,217 Don Perkins (1961-68)
5,009 Calvin Hill (1969-74)
4,784 Robert Newhouse (1972-83)
Season
1,646 Tony Dorsett (1981), 4.8 per carry
1,325 Tony Dorsett (1978), 4.6 per carry
1,321 Tony Dorsett (1983), 4.6 per carry
1,189 Tony Dorsett (1984), 3.9 per carry
1,185 Tony Dorsett (1980), 4.3 per carry
1,142 Calvin Hill (1973), 4.2 per carry
1,107 Tony Dorsett (1979), 4.4 per carry
1,036 Calvin Hill (1972), 4.2 per carry
Game
206 Tony Dorsett (12/4/77 vs. Philadelphia) on 23 carries
183 Tony Dorsett (11/9/80 @ N.Y. Giants) on 24 carries
175 Tony Dorsett (12/6/81 @ Baltimore) on 30 carries
162 Tony Dorsett (9/21/81 @ New England) on 19 carries
159 Tony Dorsett (10/18/81 vs. L.A. Rams) on 27 carries
Opponent/Game
232 Jim Brown, Cleveland (9/22/63)
206 Greg Bell, @ Buffalo (11/18/84)
195 Earl Campbell, Houston (11/22/79)

ATTEMPTS

Career
2,136 Tony Dorsett (1977-84)
1,500 Don Perkins (1961-68)
1,166 Calvin Hill (1969-74)
1,160 Robert Newhouse (1972-83)
Season
342 Tony Dorsett (1981)
302 Tony Dorsett (1984)
290 Tony Dorsett (1978)
289 Tony Dorsett (1983)
Game
32 Calvin Hill (11/10/74 vs. San Francisco)
31 Calvin Hill (9/16/73 @ Chicago)
Opponent/Game
32 John Riggins, Washington (10/14/84), 165 yards

TOUCHDOWNS RUSHING

Career
59 Tony Dorsett (1977-84)
42 Don Perkins (1961-68)
39 Calvin Hill (1969-74)
31 Robert Newhouse (1972-83)
Season
12 Tony Dorsett (1977)
11 Tony Dorsett (1980)
11 Duane Thomas (1971)
Game
4 Calvin Hill (9/19/71 @ Buffalo)
Opponent/Game
3 Jim Taylor, @ Green Bay (11/13/60)
3 Dick James, @ Washington (12/17/61)

RUSHING AVERAGE

Career (700 attempts)
4.5 Tony Dorsett (1977-84), 2,136 attempts
4.3 Walt Garrison (1966-74), 899 attempts
4.3 Calvin Hill (1969-74), 1,166 attempts
Season
5.6 Amos Marsh (1962), 144-802
5.3 Duane Thomas (1970), 151-803
4.8 Tony Dorsett (1981), 342-1,646
4.8 Tony Dorsett (1977), 208-1,007
Game (10 attempts)
12.1 Walt Garrison (12/9/72 vs. Washington), 10-121
10.9 Amos Marsh (11/4/62 @ Washington), 10-109
10.8 Dan Reeves (12/11/66 vs. Washington), 10-108
Longest Runs
99 Tony Dorsett (1/3/83 @ Minnesota) TD
84 Tony Dorsett (12/4/77 vs. Philadelphia) TD
77 Tony Dorsett (10/9/77 @ St. Louis) TD
77 Tony Dorsett (9/5/83 @ Washington)
75 Tony Dorsett (9/21/81 @ New England) TD
73 Amos Bullocks (11/18/62 vs. Chicago) TD
Opponent/Longest Run
85 Greg Bell, @ Buffalo (11/18/84) TD

PASSING

TOTAL YARDS

Career
22,700 Roger Staubach (1969-79)
17,199 Don Meredith (1960-68)
14,754 Danny White (1976-84)
Season
3,980 Danny White (1983)
3,586 Roger Staubach (1979)
3,287 Danny White (1980)
3,190 Roger Staubach (1978)
3,098 Danny White (1981)
Game
460 Don Meredith (11/10/63 @ San Francisco), 30 of 48
406 Don Meredith (11/13/66 @ Washington), 21 of 29
394 Don Meredith (11/6/66 @ Philadelphia), 14 of 24
Opponent/Game
466 Bill Wade, Chicago (11/18/62), 28 of 46
411 Sonny Jurgensen, @ Washington (11/28/65)
408 David Woodley, Miami (10/25/81)
388 Neil Lomax, @ St. Louis (11/11/84)
377 Ed Brown, @ Pittsburgh (10/27/63)

PASS ATTEMPTS

Career
2,958 Roger Staubach (1969-79)
2,308 Don Meredith (1960-68)
Season
533 Danny White (1983), 334 completions
461 Roger Staubach (1979), 267 completions
436 Danny White (1980), 260 completions
413 Roger Staubach (1978), 231 completions
Game
49 Roger Staubach (10/26/75 @ Philadelphia), 27 completions
48 Don Meredith (11/10/63 @ San Francisco), 30 completions
Opponent/Game
52 Neil Lomax, @ St. Louis (11/11/84)
49 Marc Wilson, L.A. Raiders (10/23/83)

PASS COMPLETIONS

Career
1,685 Roger Staubach (1969-79)
1,170 Don Meredith (1960-68)
Season
334 Danny White (1983), 533 attempts
267 Roger Staubach (1979), 461 attempts
260 Danny White (1980), 436 attempts
231 Roger Staubach (1978), 413 attempts
223 Danny White (1981), 391 attempts
Game
33 Gary Hogeboom (9/3/84 @ L.A. Rams), 47 attempts
31 Danny White (11/13/83 @ San Diego), 47 attempts
30 Don Meredith (11/10/63 @ San Francisco), 48 attempts
29 Danny White (10/9/83 vs. Tampa Bay), 44 attempts
Opponent/Game
28 Bill Wade, Chicago (11/18/62), 46 attempts
28 Kent Nix, @ Pittsburgh (10/22/67), 45 attempts
28 Joe Theismann, @ Washington (9/5/83), 38 attempts

TOUCHDOWN PASSES

Career
153 Roger Staubach (1969-79)
135 Don Meredith (1960-68)
Season
29 Danny White (1983) of 334 completions
28 Danny White (1980) of 260 completions
27 Roger Staubach (1979) of 267 completions
25 Roger Staubach (1978) of 231 completions
Game
5 Eddie LeBaron (10/21/62 @ Pittsburgh)
5 Don Meredith (9/18/66 vs. N.Y. Giants)
5 Don Meredith (10/9/66 vs. Philadelphia)
5 Don Meredith (9/29/68 @ Philadelphia)
5 Craig Morton (10/19/69 vs. Philadelphia)
5 Craig Morton (12/20/70 vs. Houston)
5 Danny White (10/30/83 @ N.Y. Giants)
Opponent/Game
6 Y. A. Tittle, @ N.Y. Giants (12/16/62)

PASSES HAD INTERCEPTED

Career
111 Don Meredith (1960-68)
109 Roger Staubach (1969-79)
Season
25 Eddie LeBaron (1960), 225 attempts
25 Danny White (1980), 436 attempts
23 Danny White (1983), 533 attempts
21 Craig Morton (1972), 339 attempts
Game
5 Eddie LeBaron (9/30/60 vs. Philadelphia), 29 attempts
5 Eddie LeBaron (11/5/61 vs. St.Louis), 33 attempts
5 Danny White (11/9/80 @ N.Y. Giants), 23 attempts
Opponent/Game
6 Pete Liske, @ Philadelphia (9/26/71), 29 attempts

LOWEST INTERCEPTION RATE (150 or more attempts)

Season
1.9 Roger Staubach (1971), 4 of 211
2.4 Roger Staubach (1979), 11 of 461
2.5 Roger Staubach (1977), 9 of 361
3.0 Roger Staubach (1976), 11 of 369

COMPLETION PERCENT

Career (1500 attempts)
59.4 Danny White (1976-84), 1,155 of 1,943
57.0 Roger Staubach (1969-79), 1,685 of 2,958
50.7 Don Meredith (1960-68), 1,170 of 2,308
Season
63.2 Danny White (1982), 156 of 247
62.7 Danny White (1983), 334 of 533
62.6 Roger Staubach (1973), 179 of 286
59.7 Roger Staubach (1971), 126 of 211
Game (12 or more completions)
87.5 Danny White (11/6/83 @ Philadelphia), 21 of 24
84.2 Don Meredith (9/15/68 vs. Detroit), 16 of 19
81.2 Eddie LeBaron (9/16/62 vs. Washington), 13 of 16

LONGEST PASS PLAYS

95 Don Meredith to Bob Hayes (11/13/66 vs. Washington) TD
91 Roger Staubach to Tony Dorsett (9/4/78 vs. Baltimore) TD
89 Craig Morton to Bob Hayes (10/25/70 @ Kansas City) TD
Opponent/Longest Pass Play
94 Norm Snead to Rich Houston, @ N.Y. Giants (9/24/72) TD

PASS RECEIVING

TOTAL RECEPTIONS

Career
489 Drew Pearson (1973-83)
365 Bob Hayes (1965-74)
356 Tony Hill (1977-84)
292 Tony Dorsett (1977-84)

Season
73 Ron Springs (1983), 589 yards
65 Frank Clarke (1964), 973 yards
64 Bob Hayes (1966), 1,232 yards

Game
13 Lance Rentzel (11/19/67 vs. Washington), 223 yards
11 Bill Howton (11/25/62 @ Philadelphia), 102 yards
11 Ron Springs (9/21/81 @ New England), 72 yards
11 Ron Springs (10/9/83 vs. Tampa Bay), 126 yards

Opponent/Game
12 J. R. Wilburn, @ Pittsburgh (10/22/67), 142 yards

TOTAL RECEIVING YARDS

Career
7,822 Drew Pearson (1973-83)
7,295 Bob Hayes (1965-74)
6,105 Tony Hill (1977-84)
5,214 Frank Clarke (1960-67)
3,565 Billy Joe DuPree (1973-83)
3,521 Lance Rentzel (1967-70)

Season
1,232 Bob Hayes (1966), 64 receptions
1,087 Drew Pearson (1974), 62 receptions
1,062 Tony Hill (1979), 60 receptions
1,055 Tony Hill (1980), 60 receptions
1,043 Frank Clarke (1962), 47 receptions
1,026 Drew Pearson (1979), 55 receptions
1,009 Lance Rentzel (1968), 54 receptions

Game
246 Bob Hayes (11/13/66 @ Washington), 9 receptions
241 Frank Clarke (9/16/62 vs. Washington), 10 receptions
223 Lance Rentzel (11/19/67 vs. Washington), 13 receptions
213 Tony Hill (11/12/79 vs. Philadelphia), 7 receptions

Opponent/Game
238 Harold Jackson, @ L.A. Rams (10/14/73), 7 receptions

TOUCHDOWNS RECEIVING

Career
71 Bob Hayes (1965-74)
50 Frank Clarke (1960-67)
48 Drew Pearson (1973-83)
41 Billy Joe DuPree (1973-83)
41 Tony Hill (1977-84)

Season
14 Frank Clarke (1962), 47 receptions
13 Bob Hayes (1966), 64 receptions
12 Lance Rentzel (1969), 43 receptions
12 Bob Hayes (1965), 46 receptions

Game
4 Bob Hayes (12/20/70 vs. Houston)

Opponent/Game
4 Harold Jackson, @ L.A. Rams (10/14/73)

RUSHING — RECEIVING

Career
12,064 Tony Dorsett (1977-84), 9,525 rushing, 2,539 receiving
8,012 Drew Pearson (1973-83), 7,822 receiving, 190 rushing
7,527 Don Perkins (1961-68), 6,217 rushing, 1,310 receiving
7,365 Bob Hayes (1965-74), 7,295 receiving, 70 rushing
6,368 Calvin Hill (1969-74), 5,009 rushing, 1,359 receiving

Season
1,971 Tony Dorsett (1981), 1,646 rushing, 325 receiving
1,703 Tony Dorsett (1978), 1,325 rushing, 378 receiving
1,648 Tony Dorsett (1984), 1,189 rushing, 459 receiving
1,608 Tony Dorsett (1983), 1,321 rushing, 287 receiving
1,482 Tony Dorsett (1979), 1,107 rushing, 375 receiving

Game
254 Tony Dorsett (9/4/78 vs. Baltimore), 147 rushing, 107 receiving
246 Bob Hayes (11/13/66 @ Washington), 246 receiving
241 Frank Clarke (9/16/62 vs. Washington), 241 receiving
230 Tony Dorsett (12/4/77 vs. Philadelphia), 206 rushing, 24 receiving

COMBINED YARDAGE

Career
12,118 Tony Dorsett (1977-84), 54 return yards
9,104 Bob Hayes (1965-74), 1,739 return yards
8,180 Drew Pearson(1973-83), 168 return yards
7,978 Don Perkins (1961-68), 451 return yards
6,559 Tony Hill (1977-84), 364 return yards
6,493 Calvin Hill (1969-74), 125 return yards
6,493 Walt Garrison (1966-74), 813 return yards

Season
1,998 Amos Marsh (1962), 729 return yards
1,971 Tony Dorsett (1981), no return yards
1,757 Tony Dorsett (1978), 54 return yards
1,648 Tony Dorsett (1984), no return yards
1,608 Tony Dorsett (1983), no return yards

Game
285 Bob Hayes (12/24/67 vs. Cleveland — playoff game) 5/144 receiving, 3/141 punt returns
285 Calvin Hill (11/16/69 @ Washington) 3/100 kickoff return, 27/150 rushing, 2/35 receiving

PUNTING

TOTAL PUNTS

Career
611 Danny White (1976-84)
247 Ron Widby (1968-71)
192 Danny Villanueva (1965-67)

Season
82 Danny White (1984), 38.4 average
81 Danny White (1981), 40.8 average
80 Danny White (1977), 39.6 average

Game
11 Danny White (9/23/84 vs. Philadelphia) 40.5 average

AVERAGE YARDS

Career
45.1 Sam Baker (1962-63)

Season
45.4 Sam Baker (1962), 57 punts
44.2 Sam Baker (1963), 71 punts
43.3 Ron Widby (1969), 63 punts

Game (4 or more punts)
53.4 Ron Widby (11/3/68 @ New Orleans)
53.0 Marv Bateman (11/4/73 vs. Cincinnati)

LONGEST PUNT
84 Ron Widby (11/3/68 @ New Orleans)

PUNT RETURNS

TOTAL RETURNS

Career
146 Butch Johnson (1976-83)
109 Mel Renfro (1964-77)
104 Bob Hayes (1965-74)

Season
54 Gary Allen (1984), 8.3 average
54 James Jones (1980), 10.1 average
51 Butch Johnson (1978), 7.9 average

Game
9 Butch Johnson (11/15/76 vs. Buffalo)

PUNT RETURN YARDAGE

Career
1,313 Butch Johnson (1976-83)
1,158 Bob Hayes (1965-74)

Season
548 James Jones (1980), 10.1 average
489 Butch Johnson (1976), 10.9 average
446 Gary Allen (1984), 8.3 average

Game
141 Bob Hayes (12/24/67 vs. Cleveland — playoff game), 3 returns
122 Bob Hayes (12/8/68 vs. Pittsburgh), 3 returns

Longest Punt Return
98 Dennis Morgan (10/13/74 vs. St. Louis)
90 Bob Hayes (12/6/68 vs. Pittsburgh)

AVERAGE YARDS

Career
11.1 Bob Hayes (1965-74), 104 returns
9.5 Gary Allen (1983-84), 63 returns
9.0 Butch Johnson (1976-83), 146 returns
8.5 James Jones (1980-82), 87 returns

Season (14 or more returns)
20.8 Bob Hayes (1968), 15 returns
15.1 Dennis Morgan (1974), 19 returns
13.1 Mel Renfro (1964), 32 returns

Game
47.0 Bob Hayes (12/24/67 vs. Cleveland — playoff game), 3 for 141 yards

FAIR CATCHES

Career
38 Mel Renfro (1964-77)
38 Butch Johnson (1976-83)
35 Golden Richards (1973-78)

Season
18 Golden Richards (1973)
16 Cliff Harris (1972)
15 Butch Johnson (1977)
15 Gary Allen (1984)

Game
4 Golden Richards (11/16/75 @ New England)
4 Golden Richards (11/17/74 @ Washington)
4 Lance Rentzel (12/21/68 vs. Cleveland — playoff game)
4 Cliff Harris (12/23/72 @ San Francisco — playoff game)

KICKOFF RETURNS

TOTAL RETURNS

Career
85 Mel Renfro (1964-77)
79 Butch Johnson (1976-83)

Season
43 Ron Fellows (1983), 19.9 average
40 Mel Renfro (1964), 25.4 average
38 Ron Springs (1979), 20.5 average

Game
8 Mel Renfro (10/29/64 vs. Green Bay), 156 yards

KICKOFF RETURN YARDAGE

Career
2,246 Mel Renfro (1964-77)
1,832 Butch Johnson (1976-83)

Season
1,017 Mel Renfro (1964), 25.4 average
855 Ron Fellows (1983), 19.9 average
823 Cliff Harris (1971), 28.4 average
823 Dennis Morgan (1974), 23.5 average

Game
168 Mel Renfro (11/22/64 @ Washington), 4 returns
157 Amos Marsh (10/14/62 vs. Philadelphia), 4 returns

Longest Kickoff Return
101 Amos Marsh (10/14/62 vs. Philadelphia)
101 Ike Thomas (12/4/71 vs. N.Y. Jets)
100 Mark Washington (11/22/70 @ Washington)
100 Mel Renfro (11/7/65 vs. San Francisco)

AVERAGE YARDS

Career
26.4 Mel Renfro (1964-77), 85 returns
25.7 Cliff Harris (1970-79), 63 returns

Season
30.0 Mel Renfro (1965), 21 returns
28.4 Cliff Harris (1971), 29 returns

Game (4 or more)
42.0 Mel Renfro (11/22/64 @ Washington), 4 for 168 yards

INTERCEPTIONS

TOTAL INTERCEPTIONS

Career
52 Mel Renfro (1964-77)
41 Charlie Waters (1970-78, 1980-81)
34 Cornell Green (1962-74)
32 Lee Roy Jordan (1963-76)

Season
11 Everson Walls (1981), 133 yards
10 Mel Renfro (1969), 118 yards
9 Dennis Thurman (1981), 187 yards

Game
3 Herb Adderley (9/26/71 @ Philadelphia), 102 yards
3 Lee Roy Jordan (11/4/73 vs. Cincinnati), 49 yards
3 Dennis Thurman (12/13/81 vs. Philadelphia), 37 yards

INTERCEPTION YARDAGE

Career
626 Mel Renfro (1964-77)
584 Charlie Waters (1970-78, 1980-81)
552 Cornell Green (1962-74)

Season
211 Cornell Green (1963), 7 for 30.1 average
187 Dennis Thurman (1981), 9 for 20.8 average
182 Herb Adderley (1971), 6 for 30.3 average

Game
121 Mike Gaechter (11/3/63 vs. Washington) on 2 int.

Longest Interception Return
100 Mike Gaechter (10/14/62 vs. Philadelphia)
96 Dennis Thurman (9/6/81 @ Washington)
90 Mel Renfro (10/4/65 @ St. Louis)

TOUCHDOWN INTERCEPTIONS

Career
3 Dennis Thurman (1977-84)
3 Mel Renfro (1964-77)
3 Lee Roy Jordan (1963-76)
3 Larry Cole (1968-80)

Cowboys Team Records

1960: 12 games
1961-77: 14 games
1978-81, 1983: 16 games

NOTE: The 1982 regular season was reduced from 16 games to 9 because of a players' strike.

SCORING

MOST POINTS SCORED
Season
479 1983
445 1966**
Game
59 9/15/68 vs. Detroit
59 10/12/80 vs. San Francisco

FEWEST POINTS SCORED
Season
177 1960
236 1961**
308 1984*
Game
0 11/16/70 vs. St. Louis

OPPONENT/MOST POINTS SCORED
Season
402 1962
Game
54 10/18/70 @ Minnesota

OPPONENT/FEWEST POINTS SCORED
Season
186 1968
208 1978*
Game
0 9 times, last 9/4/78 vs. Baltimore

MOST POINTS, BOTH TEAMS
Game
86 9/19/71 @ Buffalo, (Dallas 49, Buffalo 37)
78 10/23/83 vs. L.A. Raiders, (Raiders 40, Dallas 38)

FEWEST POINTS, BOTH TEAMS
Game
8 12/12/70 @ Cleveland, (Dallas 6, Cleveland 2)

MOST DECISIVE WIN
Game
49 10/9/66 vs. Philadelphia, (Dallas 56, Philadelphia 7)
46 9/15/68 vs. Detroit, (Dallas 59, Detroit 13)
45 9/18/66 vs. N.Y. Giants, (Dallas 52, Giants 7)
45 10/12/80 vs. San Fran., (Dallas 59, San Fran. 14)

MOST DECISIVE LOSS
Game
41 10/16/60 vs. Cleveland, (Cleveland 48, Dallas 7)
41 10/18/70 @ Minnesota, (Minnesota 54, Dallas 13)

MOST TOUCHDOWNS SCORED
Season
60 1980
56 1966**
Game
8 10/9/66 vs. Philadelphia
8 9/15/68 vs. Detroit
8 10/12/80 vs. San Francisco

FEWEST TOUCHDOWNS SCORED
Season
23 1960
29 1961**
34 1984*

OPPONENT/MOST TDS SCORED
Season
52 1962
Game
7 12/9/62 @ St. Louis

OPPONENT/FEWEST TDS SCORED
Season
22 1973
25 1978*

MOST TOUCHDOWNS BY:
RUSHING
Season
26 1980
25 1971**
Game
5 9/19/71 @ Buffalo
PASSING
Season
31 1962, 1983
Game
5 6 times, last 10/30/83 @ N.Y. Giants
INTERCEPTIONS
Season
3 1966, 67, 68, 75
Game
1 29 times, last 12/2/84 @ Philadelphia
KO RETURNS
Season
2 1971
PUNT RETURN
Season
2 1968

FEWEST TOUCHDOWNS BY:
RUSHING
Season
6 1960
6 1961**
12 1984*
PASSING
Season
10 1964
19 1984*

OPPONENT/MOST TOUCHDOWNS BY:
RUSHING
Season
24 1960
Game
5 4 times, last 10/10/65 vs. Philadelphia
PASSING
Season
33 1962
Game
5 10/30/60 vs. Baltimore
5 11/2/69 @ Cleveland
INTERCEPTIONS
Season
6 1961
KO RETURN
Season
3 1966
PUNT RETURNS
Game
1 7 times, last 12/19/83 @ San Francisco

OPPONENT/FEWEST TDS BY:
RUSHING
Season
2 1968
3 1969
8 1984*
PASSING
Season
10 1970
11 1978*

MOST PATS SCORED
Season
59 1980
56 1966**
Game
8 9/15/68 vs. Detroit
8 10/12/80 vs. San Fran.

OPPONENT/MOST PATS SCORED
Season
49 1962
Game
7 12/9/62 @ St. Louis

MOST FGS SCORED
Season
27 1981
23 1984
Game
4 11/24/66 vs. Cleveland
4 11/12/72 vs. St. Louis
4 9/21/75 vs. L.A. Rams
4 9/6/81 @ Washington
4 9/21/81 @ New England

SCORE BY QUARTERS
1st Quarter
28 10/19/69 vs. Philadelphia
28 12/4/71 vs. N.Y. Jets
2nd Quarter
24 9/18/66 vs. N.Y. Giants
24 10/30/66 vs. Pittsburgh
24 9/15/68 vs. Detroit
24 10/24/71 vs. New England
24 10/12/80 vs. San Francisco
3rd Quarter
21 10/30/66 vs. Pittsburgh
21 9/24/73 vs. New Orleans
21 12/7/74 vs. Cleveland
21 9/28/75 vs. St. Louis
21 10/26/80 vs. San Diego
4th Quarter
21 12/19/65 @ N.Y. Giants
21 9/15/68 vs. Detroit
21 10/6/75 @ Detroit
21 10/21/73 vs. N.Y. Giants
21 11/27/80 vs. Seattle
21 10/21/84 vs. New Orleans

SCORE BY HALVES
1st Half
42 10/19/69 vs. Philadelphia
2nd Half
31 9/29/68 @ Philadelphia
31 11/17/68 @ Washington

OPPONENT/SCORE BY QUARTERS
1st Quarter
21 12/3/60 vs. Cleveland
21 10/11/81 @ San Francisco
21 12/19/83 @ San Francisco
2nd Quarter
28 12/16/62 @ N.Y.Giants
3rd Quarter
21 12/17/61 @ Washington
4th Quarter
21 12/9/62 @ St. Louis
21 11/28/65 @ Washington
21 11/16/70 vs. St. Louis
21 11/5/72 @ San Diego

OPPONENT/SCORE BY HALVES
1st Half
35 12/16/62 @ N.Y. Giants
2nd Half
38 12/9/62 @ St. Louis

SCORE BY QUARTERS, BOTH TEAMS
1st Quarter
35 10/19/69 vs. Philadelphia
2nd Quarter
38 11/10/75 vs. Kansas City
38 10/23/83 vs. L.A. Raiders
3rd Quarter
35 9/28/75 vs. St. Louis
4th Quarter
35 10/21/73 vs. N.Y. Giants

SCORE BY HALVES, BOTH TEAMS
1st Half
59 12/16/62 @ N.Y. Giants
2nd Half
52 9/28/75 vs. St. Louis

FIRST DOWNS

MOST FIRST DOWNS
Season
342 1978, 1983
Game
32 10/9/66 vs. Philadelphia
32 9/10/78 @ N.Y. Giants
32 11/12/78 @ Green Bay
32 10/16/83 vs. Philadelphia

FEWEST FIRST DOWNS
Season
180 1960
211 1965**
321 1981*
Game
8 10/16/60 vs. Cleveland
8 11/12/61 @ Pittsburgh
8 12/10/61 @ St. Louis
8 11/29/64 vs. Green Bay
8 11/1/70 vs. Philadelphia

OPPONENT/MOST FIRST DOWNS
Season
296 1980
Game
31 10/23/83 vs. L.A. Raiders

OPPONENT/FEWEST FIRST DOWNS
Season
199 1974
232 1978*
Game
5 11/6/66 @ Philadelphia
5 10/20/74 vs. Philadelphia

MOST FIRST DOWNS, BOTH TEAMS
633 1980
Game
55 10/1/67 vs. L.A. Rams

MOST FIRST DOWNS BY:
RUSHING
Season
147 1974

Game
19 12/6/81 @ Baltimore
PASSING
Season
205 1983
Game
23 11/10/63 @ San Francisco
PENALTY
Season
29 1978
Game
6 10/9/83 vs. Tampa Bay
FEWEST FIRST DOWNS BY:
RUSHING
Season
57 1960
87 1965**
93 1984*
Game
0 11/16/70 vs. St. Louis
PASSING
Season
95 1970
158 1981*
Game
3 8 times, last 9/23/74 @ Philadelphia
PENALTY
Season
9 1961
9 1962**
9 1971**
OPPONENT/MOST FIRST DOWNS BY:
RUSHING
Season
122 1961
Game
17 9/30/84 @ Chicago
PASSING
Season
181 1983
Game
21 11/18/62 vs. Chicago
21 11/20/83 vs. Kansas City
21 11/11/84 @ St. Louis
PENALTY
Season
28 1980
Game
5 11/21/65 vs. Cleveland
5 12/7/74 vs. Cleveland
5 11/20/83 vs. Kansas City
OPPONENT/FEWEST FIRST DOWNS BY:
RUSHING
Season
52 1969
82 1983*
PASSING
Season
94 1977
128 1978*
PENALTY
Season
10 1969
18 1981*

TOTAL YARDS

MOST NET YARDS GAINED
Season
5,968 1979
Game
652 10/6/66 vs. Philadelphia
583 9/4/78 vs. Baltimore
578 9/30/73 vs. St. Louis
FEWEST NET YARDS GAINED
Season
3,153 1960
3,704 1964**
5,320 1984*
Game
126 12/10/61 @ St. Louis
OPPONENT/MOST NET YARDS GAINED
Season
5,427 1983
Game
529 10/25/81 vs. Miami
527 12/9/62 @ St. Louis
OPPONENT/FEWEST NET YDS. GAINED
Season
3,213 1977
4,009 1978**
Game
63 10/24/65 @ Green Bay
80 12/10/67 vs. Philadelphia
MOST NET YARDS, BOTH TEAMS
Season
11,386 1983
Game
995 10/25/81 vs. Miami
926 11/10/63 @ San Francisco

RUSHING

MOST YARDS RUSHING
Season
2,783 1978
Game
354 12/6/81 @ Baltimore
FEWEST YARDS RUSHING
Season
1,049 1960
1,608 1965**
1,714 1984*
Game
33 12/11/83 vs. Washington
OPPONENT/MOST YARDS RUSHING
Season
2,242 1960
2,226 1984*
Game
289 10/22/61 vs. Philadelphia
OPPONENT/FEWEST YARDS RUSHING
Season
1,050 1969
1,499 1983*
Game
7 10/30/66 vs. Pittsburgh
MOST YARDS RUSHING, BOTH TEAMS
Season
5,760 1981
Game
510 12/6/81 @ Baltimore
466 10/22/61 vs. Philadelphia
MOST ATTEMPTS RUSHING
Season
630 1981
Game
66 12/6/81 @ Baltimore
FEWEST RUSHING ATTEMPTS
Season
311 1960
416 1961**
469 1984*
Game
16 11/7/65 vs. San Francisco
OPPONENT/MOST ATMPTS. RUSHING
Season
510 1984
Game
54 10/11/70 vs. Atlanta
OPPONENT/FEWEST ATMPTS. RUSHING
Season
313 1969
410 1983*
Game
12 10/16/83 vs. Philadelphia
12 9/24/67 vs. N.Y. Giants
12 10/30/66 vs. Pittsburgh

PASSING

MOST NET YARDS PASSING
Season
3,842 1983
Game
440 10/9/66 vs. Philadelphia
FEWEST NET YARDS PASSING
Season
2,013 1964
3,104 1980*
Game
-10 10/24/65 @ Green Bay
OPPONENT/MOST NET YDS. PASSING
Season
3,928 1983
Game
437 11/18/62 vs. Chicago
OPPONENT/FEWEST NET YDS. PASS.
Season
1,562 1977
2,288 1980*
Game
-1 10/24/65 @ Green Bay
-1 12/21/75 @ N.Y. Jets
MOST GROSS YARDS PASSING
Season
4,156 1983
Game
460 11/10/63 @ San Francisco
FEWEST GROSS YARDS PASSING
Season
2,388 1960
2,445 1970**
3,356 1980*
Game
42 10/24/65 @ Green Bay
OPPONENT/MOST GROSS YDS. PASS.
Season
4,365 1983
Game
466 11/18/62 vs. Chicago
OPPONENT/FEWEST GROSS YDS. PASS.
Season
1,991 1977
2,730 1978*
Game
-15 12/21/75 @ N.Y. Jets
MOST PASS ATTEMPTS
Season
604 1984
Game
50 10/26/75 @ Philadelphia
FEWEST PASS ATTEMPTS
Season
297 1970
439 1981*
Game
11 10/21/73 vs. N.Y. Giants
11 10/11/70 vs. Atlanta
OPPONENT/MOST PASS ATTEMPTS
Season
558 1983
Game
59 11/20/83 vs. Kansas City
OPPONENT/FEWEST PASS ATTEMPTS
Season
293 1960
326 1961**
432 1978*
Game
10 10/3/71 vs. Washington
10 11/22/73 vs. Miami
MOST PASS COMPLETIONS
Season
346 1983
Game
33 9/3/84 @ L.A. Rams
FEWEST PASS COMPLETIONS
Season
149 1970
251 1978*
Game
4 10/11/70 vs. Atlanta
OPPONENT/MOST PASS COMPLETIONS
Season
299 1983
Game
33 11/20/83 vs. Kansas City
OPPONENT/FEWEST PASS COMPLNS.
Season
146 1960
154 1977**
202 1978*
Game
2 12/21/75 @ N.Y. Jets
DEFENSE, MOST QB SACKS
Season
60 1966
58 1978*
Game
12 11/20/66 @ Pittsburgh
11 10/6/75 @ Detroit
OPPONENT/DFNS., MOST QB SACKS
Season
68 1964
Game
9 10/24/65 @ Green Bay

INTERCEPTIONS

MOST PASSES INTERCEPTED
Season
37 1981
Game
7 9/30/60 vs. Philadelphia
7 9/26/71 @ Philadelphia
FEWEST PASSES INTERCEPTED
Season
13 1974, 1979
OPPONENT/MOST PASSES INTER.
Season
33 1960
Game
5 9/30/60 vs. Philadelphia
5 11/5/61 vs. St. Louis
5 11/9/80 @ N.Y. Giants
5 12/2/84 @ Philadelphia
OPPONENT/FEWEST PASSES INTER.
Season
10 1977
13 1979*

PENALTIES

MOST PENALTIES
Season
107 1980
Game
15 10/18/81 vs. L.A. Rams
14 11/6/77 @ N.Y. Giants
14 9/9/79 @ San Francisco
FEWEST PENALTIES
Season
47 1961
96 1978**
Game
0 12/10/61 @ St. Louis
0 11/23/80 vs. Washington
OPPONENT/MOST PENALTIES
Season
106 1980
Game
14 10/9/83 vs. Tampa Bay
OPPONENT/FEWEST PENALTIES
Season
38 1961
70 1979*
Game
0 10/21/62 @ Pittsburgh
0 12/5/65 @ Philadelphia

MOST YARDS PENALIZED
Season
952 1964, 1971
Game
161 11/2/70 @ Washington
159 10/13/68 vs. Philadelphia
FEWEST YARDS PENALIZED
Season
427 1961
704 1978*
Game
0 12/10/61 @ St. Louis
0 11/23/80 vs. Washington
OPPONENT/MOST YARDS PENALIZED
Season
989 1980
Game
185 10/9/83 vs. Tampa Bay
166 10/9/77 @ St. Louis
OPPONENT/FEWEST YARDS PENALIZED
Season
362 1961
704 1979*
Game
0 10/21/62 @ Pittsburgh
0 12/5/65 @ Philadelphia
BOTH TEAMS, FEWEST YDS. PENAL.
Season
789 1961
1,549 1979
Game
10 12/10/61 @ St. Louis

PUNTING

MOST PUNTS
Season
108 1984
Game
11 9/23/84 vs. Philadelphia
OPPONENT/MOST PUNTS
Season
108 1978
Game
11 9/30/62 @ L.A. Rams
11 9/15/74 @ Atlanta
11 11/15/76 vs. Buffalo
11 11/22/84 vs. New England
HIGHEST AVERAGE
Season
45.4 1962
Game
53.4 11/3/68 vs. New Orleans (4)
OPPONENT/HIGHEST AVERAGE
Season
45.5 1961
Game
54.3 10/17/65 @ Cleveland (6)

PUNT RETURNS

MOST PUNT RETURNS
Season
63 1978
Game
9 11/15/76 vs. Buffalo
MOST PUNT RETURN YARDS
Season
573 1974
556 1980*
Game
122 12/8/68 vs. Pittsburgh
OPPONENT/MOST PUNT RETURNS
Season
55 1984
Game
8 11/4/84 vs. N.Y. Giants
OPPONENT/MOST PUNT RETURN YDS.
Season
588 1983
Game
109 11/16/70 vs. St. Louis

KICKOFF RETURNS

MOST KICKOFF RETURNS
Season
70 1983
Game
9 10/18/70 @ Minnesota
MOST KICKOFF RETURN YARDS
Season
1,376 1971
1,351 1983*
Game
260 11/7/65 vs. San Francisco
OPPONENT/MOST KICKOFF RETURNS
Season
78 1966, 1983*
Game
10 9/15/68 vs. Detroit
OPPONENT/MOST KICKOFF RET. YDS.
Season
1,806 1983
Game
261 11/6/66 @ Philadelphia

FUMBLES

MOST FUMBLES
Season
46 1961
45 1981*
Game
7 10/11/71 vs. N.Y. Giants
MOST FUMBLES LOST
Season
21 1961, 71, 79
Game
5 11/13/68 @ New Orleans
5 10/11/71 vs. N.Y. Giants
5 11/10/75 vs. Kansas City
OPPONENT/MOST FUMBLES
Season
44 1973
43 1981*
Game
7 11/28/65 @ Washington
7 11/10/75 vs. Kansas City
OPPONENT/MOST FUMBLES LOST
Season
25 1971
21 1983*
Game
5 10/11/71 vs. N.Y. Giants
5 9/16/73 @ Chicago
5 10/12/80 vs. San Francisco
5 10/23/83 vs. L.A. Raiders

*16-game record
**14-game record

Cowboys Individual Playoff Records

TOTAL POINTS
18 Craig Baynham (12/24/67 vs. Cleveland), 3 TDs
18 Preston Pearson (1/4/76 @ L.A. Rams), 3 TDs
13 Toni Fritsch (1/4/76 @ L.A. Rams) (kicker)
13 Efren Herrera (12/26/77 vs. Chicago) (kicker)
13 Rafael Septien (1/16/83 vs. Green Bay) (kicker)
TOUCHDOWNS
3 Craig Baynham (12/24/67 vs. Cleveland), 2 runs, 1 pass
3 Preston Pearson (1/4/76 @ L.A. Rams), 3 passes
FIELD GOALS MADE
3 Toni Fritsch (12/23/72 @ San Francisco)
3 Toni Fritsch (1/4/76 @ L.A. Rams)
3 Efren Herrera (12/26/77 vs. Chicago)
3 Rafael Septien (1/9/83 vs. Tampa Bay and 1/16/83 vs. Green Bay)
LONGEST FIELD GOAL
50 Rafael Septien (1/16/83 vs. Green Bay)
FIELD GOALS ATTEMPTED
5 Efren Herrera (1/15/78 vs. Denver), 2 FGs
EXTRA POINTS ATTEMPTED — MADE
7-7 Danny Villanueva (12/24/67 vs. Cleveland)

RUSHING
RUSHING YARDS
160 Tony Dorsett (12/28/80 vs. L.A. Rams), 22 carries
RUSHING ATTEMPTS
30 Duane Thomas (12/26/70 vs. Detroit)
TOUCHDOWNS RUSHING
2 Don Perkins (12/24/67 vs. Cleveland)
2 Craig Baynham (12/24/67 vs. Cleveland)
2 Tony Dorsett (12/26/77 vs. Chicago)
RUSHING AVERAGE (Min. 10 Attempts)
7.2 Tony Dorsett (12/28/80 vs. L.A. Rams), 22-160
6.9 Calvin Hill (12/23/72 @ San Francisco), 18-125
6.4 Don Perkins (1/1/67 vs. Green Bay), 17-108
LONGEST RUN
53 Tony Dorsett (1/7/79 @ Los Angeles)

PASSING
PASSING YARDS
330 Danny White (12/26/83 vs. L.A. Rams), 32 of 53
322 Danny White (1/4/81 @ Atlanta), 25 of 39
312 Danny White (1/9/83 vs. Tampa Bay), 27 of 45
246 Roger Staubach (12/28/75 @ Minnesota), 15 of 24
PASS ATTEMPTS
53 Danny White (12/26/83 vs. L.A.Rams), 32 completions
45 Danny White (1/9/83 vs.Tampa Bay), 27 completions
39 Danny White (1/4/81 @ Atlanta), 25 completions
37 Roger Staubach (12/19/76 vs. L.A. Rams), 15 completions
36 Danny White (1/16/83 vs. Green Bay), 23 completions
PASS COMPLETIONS
32 Danny White (12/26/83 vs. L.A. Rams), 53 attempts
27 Danny White (1/9/83 vs. Tampa Bay), 45 attempts
25 Danny White (1/4/81 @ Atlanta), 39 attempts
23 Danny White (1/16/83 vs. Green Bay), 36 attempts
17 Roger Staubach (12/28/75 @ Minnesota), 29 attempts
17 Roger Staubach (1/15/78 vs. Denver), 25 attempts
17 Roger Staubach (1/21/79 vs. Pittsburgh), 30 attempts
TOUCHDOWN PASSES
4 Roger Staubach (1/4/76 @ L.A. Rams)
PASSES HAD INTERCEPTED
4 Roger Staubach (12/30/73 vs. Minnesota)
COMPLETION PERCENTAGE (Min. 12 completions)
68.0 Roger Staubach (1/15/78 vs. Denver), 17 of 25
66.7 Danny White (1/10/82 @ San Francisco), 16 of 24
64.1 Danny White (1/4/81 @ Atlanta), 25 of 39
LONGEST COMPLETION
86 Don Meredith to Bob Hayes (12/24/67 vs. Cleveland), TD
83 Roger Staubach to Drew Pearson (12/23/73 vs. L.A.), TD
MOST TIMES SACKED
7 Roger Staubach (12/23/73 vs. L.A. Rams)
7 Roger Staubach (1/18/76 vs. Pittsburgh)
Miscellaneous Individual Records

PLAYOFFS
Most Games Played
26 — Larry Cole
25 — D.D. Lewis
23 — Jethro Pugh
Charlie Waters
Most Super Bowls Played
5 — Larry Cole, Cliff Harris, D. D. Lewis, Charlie Waters, Rayfield Wright
Most Consecutive Passes Without Interception
99 — Roger Staubach (began vs. Minnesota, 12/25/71, ended vs. Minnesota, 12/30/73).
Most Consecutive Games Rushing for TD
3 — Duane Thomas (began 12/25/71 vs. Minnesota, ended 1/16/72 after Super Bowl victory).
3 — Tony Dorsett (began 12/26/77 vs. Chicago, ended 12/30/78 vs. Atlanta).
Most Consecutive Games Catch TD Pass
2 — Golden Richards (vs. Minnesota, 1/1/78 and vs. Denver, 1/15/78).
Drew Pearson (vs. Los Angeles, 12/28/80 and vs. Atlanta, 1/4/81).
Most Consecutive Games Intercept Pass
3 — Mel Renfro (vs. Detroit, 12/26/70; vs. San Francisco, 1/3/71; and vs. Baltimore, 1/17/71)
3 — Randy Hughes (vs. Denver, 1/15/78; vs. Atlanta, 12/30/78; and vs. Los Angeles, 1/7/79).
Most Consecutive Games at Least One Pass Catch
16 — Drew Pearson (began vs. Los Angeles, 12/23/73, ongoing).
Most Consecutive Games Kick FG
7 — Toni Fritsch (started vs. San Francisco, 12/23/72, ended after 1/18/76, vs. Pittsburgh).
Most Consecutive Games Played
22 — Jethro Pugh (started 1/1/67 vs. Green Bay, ended 12/30/78 vs. Atlanta).

PASS RECEIVING
RECEPTIONS
9 Tony Hill (12/26/83 vs. L.A. Rams), 115 yards
7 Billy Parks (12/23/72 @ San Francisco), 136 yards
7 Preston Pearson (1/4/76 @ L.A. Rams), 123 yards
7 Drew Pearson (1/9/83 vs. Tampa Bay), 95 yards
7 Tony Hill (1/16/83 vs. Green Bay), 142 yards
7 Timmy Newsome (1/16/83 vs. Green Bay), 70 yards
RECEIVING YARDS
144 Bob Hayes (12/24/67 vs. Cleveland), 5 receptions
142 Tony Hill (1/16/83 vs. Green Bay), 7 receptions
TOUCHDOWNS RECEIVING
3 Preston Pearson (1/4/76 @ L.A. Rams)
RUSHING — RECEIVING
188 Tony Dorsett (12/28/80 vs. L.A. Rams), 160 rushing, 28 receiving
167 Duane Thomas (1/3/71 vs. San Francisco), 143 rushing, 24 receiving
COMBINED YARDAGE
285 Bob Hayes (12/24/67 vs. Cleveland), 5/144 receiving, 3/141 punt returns

PUNTING
PUNTS
9 Ron Widby (1/17/71 vs. Baltimore), 38.6 average
PUNT AVERAGE
46.7 Marv Bateman (12/23/73 vs. L.A. Rams), 7 punts

PUNT RETURNS
PUNT RETURNS
5 James Jones (12/28/80 vs. L.A. Rams)
PUNT RETURN YARDAGE
141 Bob Hayes (12/24/67 vs. Cleveland), 3 returns
LONGEST PUNT RETURN
68 Bob Hayes (12/24/67 vs. Cleveland)
PUNT RETURN AVERAGE
47.0 Bob Hayes (12/24/67 vs. Cleveland), 3 for 141 yards
FAIR CATCHES
4 Lance Rentzel (12/21/68 @ Cleveland)
4 Cliff Harris (12/23/72 @ San Francisco)

KICKOFF RETURNS
KICKOFF RETURNS
5 Mel Renfro (1/1/67 vs. Green Bay), 124 yards
KICKOFF RETURN YARDAGE
124 Mel Renfro (1/1/67 vs. Green Bay), 5 returns
LONGEST KICKOFF RETURN
48 Thomas Henderson (1/18/76 vs. Pittsburgh)
KICKOFF RETURN AVERAGE
24.8 Mel Renfro (1/1/67 vs. Green Bay), 5 for 124 yards

INTERCEPTIONS
INTERCEPTIONS
3 Charlie Waters (12/26/77 vs. Chicago)
INTERCEPTION RETURN YARDAGE
68 Thomas Henderson (1/8/79 @ L.A. Rams), on 1 int.
LONGEST INTERCEPTION RETURN
68 Thomas Henderson (1/8/79 @ L.A. Rams)
PASSES HAD INTERCEPTED
4 Roger Staubach (12/30/73 vs. Minnesota)
COMPLETION PERCENTAGE (Min. 12 completions)
68.0 Roger Staubach (1/15/78 vs. Denver), 17 of 25
66.7 Danny White (1/10/82 @ San Francisco), 16 of 24
64.1 Danny White (1/4/81 @ Atlanta), 25 of 39
LONGEST COMPLETION
86 Don Meredith to Bob Hayes (12/24/67 vs. Cleveland), TD
83 Roger Staubach to Drew Pearson (12/23/73 vs. L.A. Rams), TD
MOST TIMES SACKED
7 Roger Staubach (12/23/73 vs. L.A. Rams)
7 Roger Staubach (1/18/78 vs. Pittsburgh)

Cowboys Team Playoff Records

SCORING

MOST POINTS SCORED
52 12/24/67 vs. Cleveland, (Dallas 52, Cleveland 14)

FEWEST POINTS SCORED
3 12/31/72 @ Washington, (Washington 26, Dallas 3)

OPPONENT/MOST POINTS SCORED
38 12/28/69 vs. Cleveland, (Cleveland 38, Dallas 14)

OPPONENT/FEWEST POINTS SCORED
0 12/26/70 vs. Detroit, (Dallas 5, Detroit 0)
0 1/7/79 @ L.A. Rams, (Dallas 28, L.A. Rams 0)
0 1/2/82 vs. Tampa Bay (Dallas 38, Tampa Bay 0

MOST DECISIVE WIN
38 1/2/82 vs. Tampa Bay, (Dallas 38, Tampa Bay 0)
38 12/24/67 vs. Cleveland, (Dallas 52, Cleveland 14)

MOST DECISIVE LOSS
24 12/28/69 vs. Cleveland, (Cleveland 38, Dallas 14)

MOST POINTS COMBINED
66 12/24/67 vs. Cleveland, (Dallas 52, Cleveland 14)
66 1/21/79 vs. Pittsburgh, (Pittsburgh 35, Dallas 31)

FIRST DOWNS

MOST FIRST DOWNS
29 12/28/80 vs. L.A. Rams
29 1/9/83 vs. Green Bay

FEWEST FIRST DOWNS
8 12/31/72 @ Washington

OPPONENT/MOST FIRST DOWNS
26 1/10/82 @ San Francisco
22 12/28/69 vs. Cleveland

OPPONENT/FEWEST FIRST DOWNS
7 12/26/70 vs. Detroit

MOST FIRST DOWNS BY:
Rushing
19 12/28/80 vs. L.A. Rams
Passing
20 12/26/83 vs. L.A. Rams
Penalty
2 8 times, last 1/10/82 @ San Francisco

FEWEST FIRST DOWNS BY:
Rushing
2 1/22/83 @ Washington
Passing
3 12/26/70 vs. Detroit
3 12/31/72 @ Washington

OPPONENT/MOST FIRST DOWNS BY:
Rushing
14 12/30/73 vs. Minnesota
Passing
17 12/28/69 vs. Cleveland
17 1/10/82 @ San Francisco
Penalty
4 1/17/71 vs. Baltimore

OPPONENT/FEWEST FIRST DOWNS BY:
Rushing
1 1/4/76 @ L.A. Rams
Passing
1 1/15/78 vs. Denver

TOTAL YARDS

MOST NET YARDS GAINED
528 12/28/80 vs. L.A. Rams

FEWEST NET YARDS GAINED
153 12/30/73 vs. Minnesota

OPPONENT/MOST NET YARDS GAINED
466 1/16/83 vs. Green Bay
393 1/10/82 @ San Francisco

OPPONENT/FEWEST NET YARDS GAINED
118 1/4/76 @ L.A. Rams

RUSHING

MOST YARDS RUSHING
345 1/2/82 vs. Tampa Bay
338 12/28/80 vs. L.A. Rams

FEWEST YARDS RUSHING
63 12/26/83 vs. L.A. Rams

OPPONENT/MOST YARDS RUSHING
263 1/11/81 @ Philadelphia

OPPONENT/FEWEST YARDS RUSHING
22 1/4/76 vs. L.A. Rams

PASSING

MOST NET YARDS PASSING
310 1/4/81 @ Atlanta

FEWEST NET YARDS PASSING
22 12/26/70 vs. Detroit

OPPONENT/MOST NET YARDS PASSING
308 1/16/83 vs. Green Bay

OPPONENT/FEWEST NET YARDS PASSING
35 12/30/78 vs. Atlanta

MOST GROSS YARDS PASSING
330 12/26/83 vs. L.A. Rams

FEWEST GROSS YARDS PASSING
38 12/26/70 vs. Detroit

OPPONENT/MOST GROSS YARDS PASSING
322 1/16/83 vs. Green Bay
320 1/4/81 @ Atlanta

OPPONENT/FEWEST GROSS YARDS PASSING
61 1/15/78 vs. Denver

MOST PASS ATTEMPTS
53 12/26/83 vs. L.A. Rams
45 1/9/83 vs.Tampa Bay

FEWEST PASS ATTEMPTS
14 12/25/71 @ Minnesota
14 12/24/77 vs. Chicago

OPPONENT/MOST PASS ATTEMPTS
40 1/3/71 vs. San Francisco

OPPONENT/FEWEST PASS ATTEMPTS
18 12/31/72 @ Washington

MOST PASS COMPLETIONS
32 12/26/83 vs. L.A. Rams
27 1/9/83 vs. Tampa Bay

FEWEST PASS COMPLETIONS
4 12/26/70 vs. Detroit

OPPONENT/MOST COMPLETIONS
22 1/10/82 @ San Francisco
20 12/28/69 vs. Cleveland

OPPONENT/FEWEST PASS COMPLETIONS
7 12/26/70 vs. Detroit
7 12/23/73 vs. L.A. Rams

DEFENSE, MOST QB SACKS
8 12/31/67 @ Green Bay, (76 yards)

OPPONENT/DFNS., MOST QB SACKS
7 12/23/73 vs. L.A. Rams
7 1/18/76 vs. Pitt. (52 yds.)

INTERCEPTIONS

MOST PASSES INTERCEPTED BY COWBOYS
5 1/7/79 @ L.A. Rams

OPPONENT/MOST PASSES INTERCEPTED BY
4 12/21/68 @ Cleveland
4 12/30/73 vs. Minnesota

PENALTIES

MOST PENALTIES
12 1/15/78 vs. Denver

FEWEST PENALTIES
2 7 times, last 1/18/76 vs. Pittsburgh

OPPONENT/MOST PENALTIES
10 1/2/82 vs.Tampa Bay
8 1/19/76 @ L.A. Rams
8 1/15/78 vs. Denver

OPPONENT/FEWEST PENALTIES
0 3 times, last 1/18/76 vs. Pittsburgh

MOST YARDS PENALIZED
133 1/17/71 vs. Baltimore

FEWEST YARDS PENALIZED
10 12/24/67 vs. Cleveland
10 12/25/71 @ Minnesota

OPPONENT/MOST YARDS PENALIZED
94 1/19/76 @ L.A. Rams

PUNTING

MOST PUNTS
9 1/17/71 vs. Baltimore

FEWEST PUNTS
2 12/24/67 vs. Cleveland
2 12/28/80 vs. L.A. Rams

OPPONENT/MOST PUNTS
8 3 times, last 1/1/78 vs. Minnesota

OPPONENT/FEWEST PUNTS
1 12/28/69 vs. Cleveland

HIGHEST COWBOYS AVERAGE
46.7 12/23/73 vs. L.A. Rams

HIGHEST OPPONENT AVERAGE
48.8 12/26/70 vs. Detroit

PUNT RETURNS

MOST PUNT RETURNS
5 1/1/78 vs. Minnesota
5 12/28/80 vs. L.A. Rams
5 1/19/83 vs. Tampa Bay

MOST PUNT RETURN YARDS
155 12/24/67 vs. Cleveland

OPPONENT/MOST PUNT RETURNS
6 12/26/70 vs. Detroit
6 1/11/81 @ Philadelphia

OPPONENT/MOST PUNT RETURN YARDS
69 1/11/81 @ Philadelphia

KICKOFF RETURNS

MOST KICKOFF RETURNS
6 4 times, last 1/16/83 vs. Green Bay

MOST KICKOFF RETURN YARDS
173 1/16/83 vs. Green Bay

OPPONENT/MOST KICKOFF RETURNS
8 1/4/76 @ L.A. Rams
8 12/26/77 vs. Chicago

OPPONENT/MOST KICKOFF RETURN YARDS
188 12/25/71 @ Minnesota

FUMBLES

MOST FUMBLES
6 12/30/78 vs. Atlanta
6 1/15/78 vs. Denver

MOST FUMBLES LOST
3 12/23/72 @ San Francisco
3 12/28/78 vs. Atlanta

OPPONENT/MOST FUMBLES
5 1/17/71 vs. Baltimore
5 12/23/72 @ San Francisco
5 1/1/78 @ Minnesota

OPPONENT/MOST FUMBLES LOST
4 1/17/71 @ Baltimore
4 1/15/78 vs. Denver
3 1/10/82 @ San Francisco

Cowboys Big Days

RUSHING

(includes all 100-yard days)

206 — Tony Dorsett vs. Philadelphia, Dec. 4, 1977 (23 carries).
183 — Tony Dorsett @ N.Y. Giants, Nov. 9, 1980 (24 carries).
175 — Tony Dorsett @ Baltimore, Dec. 6, 1981 (30 carries).
162 — Tony Dorsett @ New England, Sept. 21, 1981 (19 carries).
*160 — Tony Dorsett vs. L.A. Rams, Dec. 28, 1980 (22 carries).
159 — Tony Dorsett vs. L.A. Rams, Oct. 18, 1981 (27 carries).
154 — Tony Dorsett vs. St. Louis, Sept. 24, 1978 (21 carries).
153 — Tony Dorsett @ Minnesota, Jan. 3, 1983 (16 carries).
153 — Calvin Hill vs. San Francisco, Nov. 10, 1974 (32 carries).
152 — Tony Dorsett vs. New Orleans, Nov. 19, 1978 (25 carries).
151 — Tony Dorsett @ Washington, Sept, 5, 1983 (14 carries).
150 — Calvin Hill @ Washington, Nov. 16, 1969 (27 carries).
149 — Tony Dorsett @ Green Bay, Nov. 12, 1978 (23 carries).
147 — Tony Dorsett vs. Baltimore, Sept. 4, 1978 (15 carries).
145 — Tony Dorsett @ Minnesota, Oct. 7, 1979 (21 carries).
*143 — Duane Thomas vs. San Francisco, Jan. 3, 1971 (27 carries).
141 — Tony Dorsett @ Minnesota, Oct. 2, 1983 (26 carries).
141 — Tony Dorsett @ St. Louis, Oct. 9, 1977 (14 carries).
140 — Calvin Hill vs. Philadelphia, Oct. 20, 1974 (26 carries).
138 — Calvin Hill @ New Orleans, Sept. 28, 1969 (23 carries).
137 — Don Perkins vs. St. Louis, Oct. 28, 1962 (24 carries).
137 — Don Perkins vs. N.Y. Giants, Oct. 11, 1964 (17 carries).
*135 — Duane Thomas vs. Detroit, Dec. 26, 1970 (30 carries).
134 — Duane Thomas @ Kansas City, Oct. 25, 1970 (20 carries).
133 — Don Perkins @ Green Bay, Oct. 24, 1965 (22 carries).
132 — Tony Dorsett @ Washington, Sept. 6, 1981 (20 carries).
130 — Calvin Hill @ Chicago, Sept. 16, 1973 (31 carries).
129 — Tony Dorsett vs. St. Louis, Sept. 13, 1981 (16 carries).
*125 — Calvin Hill @ San Francisco, Dec. 23, 1972 (18 carries).
124 — Robert Newhouse @ St. Louis, Dec. 16, 1973 (19 carries).
124 — Tony Dorsett vs. New Orleans, Sept. 25, 1983 (16 carries).
123 — Don Perkins vs. Cleveland, Dec. 3, 1961 (20 carries).
123 — Duane Thomas vs. Washington, Dec. 6, 1970 (19 carries).
123 — Calvin Hill vs. N.Y. Giants, Oct. 21, 1973 (23 carries).
122 — Tony Dorsett vs. Miami, Oct. 25, 1981 (24 carries).
122 — Scott Laidlaw vs. Washington, Nov. 23, 1978 (16 carries).
122 — Tony Dorsett vs. St. Louis, Nov. 16, 1980 (26 carries).
121 — Walt Garrison vs. Washington, Dec. 9, 1972 (10 carries).
121 — Tony Dorsett @ N.Y. Jets, Dec. 17, 1978 (29 carries).
120 — Robert Newhouse @ Seattle, Oct. 3, 1976 (19 carries).
120 — Calvin Hill @ St. Louis, Dec. 3, 1972 (26 carries).
119 — Tony Dorsett vs. Cincinnati, Sept. 30, 1979 (20 carries).
117 — Tony Dorsett @ Seattle, Dec. 4, 1983 (26 carries).
117 — Tony Dorsett vs. Buffalo, Nov. 9, 1981 (28 carries).
117 — Amos Marsh vs. Cleveland, Dec. 2, 1962 (17 carries).
117 — Calvin Hill @ Philadelphia, Sept. 20, 1970 (25 carries).
117 — Calvin Hill vs. Atlanta, Oct.11, 1970 (29 carries).
116 — Tony Dorsett vs. Cleveland, Nov. 25, 1982 (20 carries).
115 — Tony Dorsett vs. Washington, Nov. 22, 1981 (23 carries).
115 — Duane Thomas vs. Houston, Dec. 20, 1970 (17 carries).
114 — Dan Reeves @ Cleveland, Sept. 17, 1967 (18 carries).
112 — Duane Thomas vs. N.Y. Jets, Dec. 4, 1971 (14 carries).
111 — Don Perkins vs. Cleveland, Nov. 24, 1966 (23 carries).
111 — Don Perkins vs. Atlanta, Nov. 5, 1967 (21 carries).
111 — Calvin Hill vs. Washington, Dec. 9, 1972 (24 carries).
111 — Tony Dorsett @ N.Y. Giants, Sept. 10, 1978 (24 carries).
111 — Tony Dorsett vs. St. Louis, Oct. 21, 1979 (20 carries).
110 — Tony Dorsett @ Philadelphia, Dec. 2, 1984 (22 carries).
*110 — Tony Dorsett vs.Tampa Bay, Jan. 9, 1983 (26 carries).
110 — Calvin Hill vs. Washington, Dec. 9, 1973 (27 carries).
109 — Amos Marsh @ Washington, Nov. 4, 1962 (10 carries).
109 — Don Perkins @ Washington, Sept. 29, 1963 (25 carries).
109 — Calvin Hill vs. New Orleans, Nov. 9, 1969 (13 carries).
108 — Don Perkins vs. Minnesota, Sept. 24, 1961 (17 carries).
108 — Don Perkins @ Pittsburgh, Oct. 21, 1962 (20 carries).
108 — Dan Reeves vs. Washington, Dec. 11, 1966 (10 carries).
*108 — Don Perkins vs. Green Bay, Jan. 1, 1967 (17 carries).
108 — Calvin Hill vs. Pittsburgh, Oct. 8, 1972 (23 carries).
108 — Robert Newhouse @ N.Y. Jets, Dec. 21, 1975 (19 carries).
108 — Robert Newhouse @ St. Louis, Sept. 2, 1979 (18 carries).
108 — Tony Dorsett vs. Chicago, Sept. 16, 1979 (20 carries).
108 — Tony Dorsett vs. N.Y. Giants, Dec. 2, 1979 (29 carries).
108 — Tony Dorsett vs. Kansas City, Nov. 20, 1983 (18 carries).
107 — Tony Dorsett vs. Seattle, Nov. 27, 1980 (24 carries).
105 — Tony Dorsett vs. New Orleans, Dec. 19, 1982 (25 carries).
104 — Tony Dorsett vs. Indianapolis, Oct. 28, 1984 (24 carries).
104 — Duane Thomas @ Washington, Nov. 22, 1970 (16 carries).
104 — Scott Laidlaw vs. Philadelphia, Sept. 12, 1976 (19 carries).
103 — Don Perkins @ Washington, Nov. 17, 1968 (13 carries).
103 — Calvin Hill @ Washington, Oct. 8, 1973 (21 carries).
103 — Tony Dorsett vs. L.A. Rams, Oct. 14, 1979 (24 carries).
102 — Walt Garrison vs. N.Y. Giants, Oct. 27, 1969 (16 carries).
102 — Tony Dorsett vs. St. Louis, Nov. 24, 1983 (17 carries).
101 — Tony Dorsett vs. Philadelphia, Dec. 13, 1981 (28 carries).
*101 — Tony Dorsett @ L.A. Rams, Jan. 8, 1979 (17 carries).
101 — Duane Thomas @ St. Louis, Nov. 7, 1971 (26 carries).
101 — Preston Pearson vs. Green Bay, Oct. 19, 1975 (15 carries).
101 — Robert Newhouse @ Green Bay, Nov. 12, 1978 (18 carries).
100 — Calvin Hill @ Philadelphia, Nov. 19, 1972 (15 carries).
100 — Calvin Hill @ Philadelphia, Oct. 28, 1973 (25 carries).
100 — Tony Dorsett vs. Tampa Bay, Sept. 21, 1980 (20 carries).

*Playoff Game

PASSING

460 — Don Meredith @ San Francisco, Nov. 10, 1963 (30 of 48).
406 — Don Meredith @ Washington, Nov. 13, 1966 (21 of 29).
394 — Don Meredith @ Philadelphia, Nov. 6, 1966 (14 of 24).
377 — Danny White vs. Tampa Bay, Oct. 9, 1983 (29 of 44).
358 — Don Meredith vs. N.Y. Giants, Sept. 18, 1966 (14 of 24).
354 — Danny White vs. Miami, Oct. 25, 1981 (22 of 32).
349 — Craig Morton vs. Houston, Dec. 20, 1970 (13 of 17).
347 — Danny White vs. Pittsburgh, Sept. 13, 1982 (25 of 36).
345 — Eddie LeBaron vs. Pittsburgh, Sept. 24, 1960 (15 of 28).
343 — Gary Hogeboom @ L.A. Rams, Sept. 3, 1984 (33 of 47).
339 — Roger Staubach vs. Baltimore, Sept. 26, 1976 (22 of 28).
336 — Roger Staubach vs. Washington, Dec. 16, 1979 (24 of 42).
*330 — Danny White vs. L.A. Rams, Dec. 26, 1983 (32 of 53).
327 — Danny White vs. Washington, Dec. 9, 1984 (22 of 42).
326 — Don Meredith vs. St. Louis, Dec. 11, 1965 (16 of 30).
*322 — Danny White @ Atlanta, Jan. 4, 1981 (25 of 39).
320 — Gary Hogeboom vs. Philadelphia, Sept. 16, 1984 (22 of 40).
314 — Roger Staubach @ Philadelphia, Oct. 26, 1975 (27 of 49).
308 — Roger Staubach vs. Philadelphia, November 12, 1979 (17 of 28).
307 — Roger Staubach vs. St. Louis, Sept. 28, 1975 (23 of 34).
306 — Don Meredith @ Philadelphia, Oct. 13, 1968 (21 of 38).
304 — Danny White @ N.Y. Giants, Oct. 30, 1983 (15 of 33).
303 — Roger Staubach @ Cleveland, Sept. 24, 1979 (21 of 39).
302 — Don Meredith vs. Philadelphia, Nov. 17, 1963 (25 of 33).

RECEIVING

246 — Bob Hayes @ Washington, Nov. 13, 1966 (9 catches).
241 — Frank Clarke vs. Washington, Sept. 16, 1962 (10 catches).
223 — Lance Rentzel vs. Washington, Nov. 19, 1967 (13 catches).
213 — Tony Hill vs. Philadelphia, Nov. 12, 1979 (7 catches).
195 — Bob Hayes vs. N.Y. Giants, Sept. 18, 1966 (6 catches).
190 — Frank Clarke @ San Francisco, Nov. 10, 1963 (8 catches).
188 — Drew Pearson @ Detroit, Oct. 6, 1975 (6 catches).
187 — Bob Hayes vs. Houston, Dec. 20, 1970 (6 catches).
177 — Bob Hayes vs. Philadelphia, Oct. 10, 1965 (8 catches).
170 — Bob Hayes @ Pittsburgh, Oct. 22, 1967 (7 catches).
168 — Frank Clarke @ N.Y. Giants, Oct. 20, 1963 (4 catches).
161 — Drew Pearson @ Philadelphia, Sept. 23, 1974 (10 catches).

*Playoff Game

Cowboys Longest Plays

LONG RUNS FROM SCRIMMAGE

99 — Tony Dorsett @ Minnesota, Jan. 3, 1983 (TD).
84 — Tony Dorsett vs. Philadelphia, Dec. 4, 1977 (TD).
77 — Tony Dorsett vs. St. Louis, Oct. 9, 1977 (TD).
77 — Tony Dorsett @ Washington, Sept. 5, 1983.
75 — Tony Dorsett vs. New England, Sept. 21, 1981 (TD).
73 — Amos Bullocks vs. Chicago, Nov. 18, 1962 (TD).
71 — Amos Marsh vs. New York, Oct. 15, 1961.
70 — Amos Marsh vs. Washington, Nov. 4, 1962.
68 — Les Shy vs. Philadelphia, Oct. 9, 1966.
67 — Dan Reeves vs. Washington, Dec. 11, 1966 (TD).
64 — Jim Stiger vs. Washington, Nov. 22, 1964.
63 — Tony Dorsett vs. New Orleans, Nov. 19, 1978.
59 — James Jones vs. Baltimore, Dec. 6, 1981 (TD).
59 — Don Perkins vs. Pittsburgh, Sept. 27, 1964.
59 — Scott Laidlaw vs. Washington, Nov. 23, 1978.
56 — Frank Clarke vs. New Orleans, Nov. 12, 1967.
56 — Duane Thomas vs. New England, Oct. 24, 1971 (TD).
56 — Tony Dorsett vs. N.Y. Giants, Nov. 9, 1980.
55 — Calvin Hill vs. New Orleans, Nov. 9, 1969.
55 — Tony Dorsett vs. St. Louis, Nov. 24, 1983 (TD).

LONG FORWARD PASSES

95 — Don Meredith to Bob Hayes vs. Washington, Nov. 13, 1966 (TD).
91 — Roger Staubach to Tony Dorsett vs. Baltimore, Sept. 4, 1978 (TD).
89 — Craig Morton to Bob Hayes vs. Kansas City, Oct. 25, 1970 (TD).
*86 — Don Meredith to Bob Hayes vs. Cleveland, Dec. 24, 1967 (TD).
86 — Craig Morton to Lance Rentzel vs. Philadelphia, Nov. 1, 1970 (TD).
85 — Eddie LeBaron to Amos Marsh vs. L.A. Rams, Sept. 30, 1962 (TD).
85 — Roger Staubach to Bob Hayes vs. N.Y. Giants, Dec. 12, 1971 (TD).
84 — Don Meredith to Pete Gent vs. Pittsburgh, Oct. 30, 1966 (TD).

LONG PUNTS

84 — Ron Widby vs. New Orleans, Nov. 3, 1968.
75 — Billy Lothridge vs. New York, Oct. 11, 1964.
75 — Sam Baker vs. L.A. Rams, Sept. 30, 1962.
73 — Danny White vs. L.A. Rams, Oct. 14, 1979.
71 — Billy Lothridge vs. St. Louis, Sept. 12, 1964.
71 — Sam Baker vs. New York, Dec. 16, 1962.

LONG PUNT RETURNS

98 — Dennis Morgan vs. St. Louis, Oct. 13, 1974 (TD).
90 — Bob Hayes vs. Pittsburgh, Dec. 8, 1968 (TD).
69 — Bob Hayes vs. St. Louis, Nov. 23, 1967 (TD).
69 — Mel Renfro vs. Green Bay, Nov. 29, 1964 (TD).
*68 — Bob Hayes vs. Cleveland, Dec. 24, 1967.
68 — Gary Allen vs. Kansas City, Nov. 20, 1983 (TD).
63 — Bob Hayes vs. New York, Dec. 15, 1968 (TD).
*63 — Golden Richards vs. Minnesota, Dec. 30, 1973 (TD).
55 — Butch Johnson vs. Philadelphia, Dec. 5, 1976.
52 — James Jones vs. Washington, Nov. 23, 1980.
51 — Mel Renfro vs. Cleveland, Oct. 4, 1964.
50 — Bob Hayes vs. Washington, Nov. 16, 1969.

LONG KICKOFF RETURNS

101 — Amos Marsh vs. Philadelphia, Oct. 14, 1962 (TD).
101 — Ike Thomas vs. New York Jets, Dec. 4, 1971 (TD).
100 — Mark Washington vs. Washington, Nov. 22, 1970 (TD).
100 — Mel Renfro vs. San Francisco, Nov. 7, 1965 (TD).
97 — Thomas Henderson vs. St. Louis, Sept. 28, 1975 (TD).
89 — Ike Thomas vs. L.A. Rams, Nov. 25, 1971 (TD).
87 — Mel Renfro vs. Pittsburgh, Oct. 30, 1966 (TD).

LONG INTERCEPTION RETURNS

100 — Mike Gaechter vs. Philadelphia, Oct. 14, 1962 (TD).
96 — Dennis Thurman vs. Washington, Sept. 6, 1981.
90 — Mel Renfro vs. St. Louis, Oct. 4, 1965 (TD).
86 — Mike Gaechter vs. Washington, Nov. 3, 1963.

LONG FUMBLE RETURNS

97 — Chuck Howley vs. Atlanta, Oct. 2, 1966 (TD).
86 — Michael Downs vs. Houston, Dec. 13, 1982 (TD).
84 — Don Bishop vs. St. Louis, Oct. 28, 1962 (TD).
72 — Benny Barnes vs. San Francisco, Oct. 11, 1981 (TD).
63 — Jim Ridlon vs. Philadelphia, Dec. 6, 1964 (TD).

LONG RETURNS OF FIELD-GOAL ATTEMPTS

94 — Jerry Norton vs. St. Louis, Dec. 9, 1962 (TD).
62 — Ron Fellows vs. New Orleans, Sept. 25, 1983 (TD).
60 — Mike Gaechter vs. Washington, Nov. 28, 1965 (TD).
60 — Obert Logan vs. New York, Dec. 19, 1965 (TD).

*Playoff Game

Cowboys
Big Days/Playoffs

100 YARD RUSHING GAMES

160 yards — Tony Dorsett vs. L.A. Rams .... December 28, 1980
143 yards — Duane Thomas vs. San Francisco .... January 3, 1971
135 yards — Duane Thomas vs. Detroit .... December 26, 1970
125 yards — Calvin Hill vs. San Francisco .... December 23, 1972
110 yards — Tony Dorsett vs. Tampa Bay .... January 9, 1983
108 yards — Don Perkins vs. Green Bay .... January 1, 1967
101 yards — Tony Dorsett vs. L.A. Rams .... January 7, 1979

PASSING

330 yards — Danny White vs. L.A. Rams .... December 26, 1983
322 yards — Danny White vs. Atlanta .... January 4, 1981
312 yards — Danny White vs.Tampa Bay .... January 9, 1983
246 yards — Roger Staubach vs. Minnesota .... December 28, 1975
243 yards — Don Meredith vs. Minnesota .... January 5, 1969
238 yards — Don Meredith vs. Green Bay .... January 1, 1967
228 yards — Roger Staubach vs. Pittsburgh .... January 21, 1979
225 yards — Danny White vs. Green Bay .... January 16, 1983
220 yards — Roger Staubach vs. L.A. Rams .... January 4, 1976
212 yards — Don Meredith vs. Cleveland .... December 24, 1967
204 yards — Roger Staubach vs. Pittsburgh .... January 18, 1976

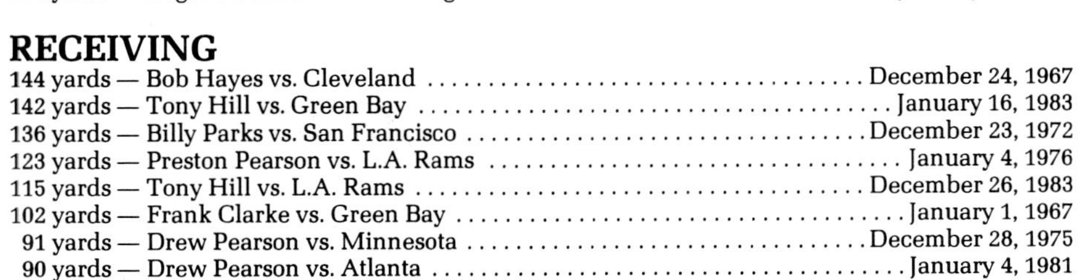

RECEIVING

144 yards — Bob Hayes vs. Cleveland .... December 24, 1967
142 yards — Tony Hill vs. Green Bay .... January 16, 1983
136 yards — Billy Parks vs. San Francisco .... December 23, 1972
123 yards — Preston Pearson vs. L.A. Rams .... January 4, 1976
115 yards — Tony Hill vs. L.A. Rams .... December 26, 1983
102 yards — Frank Clarke vs. Green Bay .... January 1, 1967
91 yards — Drew Pearson vs. Minnesota .... December 28, 1975
90 yards — Drew Pearson vs. Atlanta .... January 4, 1981

Cowboys Longest Plays/Playoffs

LONG RUNS FROM SCRIMMAGE

53 yards — Tony Dorsett vs. L.A. Rams .... January 7, 1979
48 yards — Calvin Hill vs. San Francisco .... December 23, 1972
32 yards — Ron Springs vs. Los Angeles .... December 28, 1980
29 yards — Roger Staubach vs. Washington .... December 31, 1972
29 yards — Tony Dorsett vs. Pittsburgh .... January 21, 1979
27 yards — Billy Joe DuPree vs. Los Angeles .... January 30, 1979
26 yards — Tony Dorsett vs. L.A. Rams .... December 30, 1979
26 yards — Tony Dorsett vs. Tampa Bay .... January 2, 1982

LONG FORWARD PASSES

86 yards — Don Meredith to Bob Hayes vs. Cleveland (TD) .... December 24, 1967
83 yards — Roger Staubach to Drew Pearson vs. L.A. Rams (TD) .... December 23, 1973
68 yards — Don Meredith to Frank Clarke vs. Green Bay (TD) .... January 1, 1967
51 yards — Don Meredith to Bob Hayes vs. Minnesota (TD) .... January 5, 1969
50 yards — Roger Staubach to Drew Pearson vs. Minnesota (TD) .... December 28, 1975
49 yards — Drew Pearson to Tony Hill vs. Green Bay .... January 16, 1983
45 yards — Roger Staubach to Butch Johnson vs. Denver (TD) .... January 15, 1978

LONG PUNT RETURNS

68 yards — Bob Hayes vs. Cleveland .... December 24, 1967
63 yards — Golden Richards vs. Minnesota (TD) .... December 30, 1973
44 yards — Butch Johnson vs. L.A. Rams .... December 19, 1976
43 yards — James Jones vs. L.A. Rams .... December 28, 1980

LONG KICKOFF RETURNS

89 yards — Rod Hill vs. Green Bay .... January 16, 1983
48 yards — Thomas Henderson vs. Pittsburgh .... January 18, 1976
34 yards — Cliff Harris vs. Minnesota .... December 30, 1973
33 yards — Cliff Harris vs. San Francisco .... December 23, 1972
33 yards — James Jones vs. L.A. Rams .... December 28, 1980
33 yards — Ron Fellows vs. L.A. Rams .... December 26, 1983

LONG INTERCEPTION RETURNS

68 yards — Thomas Henderson vs. L.A. Rams (TD) .... January 7, 1979
60 yards — Cornell Green vs. Cleveland (TD) .... December 24, 1967
41 yards — Chuck Howley vs. Miami .... January 16, 1972
39 yards — Dennis Thurman vs. Green Bay (TD) .... January 16, 1983
31 yards — Dennis Thurman vs. Tampa Bay .... January 2, 1982
30 yards — Cliff Harris vs. Minnesota .... December 25, 1971
27 yards — Mark Washington vs. Denver .... January 15, 1978
26 yards — Chuck Howley vs. Minnesota .... December 25, 1971

LONG FUMBLE RETURNS

44 yards — Chuck Howley vs. Cleveland (TD) .... December 21, 1968
37 yards — Mike Hegman vs. Pittsburgh (TD) .... January 21, 1979
21 yards — Randy Hughes vs. Denver .... January 15, 1978
20 yards — Charlie Waters vs. Detroit .... December 26, 1970
15 yards — D. D. Lewis vs. Chicago .... December 26, 1977

The Last Time . . .

400 Yards Total Offense
BY COWBOYS — 447 vs. Philadelphia, 9/16/84
Playoffs — 456 vs. Tampa Bay, 1/9/83
BY OPPONENT — 435, @ St. Louis, 11/11/84
Playoffs — 456 vs. Green Bay, 1/16/83

500 Yards Total Offense
BY COWBOYS — 522 vs. Philadelphia, 10/16/83
Playoffs — 528 vs. L.A. Rams, 12/28/80
BY OPPONENT — 519, L.A. Raiders, 10/23/83
Playoffs — N.A.

300 Yards Passing in Game by Player
BY COWBOYS — Danny White, 327 vs. Washington, 12/9/84
Playoffs — Danny White, 330 vs. L.A. Rams, 12/26/83
BY OPPONENT — Dan Marino, @ Miami, 340, 12/17/84
Playoffs — Lynn Dickey, Green Bay, 332, 1/16/83

4 Touchdown Passes Thrown in Game by Player
BY COWBOYS — Danny White, vs. Washington, 12/9/84
Playoffs — Roger Staubach, @ L.A. Rams, 1/4/76
BY OPPONENT — Dan Marino, @ Miami, 12/17/84
Playoffs — Terry Bradshaw, Pittsburgh, 1/21/79

100 Yards Rushing in Game by Player
BY COWBOYS — Tony Dorsett, 110, @ Philadelphia, 12/2/84
Playoffs — Tony Dorsett, 110 vs. Tampa Bay, 1/9/83
BY OPPONENT — John Riggins, 111, Washington, 12/9/84
Playoffs — John Riggins, 140 @ Washington, 1/22/83

3 Touchdowns Rushing in Game by Player
BY COWBOYS — Ron Springs (1, 4, 1) vs. St. Louis, 9/13/81
Playoffs — N.A.
BY OPPONENT — Dick James (5, 3, 39) @ Washington, 12/17/61
Playoffs — Larry Schreiber (1, 1, 1) @ San Francisco, 12/23/72

3 Touchdown Catches in Game by Player
BY COWBOYS — Drew Pearson (16, 22, 17) vs. San Francisco, 10/12/80
Playoffs — Preston Pearson (18, 15, 19) @ L.A. Rams, 1/4/76
BY OPPONENT — Mark Clayton (41, 39, 63) @ Miami, 12/17/84
Playoffs — N.A.

3 Touchdowns in Game by Player
BY COWBOYS — Ron Springs (3 rush) vs. St. Louis, 9/13/81
Playoffs — Preston Pearson (3 receive) @ L.A. Rams, 1/4/76
BY OPPONENT — Mark Clayton (3 receive) @ Miami, 12/17/84
Playoffs — Larry Schreiber (3 run) @ San Francisco, 12/23/72

4 Touchdowns in Game by Player
BY COWBOYS — Duane Thomas (3 run, 1 receive) vs. St. Louis, 12/18/71
Playoffs — N.A.
BY OPPONENT — Harold Jackson (4 receive) @ L.A. Rams, 10/14/73
Playoffs — N.A.

3 Interceptions in Game by Player
BY COWBOYS — Dennis Thurman vs. Philadelphia, 12/13/81
Playoffs — Dennis Thurman vs. Green Bay, 1/16/83
BY OPPONENT — Roger Wehrli @ St. Louis, 12/7/75
Playoffs — N.A.

Punt Returned for TD
BY COWBOYS — Gary Allen, 68 yards, vs. Kansas City, 11/20/83
Playoffs — Golden Richards, 63 yards vs. Minnesota, 12/30/73
BY OPPONENT — Dana McLemore, 56 yards, @ San Francisco, 12/19/83
Playoffs — N.A.

Kickoff Return for TD
BY COWBOYS — Thomas Henderson, 97 yards vs. St. Louis, 9/28/75
Playoffs — N.A.
BY OPPONENT — Roy Green, 106 yards, St. Louis, 10/21/79
Playoffs — Vic Washington, 97 yards, @ San Francisco, 12/23/72

Interception Returned for TD
BY COWBOYS — Dennis Thurman, 38 yards, @ Philadelphia, 12/2/84
Playoffs — Dennis Thurman, 39 yards vs. Green Bay, 1/16/83
BY OPPONENT — Darrell Green, Washington, 32 yards, 12/9/84
Playoffs — Darryl Grant, @ Washington, 10 yards, 1/22/83

Fumble Returned for TD
BY COWBOYS — Jim Jeffcoat, recovered in endzone vs. New Orleans, 10/21/84
Playoffs — Mike Hegman, 37 yards vs. Pittsburgh, 1/21/79
BY OPPONENT — Andy Headen, 81 yards, N.Y. Giants, 9/9/84
Playoffs — Hugh Green, vs. Tampa Bay, 60 yards, 1/9/83

Punt Blocked for TD
BY COWBOYS — Jay Saldi, @ Philadelphia (Waters runs 17 yards), 10/23/77
Playoffs — N.A.
BY OPPONENT — Miles McPherson, @ San Diego, (Derrie Nelson runs 21 yards), 11/13/83
Playoffs — N.A.

50 Points Scored in a Game
BY COWBOYS — Dallas 51, Seattle 7, 11/27/80
Playoffs — Dallas 52, Cleveland 14, 12/24/67
BY OPPONENT — @ Minnesota 54, Dallas 13, 10/6/70
Playoffs — N.A.

40 Points Scored in a Game
BY COWBOYS — Dallas 41, Kansas City 21, 11/20/83
Playoffs — N.A.
BY OPPONENT — @ San Francisco 42, Dallas 17, 12/19/83
Playoffs — N.A.

Shutout Scored
BY COWBOYS — Dallas 38, Baltimore 0, 9/4/78
Playoffs — Dallas 38, Tampa Bay 0, 1/2/82
BY OPPONENT — St. Louis 38, Dallas 0, 11/16/70
Playoffs — N.A.

Safety Scored
BY COWBOYS — John Dutton tackled Pisarcik in endzone, @ Philadelphia, 12/2/84
Playoffs — Randy White tackled V. Ferragamo in endzone, vs. L.A. Rams, 12/30/79
BY OPPONENT — John Thaxton, blocked punt out of endzone, St. Louis, 9/24/78
Playoffs — Reggie Harrison, blocked punt out of endzone, Pittsburgh, 1/18/76

PAT Missed
BY COWBOYS — vs. Indianapolis, 10/28/84 (Septien)
Playoffs — @ Atlanta, 1/4/81 (Septien)
BY OPPONENT — Green Bay, 9/23/84 (Garcia)
Playoffs — Green Bay, 1/16/83 (Stenerud)

Field Goal Blocked
BY COWBOYS — @ St. Louis, 11/11/84 (Downs)
Playoffs — @ Philadelphia, 1/11/81 (Mitchell)
BY OPPONENT — @ St. Louis, 11/11/84 (Art Plunkett)
Playoffs — @ San Francisco, 1/2/72 (Frank Nunley)

Punt Blocked
BY COWBOYS — Chuck McSwain, vs. New Orleans, 10/21/84
Playoffs — N.A.
BY OPPONENT — Miles McPherson, @ San Diego, 11/13/83
Playoffs — Reggie Harrison, Pittsburgh, 1/18/76

100 Yards Receiving
BY COWBOYS — Tony Hill, 115, @ Miami, 12/17/84
Playoffs — Tony Hill, 115 yards, vs. L.A. Rams, 12/26/83
BY OPPONENT — Mark Clayton, 150, @ Miami, 12/17/84
Playoffs — James Lofton, 109 yards, Green Bay, 1/16/83

PAT Blocked
BY COWBOYS — Downs vs. Green Bay, 9/23/83
Playoffs — Rod Hill vs. Green Bay, 1/16/83
BY OPPONENT — Vernon Maxwell, Indianapolis, 10/28/84
Playoffs — Carl Eller, Minnesota, 1/1/78

400 Yards Passing
BY COWBOYS — 406, Don Meredith @ San Francisco, 11/10/63
Playoffs — N.A.
BY OPPONENT — 408, David Woodley, Miami, 10/25/81
Playoffs — N.A.

200 Yards Rushing
BY COWBOYS — 206, Tony Dorsett vs. Philadelphia, 12/4/77
Playoffs — N.A.
BY OPPONENT — 206, Greg Bell, @ Buffalo, 11/18/84
Playoffs — N.A.

Miscellaneous Records

Individual

Most Consecutive Passes Completed
12 — Roger Staubach (last 11 vs. Baltimore, Sept. 4, 1978, and first one vs. N.Y. Giants, Sept. 10, 1978).
12 — Danny White (@ Philadelphia, Nov. 6, 1983).

Most Consecutive Passes Without Interception
166 — Don Meredith (began vs. Philadelphia, Dec. 5, 1965, ended vs. St. Louis, Oct. 16, 1966).

Most Consecutive Games Rush for TD
6 — Tony Dorsett in 1977.
6 — Tony Dorsett in 1980.

Most Consecutive Games Catch TD Pass
7 — Frank Clarke (final game of 1961 season, first six games in '62).
7 — Bob Hayes (final three games of 1965 season, first four games in 1966).

Most Consecutive Games Intercept Pass
5 — Don Bishop in 1961.

Most Consecutive PATs
99 — Mike Clark (last 17 in 1969, all 35 in 1970 and all 47 in 1971).

Most Consecutive Games at Least One Pass Catch
58 — Drew Pearson (final three games of 1974 season, all of 1975, 1976 and 1977, first 13 games of 1978; ended vs. New England, Dec. 3, 1978).

Most Consecutive FG
9 — Rafael Septien (began vs. New England, Sept. 21, 1981, ended vs. Miami, Oct. 25, 1981).

Most Consecutive Games Kick FG
10 — Mike Clark (final nine games of 1969 season, first game in 1970).
10 — Toni Fritsch, twice (final seven games of 1972 season, first three games in 1973; first 10 games in 1975).

Most Seasons Played
14 — Bob Lilly (1961-74)
Lee Roy Jordan (1963-76)
Jethro Pugh (1965-78)
13 — Cornell Green (1962-74)
Dave Edwards (1963-75)
D. D. Lewis (1968, 1970-81)

Most Consecutive Games Played
196 — Bob Lilly (from 1961 through 1974)
168 — Cornell Green (1962-74)
159 — Billy Joe DuPree (1973-83)

Most Tackles in a Season
167 — Bob Breunig, 1979

Most Unassisted Tackles in a Game
14 — Lee Roy Jordan vs. Philadelphia, Oct. 28, 1973.

Most Assisted Tackles in a Game
15 — Jerry Tubbs vs. Chicago, Nov. 27, 1960.

Most Tackles Combined in a Game
21 — Lee Roy Jordan vs. Philadelphia, Sept. 26, 1971.

Team

***Consecutive Winning Seasons**
19 — (1966-84)

***Consecutive Playoff Appearances**
9 — (1975-83)

***Consecutive Season-Opening Victories**
17 — (1965-81)

All-Time Texas Stadium Record
90-23 — (1971-84, regular season and playoffs)

Longest Home Winning Streak
18 games — (began Sept. 8, 1980 @ Washington, ended Sept. 13, 1982 vs. Pittsburgh)

Most Consecutive Games Intercept Pass
28 — Every game in 1962 and 1963.

Most Consecutive PATs
162 — 1969, 1970, 1971, 1972, 1973.

Most Consecutive Games Without Losing Fumble
3 — 1973, 1974, 1975, 1976 and 1977.

*NFL record

PAT Record

21 of 23 in 1960 — last 17 straight.
29 of 29 in 1961 — all 29.
50 of 51 in 1962 — first 33, last 17.
38 of 40 in 1963 — first 32.
28 of 30 in 1964 — last 23.
37 of 38 in 1965 — last 24.
56 of 56 in 1966 — all 56.
41 of 44 in 1967 — first 8, last 1.
54 of 54 in 1968 — all 54.
43 of 44 in 1969 — first 26, last 17.
35 of 35 in 1970 — all 35.
50 of 50 in 1971 — all 50.
36 of 36 in 1972 — all 36.
45 of 46 in 1973 — first 24, last 21.
37 of 38 in 1974 — first 4, last 33.
38 of 40 in 1975 — last 34.
34 of 34 in 1976 — all 34.
39 of 41 in 1977 — first 14, last 16.
46 of 48 in 1978 — first 8, last one.
40 of 45 in 1979 — first one, last 26.
59 of 60 in 1980 — first 52, last 7.
40 of 40 in 1981 — all 40.
28 of 28 in 1982 — all 28.
57 of 59 in 1983 — first 13, last 20.
33 of 34 in 1984 — first 17, last 16.

Largest Margin of Victory

1. 49 points, (56-7) vs. Philadelphia, 1966
2. 46 points, (59-13) vs. Detroit, 1968
3. 45 points, (52-7) vs. N.Y. Giants, 1966
   45 points, (59-14) vs. San Francisco, 1980
5. 44 points, (51-7) vs. Seattle, 1980
6. 42 points, (52-10) vs. Houston, 1970
   42 points, (52-10) vs. N.Y. Jets, 1971
8. 38 points, (52-14) vs. Cleveland, 1967 (Eastern Conference Championship Game)
   38 points, (38-0) vs. Baltimore, 1978
   38 points, (38-0) vs. Tampa Bay, 1982 (1981 NFC Divisional Playoff)
11. 37 points, (40-3) vs. New Orleans, 1973
    37 points, (37-0) vs. Detroit, 1977
13. 35 points, (49-14) vs. Philadelphia, 1969
    35 points, (42-7) vs. Philadelphia, 1971
    35 points, (45-10) vs. St. Louis, 1973
16. 34 points, (34-0) vs. Washington, 1970

Largest Margin of Defeat

1. 41 points, (48-7) vs. Cleveland, 1960
   41 points, (54-13) vs. Minnesota, 1970
3. 38 points, (45-7) vs. Baltimore, 1960
   38 points, (38-0) vs. St. Louis, 1970
5. 36 points, (43-7) vs. Philadelphia, 1961
6. 34 points, (41-7) vs. Green Bay, 1960
7. 32 points, (52-20) vs. St. Louis, 1962
   32 points, (42-10) vs. Cleveland, 1969
9. 31 points, (45-14) @ San Francisco, 1981
10. 30 points, (37-7) vs. Pittsburgh, 1961

Cowboys All-Time Results

All-Time Regular Season Record: 211-122-6
Playoff Record: 20-14

* — Designates Home Games

1960 (0-11-1)
Tom Landry, Head Coach

L	*28	Pittsburgh (30,000)	35
L	*25	Philadelphia (18,500)	27
L	14	Washington (21,142)	26
L	*7	Cleveland (28,500)	48
L	10	St. Louis (23,128)	12
L	*7	Baltimore (25,500)	45
L	*13	Los Angeles (16,000)	38
L	7	Green Bay (32,294)	41
L	*14	San Francisco (10,000)	26
L	7	Chicago (39,951)	17
T	31	New York (55,033)	31
L	14	Detroit (43,272)	23
	177		369

1961 (4-9-1)
Tom Landry, Head Coach

W	*27	Pittsburgh (23,500)	24
W	*21	Minnesota (20,500)	7
L	7	Cleveland (43,638)	25
W	28	Minnesota (33,070)	0
L	*10	New York (41,500)	31
L	*7	Philadelphia (25,000)	43
W	17	New York (60,254)	16
L	*17	St. Louis (20,500)	31
L	7	Pittsburgh (17,519)	37
T	*28	Washington (17,500)	28
L	13	Philadelphia (60,127)	35
L	17	Cleveland (23,500)	38
L	13	St. Louis (15,384)	31
L	24	Washington (21,451)	34
	236		380

1962 (5-8-1)
Tom Landry, Head Coach

T	*35	Washington (15,730)	35
L	*28	Pittsburgh (19,478)	30
W	27	Los Angeles (26,907)	17
L	10	Cleveland (44,040)	19
W	*41	Philadelphia (18,645)	19
W	42	Pittsburgh (23,106)	27
L	*24	St. Louis (16,027)	28
W	38	Washington (49,888)	10
L	*10	New York (45,668)	41
L	*33	Chicago (12,692)	34
L	14	Philadelphia (58,070)	28
W	*45	Cleveland (24,226)	21
L	20	St. Louis (14,102)	52
L	31	New York (62,694)	41
	398		402

1963 (4-10)
Tom Landry, Head Coach

L	*7	St. Louis (36,432)	34
L	*24	Cleveland (28,710)	41
L	17	Washington (40,101)	21
L	21	Philadelphia (60,671)	24
W	*17	Detroit (27,264)	14
L	21	New York (62,889)	37
L	21	Pittsburgh (19,047)	27
W	*35	Washington (18,838)	20
L	24	San Francisco (29,563)	31
W	*27	Philadelphia (23,694)	20
L	17	Cleveland (55,096)	27
L	*27	New York (29,653)	34
L	*19	Pittsburgh (24,136)	24
W	28	St. Louis (12,695)	24
	305		378

1964 (5-8-1)
Tom Landry, Head Coach

L	*6	St. Louis (36,605)	16
W	*24	Washington (25,158)	18
L	17	Pittsburgh (35,594)	23
L	6	Cleveland (72,062)	27
T	*13	New York (33,324)	13
L	*16	Cleveland (37,456)	20
W	31	St. Louis (28,253)	13
W	24	Chicago (47,527)	10
W	31	New York (63,031)	21
L	*14	Philadelphia (55,972)	17
L	16	Washington (49,219)	28
L	*21	Green Bay (44,975)	45
L	14	Philadelphia (60,671)	24
W	*17	Pittsburgh (35,271)	14
	250		289

1965 (7-7)
Tom Landry, Head Coach

W	*31	New York (59,366)	2
W	*27	Washington (61,577)	7
L	13	St. Louis (32,034)	20
L	*24	Philadelphia (56,249)	35
L	17	Cleveland (80,451)	23
L	3	Green Bay (48,311)	13
L	13	Pittsburgh (37,804)	22
W	*39	San Francisco (39,677)	31
W	*24	Pittsburgh (57,293)	17
L	*17	Cleveland (76,251)	24
L	31	Washington (50,205)	34
W	21	Philadelphia (54,714)	19
W	*27	St. Louis (38,499)	13
W	38	New York (62,871)	20
	325		280

PLAYOFF BOWL GAME (Miami)

L	3	Baltimore (65,569)	35

1966 (10-3-1)
Tom Landry, Head Coach

W	*52	New York (60,010)	7
W	*28	Minnesota (64,116)	17
W	47	Atlanta (56,990)	14
W	*56	Philadelphia (69,372)	7
T	10	St. Louis (50,673)	10
L	21	Cleveland (84,721)	30
W	*52	Pittsburgh (58,453)	21
L	23	Philadelphia (60,658)	24
W	31	Washington (50,927)	30
W	20	Pittsburgh (42,185)	7
W	*26	Cleveland (80,259)	14
W	*31	St. Louis (76,965)	17
L	*31	Washington (64,198)	34
W	17	New York (62,735)	7
	445		239

1966 CHAMPIONSHIP GAME (Dallas)

L	27	Green Bay (75,504)	34

1967 (9-5)
Tom Landry, Head Coach

W	21	Cleveland (81,039)	14
W	*38	New York (66,209)	24
L	*13	Los Angeles (75,229)	35
W	17	Washington (50,566)	14
W	*14	New Orleans (64,128)	10
W	24	Pittsburgh (39,641)	21
L	14	Philadelphia (69,740)	21
W	*37	Atlanta (54,751)	7
W	27	New Orleans (83,437)	10
L	*20	Washington (75,538)	27
W	*46	St. Louis (68,787)	21
L	17	Baltimore (60,238)	23
W	*38	Philadelphia (55,834)	17
L	16	San Francisco (27,182)	24
	342		268

1967 EASTERN CHAMPIONSHIP GAME (Dallas)

W	52	Cleveland (70,786)	14

1967 CHAMPIONSHIP GAME (Green Bay)

L	17	Green Bay (50,861)	21

1968 (12-2)
Tom Landry, Head Coach

W	*59	Detroit (61,382)	13
W	*28	Cleveland (68,733)	7
W	45	Philadelphia (60,858)	13
W	27	St. Louis (48,296)	10
W	*34	Philadelphia (72,083)	14
W	20	Minnesota (47,644)	7
L	*17	Green Bay (74,604)	28
W	17	New Orleans (84,728)	3
L	*21	New York (72,163)	27
W	44	Washington (50,816)	24
W	34	Chicago (46,667)	3
W	*29	Washington (66,076)	20
W	*28	Pittsburgh (55,069)	7
W	28	New York (62,617)	10
	431		186

1968 EASTERN CHAMPIONSHIP GAME (Cleveland)

L	20	Cleveland (81,497)	31

PLAYOFF BOWL GAME (Miami)

W	17	Minnesota (22,961)	13

1969 (11-2-1)
Tom Landry, Head Coach

W	*24	St. Louis (62,134)	3
W	21	New Orleans (79,567)	17
W	38	Philadelphia (60,658)	7
W	24	Atlanta (54,833)	17
W	*49	Philadelphia (71,509)	14
W	*25	New York (58,964)	3
L	10	Cleveland (84,850)	42
W	*33	New Orleans (68,282)	17
W	41	Washington (50,474)	28
L	23	Los Angeles (79,105)	24
T	*24	San Francisco (62,348)	24
W	10	Pittsburgh (24,990)	7
W	*27	Baltimore (63,191)	10
W	*20	Washington (56,924)	10
	369		223

1969 EASTERN CHAMPIONSHIP GAME (Dallas)

L	14	Cleveland (69,321)	38

PLAYOFF BOWL GAME (Miami)

L	0	Los Angeles (31,151)	31

1970 (10-4)
Tom Landry, Head Coach

W	17	Philadelphia (59,728)	7
W	*28	N.Y. Giants (57,239)	10
L	7	St. Louis (50,780)	20
W	*13	Atlanta (53,611)	0
L	13	Minnesota (47,900)	54
W	27	Kansas City (51,158)	16
W	*21	Philadelphia (55,736)	17
L	20	N.Y. Giants (62,928)	23
L	*0	St. Louis (69,323)	38
W	45	Washington (50,415)	21
W	*16	Green Bay (67,182)	3
W	*34	Washington (57,936)	0
W	6	Cleveland (75,458)	2
W	*52	Houston (50,504)	10
	299		221

1970 DIVISIONAL PLAYOFF (Dallas)

W	5	Detroit (73,167)	0

1970 NFC CHAMPIONSHIP GAME (San Francisco)

W	17	San Francisco (59,625)	10

SUPER BOWL V (Miami)

L	13	Baltimore (80,055)	16

1971 (11-3)
Tom Landry, Head Coach

W	49	Buffalo (46,206)	37
W	42	Philadelphia (65,358)	7
L	*16	Washington (72,000)	20
W	*20	N.Y. Giants (68,378)	13
L	14	New Orleans (83,088)	24
W	*44	New England (65,708)	21
L	19	Chicago (55,049)	23
W	16	St. Louis (50,486)	13
W	*20	Philadelphia (60,178)	7
W	13	Washington (53,041)	0
W	*28	Los Angeles (66,595)	21
W	*52	N.Y. Jets (66,689)	10
W	42	N.Y. Giants (62,815)	14
W	*31	St. Louis (66,672)	12
	406		222

1971 DIVISIONAL PLAYOFF (Minnesota)

W	20	Minnesota (49,100)	12

1971 NFC CHAMPIONSHIP GAME (Dallas)

W	14	San Francisco (66,311)	3

SUPER BOWL VI (New Orleans)

W	24	Miami (81,035)	3

1972 (10-4)
Tom Landry, Head Coach
W *28 Philadelphia (55,850) 6
W 23 N.Y. Giants (62,725) 14
L 13 Green Bay (47,103) 16
W *17 Pittsburgh (65,682) 13
W 21 Baltimore (58,992) 0
L 20 Washington (53,039) 24
W *28 Detroit (65,378) 24
W 34 San Diego (54,476) 28
W *33 St. Louis (65,218) 24
W 28 Philadelphia (65,720) 7
L *10 San Francisco (65,124) 31
W 27 St. Louis (49,797) 6
W *34 Washington (65,136) 24
L *3 N.Y. Giants (64,602) 23
319 240

1972 DIVISIONAL PLAYOFF
(San Francisco)
W 30 San Francisco (61,214) 28
1972 NFC CHAMPIONSHIP GAME
(Washington)
L 3 Washington (53,129) 26

1973 (10-4)
Tom Landry, Head Coach
W 20 Chicago (55,701) 17
W *40 New Orleans (53,972) 3
W *45 St. Louis (64,815) 10
L 7 Washington (54,314) 14
L 31 Los Angeles (61,428) 37
W *45 N.Y. Giants (64,898) 28
L 16 Philadelphia (65,954) 30
W *38 Cincinnati (58,802) 10
W 23 N.Y. Giants (70,128) 10
W *31 Philadelphia (61,985) 10
L *7 Miami (64,100) 14
W 22 Denver (51,706) 10
W *27 Washington (64,458 — †) 7
W 30 St. Louis (43,946) 3
382 203

1973 DIVISIONAL PLAYOFF
(Dallas)
W 27 Los Angeles (64,291) 16
1973 NFC CHAMPIONSHIP GAME
(Dallas)
L 10 Minnesota (64,524) 27

1974 (8-6)
Tom Landry, Head Coach
W 24 Atlanta (52,322) 0
L 10 Philadelphia (64,088) 13
L *6 N.Y. Giants (45,841) 14
L *21 Minnesota (57,847) 23
L 28 St. Louis (49,885) 31
W *31 Philadelphia (43,586) 24
W 21 N.Y. Giants (61,918) 7
W *17 St. Louis (64,146) 14
W *20 San Francisco (50,018) 14
L 21 Washington (54,395) 28
W 10 Houston (49,775) 0
W *24 Washington (63,243) 23
W *41 Cleveland (48,754) 17
L 23 Oakland (45,850) 27
297 235

1975 (10-4)
Tom Landry, Head Coach
W *18 Los Angeles (49,091) 7
W *37 St. Louis (52,417) (OT) 31
W 36 Detroit (79,784) 10
W 13 N.Y. Giants (56,511) 7
L *17 Green Bay (64,934) 19
W 20 Philadelphia (64,889) 17
L 24 Washington (55,004) (OT) 30
L *31 Kansas City (63,539) 34
W 34 New England (60,905) 31
W *27 Philadelphia (57,893) 17
W *14 N.Y. Giants (53,329) 3
L 17 St. Louis (49,701) 31
W *31 Washington (61,091) 10
W 31 N.Y. Jets (37,279) 21
350 268

1975 DIVISIONAL PLAYOFF
(Minnesota)
W 17 Minnesota (48,341) 14
1975 NFC CHAMPIONSHIP GAME
(Los Angeles)
W 37 Los Angeles (84,483) 7
SUPER BOWL X (Miami)
L 17 Pittsburgh (80,187) 21

1976 (11-3)
Tom Landry, Head Coach
W *27 Philadelphia (54,052) 7
W 24 New Orleans (61,413) 6
W *30 Baltimore (64,237) 27
W 28 Seattle (62,027) 13
W 24 N.Y. Giants (76,042) 14
L 17 St. Louis (50,317) 21
W *31 Chicago (61,346) 21
W 20 Washington (55,004) 7
W *9 N.Y. Giants (58,870) 3
W *17 Buffalo (51,779) 10
L 10 Atlanta (54,992) 17
W *19 St. Louis (62,498) 14
W 26 Philadelphia (55,072) 7
L *14 Washington (59,916) 27
296 194

1976 DIVISIONAL PLAYOFF
(Dallas)
L 12 Los Angeles (62,436) 14

1977 (12-2)
Tom Landry, Head Coach
W 16 Minnesota (47,678) (OT) 10
W *41 N.Y. Giants (64,215) 21
W *23 Tampa Bay (55,316) 7
W 30 St. Louis (50,129) 24
W *34 Washington (62,115) 16
W 16 Philadelphia (65,507) 10
W *37 Detroit (63,160) 0
W 24 N.Y. Giants (74,532) 10
L *17 St. Louis (64,038) 24
L 13 Pittsburgh (49,761) 28
W 14 Washington (55,031) 7
W *24 Philadelphia (60,289) 14
W 42 San Francisco (55,848) 35
W *14 Denver (63,752) 6
345 212

1977 DIVISIONAL PLAYOFF
(Dallas)
W 37 Chicago (62,920) 7
1977 NFC CHAMPIONSHIP GAME
(Dallas)
W 23 Minnesota (61,968) 6
SUPER BOWL XII (New Orleans)
W 27 Denver (76,400) 10

1978 (12-4)
Tom Landry, Head Coach
W *38 Baltimore (64,224) 0
W 34 N.Y. Giants (73,265) 24
L 14 Los Angeles (65,749) 27
W *21 St. Louis (62,760) 12
L 5 Washington (55,031) 9
W *24 N.Y. Giants (63,420) 3
W 24 St. Louis (48,991) (OT) 21
W *14 Philadelphia (60,525) 7
L *10 Minnesota (61,848) 21
L 16 Miami (69,414) 23
W 42 Green Bay (55,256) 14
W *27 New Orleans (57,920) 7
W *37 Washington (64,905) 10
W *17 New England (63,263) 10
W 31 Philadelphia (64,667) 13
W 30 N.Y. Jets (52,632) 7
384 208

1978 DIVISIONAL PLAYOFF
(Dallas)
W 27 Atlanta (60,338) 20
1978 NFC CHAMPIONSHIP GAME
(Los Angeles)
W 28 Los Angeles (67,470) 0
SUPER BOWL XIII (Miami)
L 31 Pittsburgh (78,656) 35

1979 (11-5)
Tom Landry, Head Coach
W 22 St. Louis (50,855) 21
W 21 San Francisco (56,728) 13
W *24 Chicago (64,056) 20
L 7 Cleveland (80,123) 26
W *38 Cincinnati (63,179) 13
W 36 Minnesota (47,572) 20
W *30 Los Angeles (64,462) 6
W *22 St. Louis (64,300) 13
L 3 Pittsburgh (50,199) 14
W 16 New York (76,490) 14
L *21 Philadelphia (62,417) 31
L 20 Washington (55,031) 34
L *24 Houston (63,897) 30
W *28 New York (63,787) 7
W 24 Philadelphia (71,434) 17
W *35 Washington (62,867) 34
371 313

1979 DIVISIONAL PLAYOFF
(Dallas)
L 19 Los Angeles (64,792) 21

1980 (12-4)
Tom Landry, Head Coach
W 17 Washington (55,045) 3
L 20 Denver (74,919) 41
W *28 Tampa Bay (62,750) 17
W 28 Green Bay (54,776) 7
W *24 N.Y. Giants (59,126) 3
W *59 San Francisco (63,399) 14
L 10 Philadelphia (70,696) 17
W *42 San Diego (60,639) 31
W 27 St. Louis (50,701) 24
L 35 N.Y. Giants (68,343) 38
W *31 St. Louis (52,567) 21
W *14 Washington (58,809) 10
W *51 Seattle (57,540) 7
W 19 Oakland (53,194) 13
L 14 Los Angeles (65,154) 38
W *35 Philadelphia (62,548) 27
454 311

1980 NFC WILD CARD PLAYOFF
(Dallas)
W 34 Los Angeles (64,533) 13
1980 DIVISIONAL PLAYOFF
(Atlanta)
W 30 Atlanta (60,022) 27
1980 NFC CHAMPIONSHIP GAME
(Philadelphia)
L 7 Philadelphia (70,696) 20

1981 (12-4)
Tom Landry, Head Coach
W 17 Washington (55,045) 3
W *30 St. Louis (63,602) 17
W 35 New England (60,311) 21
W *18 N.Y. Giants (63,449) 10
L 17 St. Louis (49,777) 20
L 14 San Francisco (57,574) 45
W *29 Los Angeles (64,649) 17
W *28 Miami (64,221) 27
W 17 Philadelphia (72,111) 14
W *27 Buffalo (62,583) 14
L 24 Detroit (79,694) 27
W *24 Washington (64,583) 10
W *10 Chicago (63,499) 9
W 37 Baltimore (54,871) 13
W *21 Philadelphia (64,955) 10
L 10 N.Y. Giants (73,009) (OT) 13
358 270

1981 DIVISIONAL PLAYOFF
(Dallas)
W 38 Tampa Bay (64,848) 0
1981 NFC CHAMPIONSHIP GAME
(San Francisco)
L 27 San Francisco (60,525) 28

1982 (6-3)
Tom Landry, Head Coach
L *28 Pittsburgh (63,431) 36
W 24 St. Louis (50,705) 7
Minnesota — canceled
*N.Y. Giants — canceled
*Washington — canceled
Philadelphia — canceled
Cincinnati — canceled
N.Y. Giants — canceled
*St. Louis — canceled
San Francisco — canceled
W *14 Tampa Bay (49,578) 9
W *31 Cleveland (46,267) 14
W 24 Washington (54,633) 10
W 37 Houston (51,808) 7
W *21 New Orleans (64,506) 7
L *20 Philadelphia (46,199) 24
L 27 Minnesota (60,007) 31
226 145

1982 SUPER BOWL TOURNAMENT — ROUND 1
W *30 Tampa Bay (65,042) 17
1982 SUPER BOWL TOURNAMENT — ROUND 2
W *37 Green Bay (63,972) 26
1982 SUPER BOWL TOURNAMENT — ROUND 3
L 17 Washington (55,045) 31

1983 (12-4)
Tom Landry, Head Coach
W 31 Washington (55,045) 30
W 34 St. Louis (48,532) 17
W *28 N.Y. Giants (62,347) 13
W *21 New Orleans (62,136) 20
W 37 Minnesota (60,774) 24
W *27 Tampa Bay (63,308) (OT) 24
W *37 Philadelphia (63,070) 7
L *38 L.A. Raiders (64,991) 40
W 38 N.Y. Giants (76,142) 20
W 27 Philadelphia (71,236) 20
L 23 San Diego (46,192) 24
W *41 Kansas City (64,103) 21
W *35 St. Louis (60,764) 17
W 35 Seattle (63,352) 10
L *10 Washington (65,074) 31
L 17 San Francisco (59,957) 42
479 360

1983 NFC WILD CARD GAME
(Dallas)
L 17 L.A. Rams (43,521) 24

1984 (9-7)
Tom Landry, Head Coach
W 20 L.A. Rams (65,403) 13
L 7 N.Y. Giants (75,921) 28
W *23 Philadelphia (64,521) 17
W *20 Green Bay (64,222) 6
W 23 Chicago (63,623) 14
L *20 St. Louis (61,438) 31
L 14 Washington (55,431) 34
W *30 New Orleans (50,966) (OT) 27
W *22 Indianapolis (58,724) 3
L *7 N.Y. Giants (60,235) 19
W 24 St. Louis (48,721) 17
L 3 Buffalo (74,391) 14
W *20 New England (55,341) 17
W 26 Philadelphia (66,322) 10
L *28 Washington (64,286) 30
L 21 Miami (74,139) 28
308 308

Cowboys All-Time Pre-Season Results

DAL.	Opponent (Attendance)	Site	OPP.
1960 (1-5)			
10	San Francisco (22,000)	@ Seattle	16
13	St. Louis (14,000)	@ San Antonio	20
10	Baltimore (40,000)	@ Dallas	14
14	New York (10,663)	@ Louisville	3
14	Los Angeles (13,500)	@ Pendleton	49
23	Green Bay (20,121)	@ Minn.	28
1961 (2-3)			
38	Minnesota (4,954)	@ Sioux Falls	13
7	Green Bay (30,000)	@ Dallas	30
10	N.Y. (21,500)	@ Albuquerque	28
35	Baltimore (19,000)	@ Norman	24
10	S.F. (22,130)	@ Sacramento	24
1962 (0-5)			
7	Green Bay (54,500)	@ Dallas	31
24	Detroit (77,683)	@ Cleveland	35
10	Baltimore (14,000)	@ Roanoke	24
7	S.F. (20,000)	@ Sacramento	26
26	Minnesota (12,500)	@ Atlanta	45
1963 (3-2)			
17	Los Angeles (70,675)	@ L.A.	14
10	Green Bay (53,121)	@ Dallas	31
17	Los Angeles (29,349)	@ Portland	20
37	S.F. (9,927)	@ Bakersfield	24
27	Detroit (51,218)	@ New Orleans	17
1964 (1-4)			
6	Los Angeles (57,450)	@ L.A.	17
34	S.F. (24,679)	@ Portland	23
16	Los Angeles (30,565)	@ Portland	25
3	Green Bay (60,057)	@ Dallas	35
6	Chicago (35,000)	@ New Orleans	21
1965 (2-3)			
0	Los Angeles (31,579)	@ L.A.	9
7	S.F. (24,837)	@ Portland	27
21	Green Bay (67,954)	@ Dallas	12
17	Minn. (41,500)	@ Birmingham	57
34	Chicago (33,525)	@ Tulsa	21
1966 (5-0)			
24	San Francisco (28,899)	@ S.F.	13
20	Los Angeles (44,217)	@ L.A.	10
21	Green Bay (75,504)	@ Dallas	3
20	Detroit (31,250)	@ Tulsa	10
28	Minnesota (58,316)	@ Dallas	24
1967 (2-3)			
6	Los Angeles (57,595)	@ L.A.	20
30	San Francisco (31,212)	@ S.F.	24
3	Green Bay (78,087)	@ Dallas	20
30	Houston (53,125)	@ Houston	17
7	Baltimore (58,492)	@ Dallas	33
1968 (3-3)			
24	Chicago (14,578)	@ Canton	30
16	San Francisco (27,530)	@ S.F.	14
42	Los Angeles (65,978)	@ L.A.	10
27	Green Bay (72,014)	@ Dallas	31
33	Houston (52,289)	@ Houston	19
10	Baltimore (69,520)	@ Dallas	16
1969 (4-2)			
17	Los Angeles (87,381)	@ L.A.	24
20	San Francisco (33,894)	@ S.F.	17
31	Green Bay (73,764)	@ Dallas	13
14	Houston (55,310)	@ Houston	11
25	N.Y. Jets (74,771)	@ Dallas	9
7	Baltimore (58,975)	@ Dallas	23
1970 (1-5)			
20	San Diego (39,392)	@ San Diego	10
10	Los Angeles (64,646)	@ L.A.	17
34	Green Bay (72,389)	@ Dallas	35
21	Houston (46,548)	@ Houston	37
0	Kansas City (69,055)	@ Dallas	13
21	New York Jets (55,297)	@ Dallas	29
1971 (6-0)			
45	Los Angeles (87,187)	@ L.A.	21
36	New Orleans (73,560)	@ Dallas	21
16	Cleveland (69,099)	@ Dallas	15
28	Houston (49,078)	@ Houston	20
27	Baltimore (22,921)	@ Baltimore	14
24	Kansas City (74,035)	@ Dallas	17
1972 (6-1)			
20	College All-Stars (54,162)	@ Chi.	7
26	Houston (65,405)	@ Dallas	24
27	Los Angeles (66,051)	@ L.A.	13
30	New Orleans (81,070)	@ N.O.	7
34	N.Y. Jets (65,386)	@ Dallas	27
10	Kansas City (79,592)	@ K.C.	20
16	Oakland (62,607)	@ Dallas	10
1973 (4-2)			
24	Los Angeles (75,461)	@ L.A.	7
26	Oakland (53,723)	@ Oakland	27
24	New Orleans (61,022)	@ Dallas	14
24	Houston (46,942)	@ Houston	27
27	Kansas City (57,468)	@ Dallas	16
26	Miami (61,378)	@ Dallas	23
1974 (3-3)			
7	Oakland (41,049)	@ Oakland	27
13	Los Angeles (46,468)	@ L.A	6
19	Houston (53,148)	@ Dallas (OT)	13
7	N. Orleans (56,563)	@ N. Orleans	16
25	Kansas City (43,492)	@ Dallas	16
15	Pittsburgh (43,900)	@ Dallas	41
1975 (2-4)			
7	Los Angeles (62,843)	@ L.A.	35
20	Kansas City (35,630)	@ K.C.	26
13	Minnesota (45,395)	@ Dallas	16
17	Houston (46,951)	@ Houston	14
20	Oakland (39,562)	@ Dallas	31
17	Pittsburgh (43,186)	@ Dallas	16
1976 (3-3)			
14	Oakland (52,391)	@ Oakland	17
14	Los Angeles (60,158)	@ L.A.	26
9	Denver (54,567)	@ Dallas	13
36	Detroit (30,340)	@ Memphis	16
20	Pittsburgh (64,264)	@ Dallas	10
26	Houston (58,844)	@ Dallas (OT)	20
1977 (3-3)			
34	San Diego (59,504)	@ Dallas	14
17	Seattle (58,789)	@ Seattle (OT)	23
14	Miami (56,820)	@ Dallas	20
23	Baltimore (54,835)	@ Dallas	21
14	Houston (49,777)	@ Houston	23
30	Pittsburgh (49,824)	@ Dallas	0
1978 (3-1)			
41	San Francisco (63,736)	@ Dallas	24
21	Denver (74,619)	@ Denver	14
13	Houston (62,242)	@ Dallas	27
16	Pittsburgh (59,747)	@ Dallas	13
1979 (3-2)			
13	Oakland (20,648)	@ Canton, Ohio	20
7	Denver (61,192)	@ Dallas	6
17	Seattle (59,803)	@ Seattle	27
16	Houston (62,803)	@ Dallas	13
16	Pittsburgh (64,543)	@ Dallas	14
1980 (3-1)			
17	Green Bay (54,876)	@ Dallas	14
19	Los Angeles (63,283)	@ Anaheim	16
20	Houston (63,658)	@ Dallas	13
10	Pittsburgh (62,795)	- @ Dallas	31
1981 (2-2)			
17	Green Bay (55,087)	@ Dallas	21
21	Los Angeles (61,459)	@ Anaheim	33
24	Pittsburgh (63,504)	@ Dallas	14
28	Houston (63,799)	@ Dallas	20
1982 (3-1)			
10	Buffalo (48,612)	@ Dallas	14
26	San Diego (49,182)	@ San Diego	16
36	New England (50,113)	@ Dallas	21
20	Houston (60,150)	@ Dallas	14
1983 (3-1)			
20	Miami (46,826)	@ Dallas	17
30	L.A. Rams (54,268)	@ Los Angeles	7
7	Pittsburgh (62,164)	@ Dallas	24
34	Houston (54,363)	@ Dallas	31
1984 (3-1)			
31	Green Bay (43,371)	@ Dallas	17
24	San Diego (50,740)	@ San Diego	13
10	Pittsburgh (55,658)	@ Dallas	20
31	Houston (53,877)	@ Dallas	24

1984 NFL REGULAR SEASON FINAL STANDINGS

AMERICAN FOOTBALL CONFERENCE

Eastern Division	W	L	T	Pct.	Pts.	OP
**Miami	14	2	0	.875	513	298
New England	9	7	0	.563	362	352
N.Y. Jets	7	9	0	.438	332	364
Indianapolis	4	12	0	.250	239	414
Buffalo	2	14	0	.125	250	454
Central Division						
**Pittsburgh	9	7	0	.563	387	310
Cincinnati	8	8	0	.500	339	339
Cleveland	5	11	0	.313	250	297
Houston	3	13	0	.188	240	437
Western Division						
**Denver	13	3	0	.813	353	241
*Seattle	12	4	0	.750	418	282
*L.A. Raiders	11	5	0	.688	368	278
Kansas City	8	8	0	.500	314	324
San Diego	7	9	0	.438	394	413

**Division Champion

PLAYOFFS

AFC Wild Card Game:
@ Seattle 13 L.A. Raiders 7

NFC Wild Card Game:
N.Y. Giants 16 @ L.A. Rams 13

AFC Divisional Playoffs:
@ Miami 31 Seattle 10
Pittsburgh 24 @ Denver 17

NFC Divisional Playoffs:
@ San Francisco 21 N.Y. Giants 10
Chicago 23 @ Washington 19

AFC Championship Game:
@ Miami 45 Pittsburgh 28

NFC Championship Game:
@ San Francisco 23 Chicago 0

Super Bowl XIX:
San Francisco 38 Miami 16

Pro Bowl:
AFC 22 NFC 14

NATIONAL FOOTBALL CONFERENCE

Eastern Division	W	L	T	Pct.	Pts.	OP
**Washington	11	5	0	.688	426	310
*N.Y. Giants	9	7	0	.563	299	301
St. Louis	9	7	0	.563	423	345
Dallas	9	7	0	.563	308	308
Philadelphia	6	9	1	.406	278	320
Central Division						
**Chicago	10	6	0	.625	325	248
Green Bay	8	8	0	.500	390	309
Tampa Bay	6	10	0	.375	335	380
Detroit	4	11	1	.281	283	408
Minnesota	3	13	0	.188	276	484
Western Division						
**San Francisco	15	1	0	.938	475	227
*L.A. Rams	10	6	0	.625	346	316
New Orleans	7	9	0	.438	298	361
Atlanta	4	12	0	.250	281	382

*Wild Card Playoff Team

1985 NFL Schedule

All times local.

FIRST WEEK

Sunday, September 8 (NBC-TV doubleheader)

Denver at Los Angeles Rams . . . 1:00
Detroit at Atlanta . . . 1:00
Green Bay at New England . . . 1:00
Indianapolis at Pittsburgh . . . 1:00
Kansas City at New Orleans . . . 12:00
Miami at Houston . . . 12:00
New York Jets at Los Angeles Raiders . . . 1:00
Philadelphia at New York Giants . . . 1:00
St. Louis at Cleveland . . . 1:00
San Diego at Buffalo . . . 4:00
San Francisco at Minnesota . . . 12:00
Seattle at Cincinnati . . . 1:00
Tampa Bay at Chicago . . . 12:00

Monday, September 9

Washington at Dallas . . . (ABC) 8:00

SECOND WEEK

Thursday, September 12

Los Angeles Raiders at Kansas City . . . (ABC) 7:00

Sunday, September 15 (CBS-TV doubleheader)

Atlanta at San Francisco . . . 1:00
Buffalo at New York Jets . . . 1:00
Cincinnati at St. Louis . . . 12:00
Dallas at Detroit . . . 1:00
Houston at Washington . . . 1:00
Indianapolis at Miami . . . 1:00
Los Angeles Rams at Philadelphia . . . 1:00
Minnesota at Tampa Bay . . . 4:00
New England at Chicago . . . 12:00
New Orleans at Denver . . . 2:00
New York Giants at Green Bay . . . 3:00
Seattle at San Diego . . . 1:00

Monday, September 16

Pittsburgh at Cleveland . . . (ABC) 9:00

THIRD WEEK

Thursday, September 19

Chicago at Minnesota . . . (ABC) 7:00

Sunday, September 22 (CBS-TV doubleheader)

Cleveland at Dallas . . . 12:00
Denver at Atlanta . . . 1:00
Detroit at Indianapolis . . . 12:00
Houston at Pittsburgh . . . 1:00
Kansas City at Miami . . . 4:00
New England at Buffalo . . . 1:00
New York Jets vs. Green Bay at Milwaukee . . . 3:00
Philadelphia at Washington . . . 1:00
St. Louis at New York Giants . . . 1:00
San Diego at Cincinnati . . . 1:00
San Francisco at Los Angeles Raiders . . . 1:00
Tampa Bay at New Orleans . . . 12:00

Monday, September 23

Los Angeles Rams at Seattle . . . (ABC) 6:00

FOURTH WEEK

Sunday, September 29 (NBC-TV doubleheader)

Atlanta at Los Angeles Rams . . . 1:00
Cleveland at San Diego . . . 1:00
Dallas at Houston . . . 12:00
Green Bay at St. Louis . . . 12:00
Indianapolis at New York Jets . . . 4:00
Los Angeles Raiders at New England . . . 1:00
Miami at Denver . . . 2:00
Minnesota at Buffalo . . . 1:00
New Orleans at San Francisco . . . 1:00
New York Giants at Philadelphia . . . 1:00
Seattle at Kansas City . . . 12:00
Tampa Bay at Detroit . . . 1:00
Washington at Chicago . . . 12:00

Monday, September 30

Cincinnati at Pittsburgh . . . (ABC) 9:00

FIFTH WEEK

Sunday, October 6 (NBC-TV doubleheader)

Buffalo at Indianapolis . . . 12:00
Chicago at Tampa Bay . . . 1:00
Dallas at New York Giants . . . (ABC) 9:00
Detroit at Green Bay . . . 12:00
Houston at Denver . . . 2:00
Kansas City at Los Angeles Raiders . . . 1:00
Minnesota at Los Angeles Rams . . . 1:00
New England at Cleveland . . . 1:00
New York Jets at Cincinnati . . . 4:00
Philadelphia at New Orleans . . . 12:00
Pittsburgh at Miami . . . 1:00
San Diego at Seattle . . . 1:00
San Francisco at Atlanta . . . 1:00

Monday, October 7

St. Louis at Washington . . . (ABC) 9:00

SIXTH WEEK

Sunday, October 13 (CBS-TV doubleheader)

Atlanta at Seattle . . . 1:00
Buffalo at New England . . . 1:00
Chicago at San Francisco . . . 1:00
Cleveland at Houston . . . 12:00
Denver at Indianapolis . . . 12:00
Detroit at Washington . . . 1:00
Kansas City at San Diego . . . 1:00
Los Angeles Rams at Tampa Bay . . . 1:00
Minnesota vs. Green Bay at Milwaukee . . . 12:00
New Orleans at Los Angeles Raiders . . . 1:00
New York Giants at Cincinnati . . . 1:00
Philadelphia at St. Louis . . . 12:00
Pittsburgh at Dallas . . . 12:00

Monday, October 14

Miami at New York Jets . . . (ABC) 9:00

SEVENTH WEEK

Sunday, October 20 (NBC-TV doubleheader)

Cincinnati at Houston . . . 12:00
Dallas at Philadelphia . . . 1:00
Indianapolis at Buffalo . . . 1:00
Los Angeles Raiders at Cleveland . . . 1:00
Los Angeles Rams at Kansas City . . . 12:00
New Orleans at Atlanta . . . 1:00
New York Jets at New England . . . 4:00
St. Louis at Pittsburgh . . . 1:00
San Diego at Minnesota . . . 12:00
San Francisco at Detroit . . . 1:00
Seattle at Denver . . . 2:00
Tampa Bay at Miami . . . 4:00
Washington at New York Giants . . . 1:00

Monday, October 21

Green Bay at Chicago . . . (ABC) 8:00